THE LAWLESS
AND
THE LOTUS

By the same author

ROAD IN THE WILDERNESS
DUST ON MY SHOES
WHO WANDERS ALONE
ANYWHERE BUT HERE
RIDE THE VOLCANO
RESTLESS MEN
TO CATCH A CROCODILE
TOO MANY SPEARS
THE BARBARIANS
THE GLASS CANNON
THE DEVILS GARDEN
THE ROAD TO ANYWHERE- Selected Travel Writings
SIGNALLER JOHNSTON'S SECRET WAR

First published in 1963 by
ANGUS & ROBERTSON LTD

Published by lulu.com
ISBN 978-1-84753-067-7

Copyright © Sava Pinney 2007
Cover art & design Sava Pinney
Email: sava@dustonmyshoes.com

Note: the original house style and layout matching the 1963 edition has
been followed almost entirely, as a whim and to help maintain the feel of
context in this new and later edition.

With special thanks to
Supapon & Ferenc Lantay-Lefkovich and Raggydax for encouraging
me continually in all endeavour; John Borthwick for his assistance and
fondness for PP; Tess Deyl for proofing and Diana Kalantzis for sharing
her knowledge and because she knows how to do this so well.

PETER PINNEY

The Lawless
and
The Lotus

Preface

Peter Pinney was a popular and well published author best known for his free-ranging adventure travel books of the 1950's and '60's.

He was a man who followed his own desires at a time when this set him apart from middle-class western society, and it is here in the greater landscapes that he travels.

Written in the first person Pinney journeys across continents and oceans with little or no luggage and an astonishing lack of regard for visas and border restrictions, participating and precipitating a kaleidoscope of odd and unusual events.

Deported, stowaway, hitch-hiker by sea and land, living on his wits in this manner Pinney truly travelled the continents.

Writing with descriptive wit about people and situations, and lyrically of the landscape, Pinney's interactions with locals and the law highlight the delights of nature and the folly or greatness of man and woman.

It is a great pleasure to see this book in print again.

Pinney published 9 books with the quintessential Australian publisher Angus & Robertson in the 1950's and '60's. Later years saw him writing television drama for Crawfords.

In the early 1990's a trio of his secretly-written diaries from the New Guinea jungle campaign in World War 2 were published, along with a selection of best travel excerpts, by University of Qld Press.

Peter Pinney died in 1992 and is much missed.

Sava Pinney,
PP's daughter, 2007

— LE NUMERO 25 FRANCS — JEUDI 25 MAI 1961

Paraissant à Fort - de France tous les matins, sauf samedi et dimanche

DIRECTEUR : VICTOR É. SURÉNA RÉDACTION - ADMINISTRATION - ANGLE DES RUES ISAMBERT 59 ET PÉRRINON 15

B. P. 173 - Tél. 22-48

documentation, imposaient ... planning très strict qui demandait alisations et nos possibilités.

Au Zoo du Fort St Louis 25 · 5 · 61

Un homme ouvre des cages et laisse s'enfuir des animaux

Sous prétexte que certains animaux du Zoo du Fort St Louis étaient mal soignés ou que leurs conditions de vie n'étaient pas respectés, un de nos visiteurs, d'origine australienne, a cru bon d'ouvrir leurs cages pour leur rendre leur liberté. Il a fait cette opération de nuit et le zo... perdu quelqu

préfère aller en prison plutôt que de voir souffrir ces bêtes.

Les responsables du zoo, ahuris devant un tel fait, soulignent à jus te titre que depuis plus de deux ans ces animaux sont en parfait état. Aussi, ils ont porté le fait à la connaissance de la Police qui enquête.

PRESS RELEASE

(For Immediate Release)

22 Mai '61.

An Australian visitor who admits he entered the Fort Ste. Louis one night last week and released several animals and birds from their cages, today charged Zoo officials, in an angry statement to the Press, with "callous indifference" to the "shocking" conditions of some caged creatures.

The visitor, who prefers to remain anonymous, frankly admits he released birds and animals last Thursday night as part of a one-man campaign to publicise official neglect and encourage an improvement in conditions.

Specifically, he stated that five animals (skunk, manicou, baboon, jackal, racoon) had been left without water for at east five days --- he watched a sick malfini a...

ne manicou --- .

For Sunshine

Letters from Readers

I first came across The Lawless and The Lotus in 1967. I was immediately entranced, not only by the writing, but the style of the book....The Lawless and The Lotus remains the best travel book I have ever read. Pinney managed to weave a narrative that was fast-moving, fascinating and intensely human, all at the same time. He has always remained my favourite travel writer.
Best wishes, *Michael Hall*

Many years ago I worked for a surgeon who had been a Changi prisoner and he read, over time, several of your father's books to us (me and another employee) aloud over lunch. We hung on every word and lived and relished his sang-froid and exotic adventures. Ken tried other books from time to time, but we liked the Pinneys by far and away the best!
All the best to you, kind regards, *Jan Matthews*

(on meeting PP in Europe)
I didn't know who he was until the day I and my family left in our Commer van to drive back to Australia. I was delighted because I had read Dust on My Shoes and he was a traveller's traveller. I had hitch-hiked from England to Australia when I was 21, but nobody held a candle to Peter when it came to travelling on a shoestring and living by your wits.
All the best, *Ray Neilson*

CONTENTS

CHAPTER

1

ST KITTS

The Moonshiners

"HEY, lookit white man! See, he dere!"

"What he do?"

"He walk about a road, that white fool!"

"Oh, sweet Lard, he got one rifle!"

"Eh-eh, maybe make it mischief, shoot a black man!"

One could hear their startled voices raised in wonder and speculation above the rumble of the motor as the vehicle approached. It was, the island's only fire-engine, a juggernaut of modest size resplendent with bold red, and with brass and chrome appointments sparkling in the blaze of the Caribbean sun. Two West Indian Negroes occupied the front seat, another four sat behind, and a battery of ardent stares was fixed on the lonely, barefoot figure who stood by the empty country road holding his hand aloft.

"What for he stan' dere?"

"He loss hisself. Drink it rum, done loss hisself."

"And he got no shoes. See, he feet be naked. Eh, dat crazy humbug!"

With a purposeful rumble the engine passed by, an imperious red chariot splendid with the flash of polished metal and trailing a lazy cloud of fine white dust: but, as if on second thoughts, it abruptly slowed and pulled to a halt some fifty yards ahead. Five of the crew gazed eagerly back at the stranger as if sensing some novel delight, but the driver stood up and audaciously demanded, "Hey, you white marn, you want it somet'ing?"

I was already trotting towards them with my canvas sack and speargun. Would they give me a lift? By the gods I needed one. Soon the police and immigration would be coming in their car on the way to Basseterre, and how they would laugh among themselves as I was enveloped in their dust! First their pained suspicion, then oblique insults, and finally their dust. Or they might, after all, pick me up and take me to the prison.

But coming abreast of the driver I greeted him, and said, "Could you give me a lift to Basseterre?"

The town was down on the coast, two miles distant.

"You walkin', white marn? On both feet?"

"Yes, both. Can you take me?"

He was a man of excellent appearance, perhaps forty, tall and spare, his lean ash-black face etched in rigid cast suggesting strength in dignity and discipline. His austere courtesy, legacy of British training, was emboldened to empirical arrogance by the recent independence of these islands. He viewed my dusty, bare feet with a pained frown.

"What you do, walkin' on a road? You got no shoe?"

"One of them broke, so I threw them away." His attitude was easily forgiven, for white man usually wore good, polished shoes; but one strap on my sandals had parted, so I left them both on the plane and thus arrived barefoot on St Kitts. His gaze wandered thoughtfully up my paint-stained jeans to the torn shirt, and he asked, "You all alone by you'self?"

"Yes."

Should I offer him money? He peered doubtfully up and down the road as if suspecting other white men were about to launch themselves from ambush, but there was only the lonely road slicing through green fields of sugar-cane. He glanced distrustfully at the speargun, and examined my striped canvas sack with lordly insolence.

"O.K., you can come then. Too hot for walk."

With the agreeable, but watchful condescension common to ticket inspectors and head waiters he permitted me to join his fellow on the front seat, and the brave little wagon rumbled off again. The man beside me, a stalwart young fellow of engaging candour and quick grins, laughed with the sheer delight of a foolish occasion and said, "Ho-ho, das funny, sah. White man walkin' on a road in a hot sun. wit' no shoe. You come on the aeroplane?"

"Yes." Aye, and just in time. Escape from the Virgin Islands had been arranged only minutes ahead of pursuit. I had brought only the clothes I stood in, and the speargun, and a few oddments stuffed in haste inside a canvas cushion cover.

"You come to good place, St Kitts. The fines' island in de sea. But you no find taxi, at that airport?"

"No," I replied, admiring the glittering brass bell. "By the time they'd finished with me there, all the taxis had gone." But who, among those elegant passengers who shafted their disdain at the barefoot sea-tramp, had ridden to town in such magnificence?

"They humbug you, those airport men?"

"A little," I said cautiously. They certainly would have prevented me from landing, if they could.

"Eh-heh, yes," he said with satisfaction, as if this bore out some private conviction about police and immigration. He had the fluid gaiety of the man who rides through life impelled by stimulus, and was obviously delighted by the thunder of the engine and the rush of wind which flushed the open driver's seat with the fragrance of sun-scorched sugar-cane.

"Have you been to a fire?" I asked, seeking to soften the driver's brittle silence. But the driver held his stern parade-ground pose.

"No fire," said the lad beside me. "We goes to watch the aeroplane come in, and fly away." There was the tug of disappointment in his tone. But he added, brightening, "Maybe one day dat aeroplane mash up, I t'ink. Then we have one big, important fire."

The men to the rear were leaning forward to catch the conversation, and one gaily shouted, "Hey, white marn, what for you come St Kitts?"

There were various good reasons. "To go to Basseterre," I shouted back mechanically. What a princely bell, so brilliantly golden! I had always had a secret desire to ride on such an engine and clang the bell.

"What for you go Basseterre?" he asked, in the manner of one prepared for easy laughter.

"For one thing," I shouted. "To see Big André. You know him?"

The lad beside me cried in alarm, "What? How you mean, marn? You mean dat Big André at the Royal?"

"Aye."

The fire-engine lost speed rapidly as the driver applied brakes. But why were we stopping? The main road was several hundred yards ahead, and then there was another mile to town.

"He fren' for you, that André?" said the lad, incredulous.

But the wagon stopped in a grinding skid, and the driver said, "Get down, white marn!"

I blinked at him in surprise. His expression was one of determined severity.

"What?"

"Ef you fren' for Big André," he said evenly, "you no fren' for me.

Get down, sah."

Relief bubbled inside me like a sweet-water spring.

"Friend? André is no friend of mine, chief. That man has no friends at all."

"Not your fren'? Then why you go see him? You go for fight with him?"

"Maybe."

One might hope not. No ordinary white man could fight with Big André and live, but probably something would happen when we met.

"You no can fight that ugly marn," he said, scowling. "More better you put that spear inside he belly. That André the wussess marn in arl of Basseterre. One mean, teefin' bad rascal." He sat there for a moment to reflect, and then added, "O.K., ef you no be fren' for him...."

The fire-engine moved off again and swung onto the main road.

"That marn scandalize this island, he so wicked scoundrel," shouted the voice behind me. "Make trouble arl a time. Give it money to police, teef anything he want, and break it arl young girl."

I knew about his stealing, he had stolen from me.

"Everybardy detes' that marn," the lad beside me said excitedly. "But he too big, too fierce, he can kill a marn so easy."

"You no fraid for him?" shouted the voice eagerly.

Yes, I admitted, I was afraid. For André was a man who wore evil like an armour of sabre-thorns; and even if good could combat evil, I was not a good enough man to break his lance.

"A spear in he fat belly!" The lad laughed. "Ho-ho, I like for see he wriggle so."

Even the driver laughed at such a joyful vision, and vied with the others in inventing methods to torture the malevolent André; and so it was that in happy and laughing company I was borne on to Basseterre in their splendid chariot, and they even let me ding their bell until we arrived on the outskirts of the town.

In the basement bar of the Royal Hotel I sought Big André, a man whom one might normally have little wish to meet. A gross black ghoul of a villain with a bladder of curses instead of a heart, the worms

16

of frustrated ambition gnawing his purulent brain, and a scarred and shrivelled conscience paralysed by every one of the seven deadly sins.

Big André, prince of pimps and waterfront informers, master of the clandestine and bull of Basseterre. But it was only mid afternoon, the sun was hot, few people were abroad, and there seemed to be no one at all in the downstairs bar.

No one? No barman, not even a serving wench? With mounting interest I glanced about the shadowed room, and listened for footsteps in the ball. Silence. There was only the sibilant wash of the sea on the beach outside. Why, there was no one in the room at all, the bar was undefended, any thief could walk in and—

This might be the chance to settle a certain debt. Had the girl who sold pasties noticed me walk by?

Moving with barefoot stealth, I crossed to the till. But the drawer was open, the money was all gone. Perhaps some common thief had discovered it before me. Aye, but those rows and rows of bottles—a few of them could fit inside my sack.

Gin? Rum? Brandy? Not gin: an effete drink, a purveyor of sad illusion, nothing more. And nobody in their right mind would take a seventh drink of Andre's rum. Brandy? Ah, but there was cognac; the Solariego was metal-sealed and virtually proof from even André's wiles. Better not to walk behind the bar, it would turn into a trap if someone came. Carefully I set down my canvas sack and speargun, making very little sound, and by wriggling flat across the bar managed to reach out and grasp a litre bottle. Clutching the bottle, I began wriggling back when, with startled apprehension, I saw movement in the shadows.

A few feet away the sinister black bulk of fat André was crouched behind the bar.

His attentions were devoted to a series of bottles arrayed before him on the floor. My body was rigid with sudden fear, avoiding any sound. Had he seen me? But he was facing in almost the opposite direction, busily sticking labels on the bottles. Slowly I lowered myself to the floor again, on the outside of the bar, and stowed the bottle quietly in my sack. Could I gain one more? Or was the risk too great?

But then the rasping sneer of his deep voice cut through the silence.

"Ten biwi* dollars, plus tax!"

* British West Indian

He lumbered heavily to his feet and fixed me with a disagreeable stare. "Smart bastard!"

Smart fool, at least. He had been aware of my presence all the time.

"Happy day André. So nice to see you again."

"Come on," he rumbled irritably, moving to be abreast of me on the other side of the bar. "The bottle, or ten biwi. I got no time for smart bastards!"

Damn, this was going badly. But nothing would persuade me to give him back the bottle. Or to buy it from him.

"I'll make you a trade," I offered.

"What trade?"

"Twenty fathoms of nylon line. For the bottle."

He glowered suspiciously. "You talkin' through your arse, man. Gimme the bottle, quick."

"I've got three witnesses."

"You've got horse manure. Gimme that bottle before I bus' your haid!"

"One of them was Pegleg, the caretaker. He saw you. He knows who you sold it to."

Barely a month before I had called in at Basseterre with the fifty-three-foot charter yacht *Zara*, and a party of four on board. A routine cruise down-island, one of the last runs I made with her. In a moderate swell we paid out anchor chain to let the stern ride in close to the exposed jetty, in order to take on fuel. It was a gusty, moonless night. We threw a line to two dark figures on the jetty, and instead of making the end secure they started to edge away and haul in slack. "More rope!" they shouted. We paid out more line. Twenty fathoms, twenty-five. "More!" Thirty, thirty-five. What were the idiots doing? When there was no more line, they cut it and ran off down the jetty with a hundred and twenty feet of brand-new nylon. One of them was a lard-bellied ox of a man, who could only have been André.

"Pegleg was sitting by the gate and he saw you," I lied. "So did two other men working in the port captain's office just above."

He thought about it for a moment, probably reflecting that he could easily squeeze an extra ten dollars from the charter parties I occasionally brought in. One official complaint might result in his being blacklisted by forty-two charter boats. Finally be shrugged and settled for the trade.

"So drop dead and keep the friggin' bottle." His voice had the flat, sultry growl of someone passing wind in the bottom of a well.

"It's a deal, then. Let's put it in a glass."

Mechanically he reached for a bottle of Mount Gay and poured two tots: deal or no deal, it paid to keep charter-boat skippers bringing their guests to the hotel. Picking up one of a stack of newly minted liquor labels lying on the bar, I saw they were identical with those he had been affixing to bottles. They were rum labels, and at the bottom was the legend, "Made in Trinidad". The labels were made in distant Trinidad, and stuck on bottles of local rotgut. The unsuspecting would assume the rum itself was made in Trinidad and tolerate its bite.

"Good idea," I said admiringly. "Man of enterprise, André."

"H'm." But one sensed his pleasure, for compliments were not his daily portion.

"Have you ever used a hypodermic syringe?"

His black eyes were like round beetles drowned in bloodshot custard.

"Syringe?"

"Yes. You can empty a bottle of good liquor without ever breaking the seal, and refill it with anything you like."

For a moment a flicker of interest seemed to cross his heavy face, and he idly twiddled his glass as he thought about syringes. Now would be as good a time as any to seek information I had come for.

"Have you seen Tic-Tac lately?"

"Who?"

"Tic-Tac. The French girl. The little one with the dark hair, and the curves, and the white bikini."

"Nevis," be admitted, fumbling for a cigarette. "Went on to Nevis Island."

"I heard she'd been arrested," I said with assumed indifference, but my pulse beat faster.

"H'm."

They must have let her go.

"When did she leave?"

He found the cigarette and lit it, and eyed me craftily through a haze of smoke.

"Shacked up with an Englishman now," he mumbled mockingly. No reason to fear that: Tic-Tac had an abiding distaste for anything, or anyone, even faintly English. Well, if she had gone to Nevis, I would go there too. I finished my drink, and hefted my bag, and speargun.

"Thanks for the drink. And the bottle."

"I'll make it up, smart man."

"Not with my parties, you won't."

"Whaddya mean?"

"I've quit."

With ponderous deliberation he drew himself up and rested his great, clenched fists on the bar, surveying me with a malicious stare from those cruel, bloodshot eyes.

"You quit? You ain't got no boat now?"

"That's right. The *Zara's* in St Thomas; I left her. I'm a gentleman of leisure again, on my way to join Tic-Tac."

"Why, you—gimme that bottle!"

He moved quickly around from behind the bar, but as quickly I locked the speargun rubbers taut and aimed the rusty steel barb at his belly. If he seized me, he could kill me with one hand. But he hesitated, his hate and fear in conflict, and while he stood there I nervously backed away and moved out into the street, to the sun-drenched waterfront of Basseterre.

The aboriginal Caribs used to call St Kitts Liamuiga, the Fertile One, but the Europeans slaughtered them and their name is remembered only by the Caribbean Sea. And from the sea the island rises in bold majesty to great volcanic peaks, a splendidly sculpted Leeward Islands queen with a reputation any lady of joy might envy—of predictable generosity, exquisite in repose, her whispered promises provoking men to ravish and possess. Tropical jungles clothe her thrusting bosoms, but her belly and smooth flanks are suggestively revealed by the quilted varigreens of cane and naked fields of cotton.

The Caribs were her children, but committed ethnic suicide by pitting clubs and darts against muskets and cannon. Europeans were her conquerors, and sugar is her king, but the Negro is her lover and to him her fruits are due.

South of a huge volcanic ridge, where massed phalanxes of cane sweep down towards the coast, the polyglot town of Basseterre dozes at the edge of the sea. A humble town, perhaps, of unkempt lanes buzzing with kerbside commerce, of paint-fletched wooden buildings and rusted iron rooves, of sudden little bazaars magically aglitter with assorted clinquant display, and slippery, reeking markets furnished with fly-ridden carcasses and enormous fish, and magnificent displays of island fruit. A town of many faces, Basseterre: an open roadstead without a harbour, the seafront lined with vividly painted dories; the centre of Britain's sugar commerce throughout the Leeward isles; a smugglers' roost—St Kitts has no distillery of her own, so sugar is exported during daylight and rum comes back after dark; a nest of political incest, as intriguing neophytes plot and counterplot and scurry from hole to hole as federation's shattered pillars crumble down about their heads.

But no matter how many faces, the town has a friendly heart: and through this heart there surges not only Negro blood from Africa's Guinea coast, but also Portuguese blood from Madeira, Chinese blood from migrants of a century ago, and the blood of East Indian coolies imported by the British when emancipated Negroes would not labour in the fields. French, Syrian, British, Latin—a secular salad of laughing, toiling, proud and gentle islanders, to whom a stranger is a guest and poverty no sin.

The island's economy may be primitive; its society is not.

The fishspear and the canvas bag were left for a little while in the Phoenician Store, and at ease with the world and its people I happily strolled the waterfront. The sun was low and a gentle breeze was washing away the heat, and from time to time a stranger would nod and murmur greeting. Lighters were unloading crated cargo from a steamer half a mile offshore, and a covey of fishing dories was tacking in to the long black beach.

There was money in my pocket, the adventures of the evening lay ahead. In some companionable cafe I would dine, and in this or the other bar there would be laughter, conversation, and new friends. Anything might happen and probably it would. Tomorrow was only a goatherd's song too distant to be heard. When survival holds no problems, and the sacred cow of conformity is seen to be only the hide of an ass stuffed with wind and sawdust, freedom from synthetic fears blesses the indolent man with a sense of harmony.

Was Tic-Tac down in Nevis, less than fifteen miles away? In gladness we would meet again; perhaps we would go to Curaçao, and then to Venezuela. Or Grenada? Trinidad? A thousand places and occasions waited on our pleasure, like coloured baubles on the shelf in the Thieves' Bazaar.

From across the road a confidential greeting cut through my reverie. "Hey, mistah!"

Ah, the first of the twilight hucksters. What would he be selling? Glass gems? Erotic postcards? His sister? A young man, he came trotting over.

"Mistah Peter, sir!"

I paused, searching his face as he drew close. A good-looking young fellow of twenty or so, pure Negro, clad in clean slacks and white singlet. He knew my name. But who the devil was he?

"You remembah me, sir?"

I grasped the hand he offered, but his smooth and regular features were standard equipment for so many of his race.

"Alexander Cricket, sir. You remembah me? That time I got troubles and you lif' me home?"

"Alexander! Of course," I answered warmly. "You thought I might forget?"

He had deserted an American charter boat whose empiric skipper had ill used and underpaid him, and I had carried him down-island on the *Zara* to his home. A hard-working lad of decent speech and manners, and an asset in foul weather.

"You are here, sir?" He scanned the bay. "Your boat is here?"

"No, I left her in St Thomas."

"Oh."

He was puzzled, but too well mannered to press me with a litany of questions, so I told him what had happened.

"You remember the American on board, the mate? His name was Murphy."

"Oh, yes." His tone had sobered. Neither he nor anyone else had thought very well of Murphy. Forty-two charter vessels operated out of St Thomas in the United States Virgin Islands, and the cut-throat competition bred bitter personal feuds. A report was made to the coastguard that a certain Australian was unlawfully in command of an American registered yacht which plied for hire, so Murphy was taken on to pass as skipper when entering and leaving United States waters. Accident-prone, unskilled and substantially a fool, he proved himself an actual source of danger, and his constant self-aggrandizement incurred the open scorn of many of our guests.

"Last trip," I continued, "it was just as if he had set out to wreck the ship one piece at a time. He jibbed in a squall and cracked the mizen, raised the main when the boom was fast and tore three dacron panels, then left the running backstay loose and all but ripped the mast out. Everything, from plugging the toilet with bandages to fouling the screw with a trailing line. So I marooned him. Put him ashore on Buck Island with a bottle of rum and a blanket, and left him there."

I chuckled as I recalled the scene; he had been reluctant to go. The thing had been done in the best tradition: twenty or so miles away was Treasure Island, beloved of Louis Stevenson, where unlucky buccaneers were occasionally marooned and left to fight to the death for a bottle of rum.

"All alone on a rock in the middle of the sea," I added, and Alexander laughed delightedly.

"O-oh, sir! Excuse me, I did not like that man. He vex me too much. He still there? He must die, on Buck Island. It got one lighthouse, no more, no water, nothing."

"The *Zara's* owner learnt about it after a couple of days, and went out and rescued him. But everyone was laughing by then. They laughed him right out of Yacht Haven, out of the Virgin Islands. The same afternoon he was rescued, he caught a plane back to the States."

"And then you quit?"

"Not long after. The coastguard heard about it. Murphy was skipper, on their papers. I'd mutinied against the skipper of a U.S. registered yacht. You can draw five years for that. I don't know what you'd get for marooning."

"Ah, so then you left, and came here?"

"Yes. And what about you? I thought you lived on St Lucia. What are you doing here?"

"Oh, this thing, that thing," he answered evasively, making a pattern in the dust with his toe.

"Do you have a spare room?" I suggested.

He glanced up, startled. "A room?"

"Yes. A place to sleep. You have a spare bed, or a hammock?"

"Oh-h, sir." But he was suddenly embarrassed, one could see. And why should such a simple request upset him?

"On the floor," I added. "I don't mind. Just for the night."

"Oh, but sir, it is not a good place. I live in a bad place."

"Oh? How bad?"

"Well, you see, sir, they are wicked people."

Well, here was a sorry thing, this innocent young shipmate had fallen among thieves. Perhaps I would have to rescue him again.

"What kind of wicked people?" I persisted. "Men? Women?"

"All kinds," he admitted miserably.

"Girls too?"

"Girls too."

Hah, the night held definite promise, even so early in the evening.

"But tell me, Alexander, what kind of wickedness? What do they do? Is it a cat-house? A casino? Marijuana? They print their own money? What happens there?"

"Everything happens there, sir."

Indeed. I would certainly have to visit such a fascinating place. "The Royal Hotel," he said suddenly, as one inspired. "Have you tried the Royal Hotel?"

I snorted politely, and laid a firm hand on his shoulder. "Alexander, my friend, take me to this wonderful little hell that you call home. You say everything happens there?"

He nodded unhappily. "It is not a good place for you, sir. It is a dark place, and not clean. And...and—"

"And what? Voodoo? Bugs? Jailbirds? What else?"

"The police, sir. They would not like a white man there."

"A pox on the police! What they like does not concern me."

He gazed at me inquiringly. "You do not like police?"

I took my hand from his shoulder and laughed, seeing how he might have mistaken me for an apostle of the law. And did his reluctance to take me to his private nest of lawless intrigue stem from the odd belief that I nursed policemen, like vipers, to my breast? What manner of place could it be, this seething warren of which he spoke?

"The police here," he said unexpectedly, "will try their best to help you. They wouldn't like to see you in bad places. They could help you find a room, sir. Or one of them might even take you home."

I studied him afresh, in growing alarm. Wings of Satan, was he a lover of police? Boilsuckers and buttscratchers one might learn to love: but police? The world is divided between authority and the others. Authority is comprised of those who traffic in restrictions: if they could, they would have restricted me from landing on St Kitts. Because they mistook me for a vagabond, with no hotel reservation and refusing to pay a bond, not even an onward ticket or as much as a pair of shoes, they had forbidden me to land. I would have to go on to other islands, for ever refused permission to land because of no onward ticket, around and around the Caribbean with British West Indian Airways in the manner of some modern Flying Dutchman.

But by then it was too late. I had already landed and the plane had gone, and though Negroes themselves they were reluctant to admit me to a prison full of Negroes. Immigration required that I report to them on Monday. Yet this Alexander Cricket loved police? Ah well, perhaps a child who knew no better would tongue a living snail, sucking at the bubbles it put forth. I glanced down admiringly at the new thong sandals I had bought, handsomely red and white.

"You like them?" I said.

"Oh yes, sir. The police are my best friends."

Eyes of a devil! He had seemed such a clean-living, pleasant sort of lad. What sort of a scorpion had I helped repatriate?

"They shoot dogs," he said suddenly. I blinked, wondering how the conversation had arrived at such a point. Certainly they shot dogs. The town was full of starving mongrels and the daily threat of rabies: but this was a civic duty, rather than a talent to admire.

"Personally," I said acidly, "I don't mind if they all drop dead."

"Dead? But they only eat the food that no one wants, and never cause a person any harm."

The man was raving mad. Whoever heard of policemen eating garbage, and causing no one harm? They planted fear like seeds of grain, watered them with threats, and reaped them with the sickle of suspicion.

"God made them so," he remarked.

Or the Devil hatched them out, pretending they were people.

"The worst they do is piddle on your trousers," he continued, "but they frighten robbers too."

What? This I must see, policemen piddling on other people's trousers.

"Are you discussing dogs?" I inquired suspiciously, "or policemen?"

"Dogs, of course!"

"Ah so. I was confusing them with policemen. I have nothing against dogs."

"Then—" he hesitated, sifting through our words—"you really mean it's police you don't like?"

"Exactly."

The frown which puckered his brow was smoothed away by a slow, uncertain smile.

"They are not your friends, sir? You would not invite them to my place?"

Ah, there was the rat that was blocking the drain: the white man was synonymous with control, larceny of freedom, and the law.

"I can't think of one small reason why I should. Police? They've put me in prison, shot at me, shuttled me back and forth across frontiers, forbidden me to go here and arrested me for going there, stolen money from me, deported me from half a dozen countries and blackened my character with fingerprints and photos. They've accused me of being a Communist, capitalist, Fascist, reactionary, revolutionary, and of not being a Communist, Fascist, and so on. If they find you with money they ask where you got it, and think of pretexts to take it away. If they find you without money, they call you a vagrant and put you in jail.

26

They stole my camera in Iraq and my pistol in Spain, stole my girl in Canada and my shoes in Siam. They even—"

"Your girl?" he broke in happily. "They stole your girl? What did they do to her?"

I shrugged with eloquent despair, warming to him once more.

"What do policemen do with the girls they steal? It is better not to think about it."

"Ah!" He breathed in robust sympathy. "Yes. And they shoot dogs."

Dogs, still?

"They shoot people, too," I observed pointedly. "They shot at me when I crossed into Soviet Germany, because they thought it wasn't a proper crossing place. In Columbia they destroyed my schooner with a case of dynamite, because they thought it had been carrying contraband. You must forgive me, Alexander, I do not love police."

"Fine, sir. I am glad. I don't love them too, and neither does my uncle. You know, they shot my little dog, for no reason?"

Good. Perhaps we need not mention dogs again. He glanced up the street, then down the street, and confidentially patted my arm.

"Come," he urged me happily, "let's go home to my place."

Alexander's warren of iniquity proved to differ somewhat from the hellhole I envisioned. Indeed it was not even in the town, but boldly sited on a hill beside a country track a full hour's march away; and as we walked, or sometimes rode double on the bicycle he had, balancing my sack, I cast back regretful glances at the gaily twinkling lights of Basseterre.

Amid the sweet and musky smell of canefields we came upon two houses, where an avalanche of yelping dogs and puppies poured upon us in the darkness to yap and lick his hands, and sniff my dungarees with suspicion. A Negro woman bearing a lantern came to the door of the nearest house to scold the dogs and call to Alexander, and he answered.

"That's my Aunt Bibby," he explained.

Aunt? He had mentioned an uncle, and here was an aunt as well. Doubtless there would be cousins and nieces too, and an album of family photographs, and a gaggle of children staring with thumbs stuffed in their mouths. Then where in Satan's name was the place he had described?

Bibby held the lantern high as we drew close, a fat and matronly figure whose handsome face inevitably lost its smile when she saw the white man there.

"Auntie? This is…is Mistah Peter."

"Oh."

She retreated as we approached, and we followed her inside. Faces stared in the light of the lamp: another woman, a beady-eyed old man, a teenage girl, and a pretty wee dumpling of a girl child.

There was silence. The comfortless and overstuffed silence of acute embarrassment.

"Good evening," I said guiltily to no one at all. No one said anything. They gazed unhappily at me, at my speargun, at each other. Alexander coughed dryly and crossed to a broken mirror, pretending to examine his teeth. Horns of a hairless goat, I was not prepared for this. I felt like an executioner abandoned to a nest of reproachful ghosts.

The old man, stooped and withered and all but swallowed by the sagging depths of an ancient cane-and-sacking chair, abruptly burst forth in a bellow of rage.

"Don't stand there staring like he some jumpy devil!" he roared. "Say something, you dang fool women. Let he set down, give he some tea. Show him he welcome here in this house."

Aunt Bibby slowly turned towards the kettle, the infant burst out crying and slid behind the couch.

"Dear God be with us now," someone crooned in pious despair.

"Set down, sir," the old fellow said kindly. "Take no notice of these fools, they only woman humbugs. Who you be? You be Alexander's friend?"

I wondered. He had promised to take me to some wondrous hell, and had brought me to purgatory instead.

"Gran'pa, he the man took me home St Lucia on he boat," Alexander explained belatedly. "I told you. That time I lef' my boat and got no money, he give me food and take me on he boat for free back home St Lucia."

Bibby swivelled on her heel with a gasp of surprise, and a delighted smile possessed her shining, oily face. The girl, a plump and comely wench, emitted a thin little whinny, Grandpa's dry old features crinkled in a toothless grin, and even the infant ceased her crying to peep out from the sofa.

Only the petulant scold in the corner preserved her sombre countenance, impaling me with a fixed and hostile stare.

"That man?" Bibby squealed. "And you come here? Oh, we glad for meet you!" She came to take me gently by the shoulders and kissed my cheek. "You done save our Alexander's life, he like to starve to death, he done tell us all about how you been good to he. Oh, I happy meet you. God's blessing, and arl."

"A good seaman brings good luck," I said, gratefully relaxing in a chair, "and he's brought good luck to me."

Alexander began explaining how we had met this afternoon, and how the *Zara*'s other white man had been left sitting on a rock, and while Grandpa climbed up and limped over to shake my hand the girl, with bashful glances, quickly slipped away to another room. As if she brooded on dark and occult things many centuries away, the woman in the corner, a golden-voiced misery of a shrew known as Olive, grimaced sourly.

"White marn in a black marn's house bring policeman to the door," she declared in lilting tones.

Grandpa released my hand and wheeled on her wrathfully.

"Don't vex me so, fool humbug! Every time you open a mouth, worm drop on a floor." He peered at the floor by her chair as if to discover worms.

"Be gentle, darlin'," said Bibby anxiously. "Don't make she sad."

"This marn be guest in my house for long as he can stay. If—" turning again to me—"these catermiauls don't fret you, and you don't mind for eat and sleep with carmon bardies."

I threw a searching glance about the room. "Don't see no common bodies." I smiled. "Only special folk." He chuckled as he went back to his chair.

"An' you from far Australia," Bibby said in wonder, as she brought a cup of tea. "I don't know that place. Fus' time I ever meet a people from that place. You Christian people there?"

"Some, yes."

"White folks don't keep sabbath," Olive ungraciously intoned.

"And some coloured folks," said Grandpa testily, "come home from chapel with he mouth stopped up with worms!"

"Eeh, don't be disgustehn!"

"Bibby, where them two fool sons of mine?"

"Out back bottlin', dear. Supper soon be ready, they come then. Lord, Lord," she mused, stirring something at the stove, "Australia, tha's far away. You got coloured people there?"

"Yes," I said uncomfortably, recalling that the Government had only recently, and reluctantly, admitted they were people. Why, Aunt Bibby herself was more of a human being that half of Canberra's politicians lumped together. "Supper smells good."

"Humble food," she said, but smiled her pleasure. "Rice and beans, and shark. Not so good as what you sometimes have, I could guess."

"You might be surprised. I was so hungry once I ate a dead mongoose."

"You eat a mongoose? Lord, Lord!" She glanced anxiously about the room and demanded suddenly, "Where Pussy?"

Did she suspect me of designs upon her cat? But the fat, little child came out from behind the sofa, and wandered over to clutch her mother's sturdy leg.

"Sweet darlin'," Bibby murmured. "Don't stray, now."

"Eh, mongoose," Olive muttered with distaste.

"Well, marn can eat a mongoose," Grandpa snapped. "Can eat a frog, a snake, a rat, a—"

"Eeh, you too disgustehn!" she carolled.

"Heh, You eatin' sheep's bowels an' arl, and yet you say a marn can't—" He broke off in astonishment as the teenage girl drifted forth from the other room clad in a shimmering slip of bright red satin, with a ribbon in her short, kinky hair and white shoes on her feet. "Jacqueline, what in hell you up to?"

"Lord!" Bibby cried again, catching sight of her. "You goin' to chapel, girl? This be Fridee night, not Sundee marnin'!"

Jacqueline halted in embarrassment, squirming as she clasped her hands, and grinned down at the floor. She was certainly not more than seventeen, and although pleasing to the eye had already assumed proportions suggesting overripeness at a very early date. Olive sniffed, and Grandpa winked at me.

"Jumpy* hidin' by the roadside," he said slyly. "Watch out where you walk."

Bibby glanced at me obliquely as she turned back to the stove.

"Oh-ho, yes. Jacqueline goin' eat you up, she got on her courtin' clothes."

There seemed to be nothing appropriate to say. Jacqueline fled to the door and hid half of herself in the night outside, but after a little while, when the others were not looking, she turned her head to catch my glance and gave me a frank, mischievous smile.

Alexander followed my gaze, and managed a polite, stiff smile.

"I must take you to meet my uncles," he suggested. "Outside in the shed."

"And tell them supper's ready in five minutes," Bibby said.

It was the shed outside which proved to be the focus of Alexander's concern about police: but even here there were no women, no girls, not even the hint of brimstone or so much as a human femur. Just two middle-aged uncles, who pottered about by the light of a hurricane lamp clinking jars and setting siphons, conversing softly in broad dialect to punctuate long intervals of silent industry. Their names were Littlejohn and Desmond, and here in this old shack they clandestinely bottled their own moonshine, stuffing in penny corks and adding plain, gummed labels entitled, in magnificent understatement, with the solitary word, RUM.

If bottles randomly acquired chanced to hold the dregs of turpentine, paraffin, or bleach, such accidents served to lend sophistication to an uncommonly raw provincial rum. Bottles and jars winked softly in the lamp's uncertain light, iron petrol drums and wooden boxes and litter were lined about the walls: but although we met in darkness we met well, for their love of Alexander was backed by kindred blood.

"Anybardy help our Alexander, he our fren' for true," Desmond said simply, his thick horny hand pumping mine.

"For true," chimed in Littlejohn, "for true. He done well for bring

*Devil

you."

"And better here than in that wicked town. Fightin', teefin', fornicatin' for money. Here we got no money, but we has fun jus' the same."

Jacqueline giggled from somewhere near at hand, and Alexander fidgeted. Desmond was a pious bachelor who recurrently fell victim to the power of his own rum, which reduced his morals to a dry sponge and hurled him forth to soak up the depravities of town. Littlejohn was Bibby's husband, a self-confessed and raw-boned sinner of droll humour and engaging knavery. Well, I had fallen among good company at least. One should not complain.

Later, when we all sat at food, we discussed the manufacture of bush rum. They drank Andre's cognac, I drank appalling rum for politeness' sake, and before the night was done the uncles had agreed that on the morrow I should go with them to see their secret moonshine still, hidden in the jungle at the foot of a volcano.

Littlejohn and I stood on top of a mossy, old hardwood log and peered into the clearing, straining to see over the top of a sweetmaid bush to the crude sugar-mill which belonged to Shilling Richness. Shilling and his woman were down in the town carousing, even though today was Sunday, but one never knew who else might be around.

"Nobardy," Littlejohn murmured, but his mellow West Indian drawl was touched by anxiety. "Nobardy at all, it bein' Sundee and everybardy away."

Through the trees beyond the clearing we could just glimpse distant Basseterre, candy coloured in the Caribbean sun, and Littlejohn drew comfort from the sight. Doubtless in imagination he saw Shilling Richness at wine, drinking the rough red wine he favoured and which his own sloop smuggled in, camouflaged in diesel drums, from the French port of Marigot. Shilling would spend all Sunday down there on the coast, Littlejohn assured me; and he wished now that he had brought some extra cans, which he could have filled at leisure and hidden in the bush and picked up later.

A slobbering snort in the bushes near by caused us to wheel in alarm. It was only Sweet'n-Sour, Littlejohn's ass, who in rubbing her tight muzzle against her foreleg had tickled her nose on a twig. The muzzle was an old British Army webbing belt, firmly secured about her nose so she could not shatter the Sunday peace with her brazen hee-haw.

"Watch that damn' arse," Littlejohn cautioned me. "Make more noise than ten fat women, if you let her."

He took the two empty five-gallon cans and, after final brief inspection of the clearing, he went off towards the mill, picking his way deftly among small hazards of brush and old fencing-wire and discarded hardware, half crouching, gingerly hefting the cans out of the way of obstacles. It was almost mid morning; with luck we would be back at the still by noon.

Safe within a thicket of West Indian oak I waited with Sweet'n-Sour, marvelling that daylight robbery should prove such a facile affair for one who devoted much of his time to moonshine. One might have considered the theft the more easily accomplished after dusk, but Littlejohn had once been pursued through the night by some unmannerly caretaker who leapt out at him from behind a pile of bags: his lantern had fallen and broken as he turned to flee, and in the utter darkness he had rushed this way into a fence which pricked him with barbs, that way into a stack of cans which spilled upon him with a fearful clatter, and finally charged blindly into the caretaker and escaped in a dither of excitement which left him twittering with fear and imagination.

Thereafter he avoided such excursions after dark.

Sweet'n-Sour was rolling her head rhythmically to and fro and gazing vaguely at the sky with an aspect of religious ecstasy, while she scratched her plump flank on facilities provided by a gnarled tree-trunk; and I pondered the relative merits of being man and ass. It seemed there were drawbacks to this business of being white, of being a European on an island tenanted by Negroes. One was not fully accepted as one of them, there was a colour bar, discrimination of a sort; certain things, as a white man, one was not allowed to do. Since my arrival three days ago I had found myself distinguished by the colour of my skin. Bronzed although it was, it could not match the lustrous black of its Kittsonian compeers. It was not allowed to pay for drink or food, and was discouraged from sleeping in peace alone:

indeed, it was at times embarrassed by the princely bounty of these dark and lusty Caribbean kings.

It could not even steal; this was forbidden. Littlejohn had brushed aside my pleas, declaring white men were such mighty thieves as should not stoop to snatching raw cane-juice, which be called molasses. Yet I knew the goodness of his heart would not expose his guest to danger. Someone had to stay with Sweet'n-Sour, he had insisted, and reproachfully I watched him sneak away like a questing stoat with the two five-gallon cans.

A black man could steal molasses. A white man would be stared at, the very birds would nudge one another and squawk in astonishment, asking who he was, and why he was taking black man's molasses. Could he not afford honest honey?

Littlejohn disappeared within the darkened confines of the shambling old mill. To one side was a great charred mound where the juiceless fibre of the pulverized cane was dumped, and occasionally burned; by the mill entrance, at the head of a rutted track which led in from broad canefields which swarmed the gentle hills, were several tons of uncrushed cane and the ancient diesel which supplied the plant with power. Somewhere within the gloomed shadows, which old corrugated iron and blackened timbers held in captive secrecy, Littlejohn was furtively at work dipping molasses from an old brick vat.

The minutes slowly passed, the bush was still.

Abruptly the peace was broken by a fearsome bellow of rage. "Yarrgh!"

Sweet'n-Sour started in alarm and pricked her ears, and I surveyed the mill with concern. It had not been Littlejohn who cried out. Who, then? Was he being attacked? Subdued sounds of high excitement commenced to issue from the mill; there was another terrible cry and the sound of something heavy crashing to the floor. Littlejohn appeared almost at once, bent by the weight of the two full cans, darting hunted looks about him while his bare, horny feet scissored rapidly towards our hiding-place.

A black monster of a man loomed from the shadows, behind him clutching an ancient shotgun. Why, it was Shilling Richness after all. He had doubled on his tracks and come back. Perhaps he had fought with his woman? An enormous fellow, naked except for a bedsheet which draped his massive flanks. He raised the shot-gun and took aim at the scudding Littlejohn.

"*Burry-flum-brrrr!*"

Shilling reeled and grasped at a roofing support for balance: at once it was apparent he was pickled with wine or rum. The roofing support gave way, and the bulk of Shilling Richness capsized on a pile of cane, followed by an avalanche of corrugated iron and rotten timbers.

Within seconds Littlejohn had gained the shelter of the thicket, puffing breathlessly and grunting with exertion. As he lowered the cans in relief, he glanced behind to gauge the chances of pursuit, but no one was coming. Turning from me, he directed his water against the nearest tree, for the shock had unsettled his bladder and caused him damp distress. Presently, with a vast sigh of relief, he turned to me.

"That dog Shillun' done come home!" he declared with mild reproach. "Las' night he swear he goin' Basseterre. You know, that Shillun' be jus' one damn' big liar. There ain't no greater liar," he said profoundly, stooping to heft one can, "than a man who can't tell the troot."

Sweet'n-Sour rolled her eyes wickedly and flicked her tail, farted threateningly and, being a West Indian ass, sought the merest chance to grab the seat of someone's pants in her strong yellow teeth. I steadied the rig amidships as her master swung up the first can and secured it, and then he lashed the second can on the other side. We were moving away from the scene of the crime at a brisk trot before he had tied the last knot in the rope.

The still was two hours' march away, but little more than ten-minutes' brisk walk from Shilling Richness's property we chanced upon a man and a small boy with a sturdy, little pony saddled, like Sweet'n-Sour, with a pair of tin cans. The cans were empty. As the pair came towards us, they inspected us with interest; doubtless their errand was the same as ours, but one might forgive them for wondering what the white man's mission was.

"Sundee," said the stranger, pausing on the track. He was a man of Littlejohn's age, but not so tall, and padded with more flesh: his heavy jowls and handsome belly suggested richer eating.

"Eh-eh, Sundee," Littlejohn agreed, causing Sweet'n-sour to halt.

"What you teefin', Littlejohn?" the other casually demanded. "Why you teefin' arl that sweetness, marn? For make it country liquor?"

"Pay good money for molasses, marn. Put it arn a bread."

"How you mean? How many bread you got?"

Littlejohn sucked his teeth and sulked. According to his tone, he was not pleased to meet the stranger, who studied me in speculative fashion and gave a little nod.

"Sundee," he said carefully.

"Eh-eh, Sundee," I replied. For a little while no one could think of anything to say. The stranger scratched his ear, brows raised high as he looked at this and that, and Littlejohn flicked at bees which were foundering in sticky juice, and licked his finger.

"Molasses," the other commented finally. "Whut for you use molasses, Littlejohn?"

"Pig eat it, marn, for true. Make sweet pork."

"Ah didden' know you was pig, marn. Why you pick out a bee, if molasses be for pig?"

"Pig can't eat a bee, fool," said Littlejohn, nettled. "Make he belly hot."

Benjamin darted me a quick glance, and chuckled complacently.

"You big humbug, Littlejohn. If can't tell troot, keep mouth shut." He urged his pony, crowding past us. "Take it damn' molasses go feed a bloody pig!"

As we continued on our way, Littlejohn sucked his teeth with vexation, thinking of all the things he might have said.

"That Benjamin," he confided, "can bring bad luck. He be a Judas marn, make trouble for everybardy." But then he laughed merrily, and joyfully declared, "Ho, but this time he find trouble for heself. Where he goin' now? He goin' straight to Shillun' Richness' place. For why? For steal molasses. Ho-ho, and what he goin' find, that Benjamin? He goin' find Shillun' Richness hidin' in the rubbidge with a gun!"

He slapped his thigh and danced a little jig, so that Sweet'n-Sour snorted in alarm and bared her teeth. And so in happy mood we passed on through brush and fields of cane and by solitary homesteads, making for the forests which clothed the higher slopes. As we climbed, we could look south to the regular volcano cone of Nevis Island, where Tic-Tac might or might not be, and north-west to Eustatius and Saba: the sunshot pastel flare of distant Basseterre was stippled with marigold and copper.

The moonshine still was hidden in a cleft between two hills, and housed a palm-thatch lean-to beside a sulphurous warm stream. The jungle crowded close, the thin little trail concealed in heavy undergrowth; only a soft green glow could filter through massed foliage overhead and the forest floor was perpetually sodden, choked with vines and ferns and thick with mouldering debris. Apart from muted birdcalls and the shrilling chirp of insects, the towering woods were hushed with a churchly quietude: the bubbling spring alone breathed life in the little vale, steaming with its sulphur smells and host to a thousand butterflies of jade and gold and purple, crimson and velvet black.

The still had been set up here largely because of the presence of the stream, for the temperature of the fermenting mash could be maintained easily at seventy degrees by artful use of the water's constant heat. Insufficient heat would slow the action of the yeast, and a rise of a few degrees would provoke too rapid action, so that following a brief but furious life it would yawn and go to sleep.

The fermenting tank held all of a hundred gallons. Littlejohn and Desmond usually managed to fill it every second or third week with cane-juice, bananas, mangoes, chopped cane and ears of corn and sweet potatoes stolen from here and there and brought up in sacks on Sweet'n-Sour. From the markets they gleaned bruised plums, damaged papaya, and half-rotten pineapples, even avocado pears and yellow guavas. When the mash had fermented for four and a half days, it was transferred to an old donkey-engine boiler, fired, and the steam run off through an intricate maze of old scrap piping to a series of jars and cans and buckets. Then a rickety bamboo viaduct channelled water to rinse the apparatus, and the still was left abandoned until materials for another mash could be traded for or stolen.

No charcoal was used to cleanse fusel and poisons and raw, unblended aldehydes and esters from the primary distillate. But, whatever might have happened to their customers, the uncles themselves continued to survive.

The fermenting tank was almost full that Sunday night, for on Saturday the uncles had ferried up supplies and this final ten gallons of molasses would ensure the sugar content of a healthy, robust brew. Therefore we slept in the lean-to, and on the Monday morning mixed and fired the mash, squashing up the pulpy fruit complete with skins and seeds, and piping in warm water from the bamboo viaduct.

Desmond, who read the holy book, firmly believed Thou shalt not Muzzle the Ox that Treads the Corn, and Monday's ceremony of the mash was accompanied by frequent libations of bush rum. A large gourd of the previous distillate was on hand for this very purpose. We would toil for a little while, perspiring in the forest's sultry heat, then sit to rest on an old log and share a teacup full of rum. Littlejohn drank with profane relish, but Desmond found occasion to drink more. First he blistered his ankle on a faggot's fiery end, then fell over backwards across an empty can, and finally, while tonguing at guava seeds which had lodged themselves in his mouth, he dropped his teeth in the mash itself and seemed to have a devilish time finding and fishing them out. With each such small misfortune he would repair to the old log with the teacup half full of rum, and his pious comments of early morning had changed, by noon, to guttural outbursts of blasphemous profanity.

The heat and toil and forest vapours must have overcome us, for we all fell asleep, and I woke in early afternoon to the sound of Desmond cursing.

"Damn' yam-headed fool! Bloody yam grow inside a haid."

Yams, I pondered drowsily. He had found yams growing in someone's head. I began drifting off to sleep again.

"Y'hear me?" he shouted angrily. "Ninglarn. Lazy, long damn' nogood he-mule! Ninglarn!"

Devil take his shouting. What was a ninglarn? I opened one eye and saw him sitting there. He had grasped one of Littlejohn's big feet and was banging it on the ground.

"Wake, you long fool. Tell you, ah goin' Ninglarn!"

What's this? Going to England? By the gods, the man was drunk! Who would want to go to England in this heat? Littlejohn woke, roughly kicked Desmond's hand loose, and sat up to lean tiredly against the log. His gaze wandered slowly around the clearing with the uncertainty of fleeting amnesia, and came to rest on Desmond's face.

"Ah goin' Basseterre, take big boat for goin' Ninglarn!"

Well, thousands of others had gone, to shiver in London's slums: and the lucky ones who managed to return invariably painted their journey in high colours. If one believed them, a Negro had only to land in London to clothe himself with European privilege and set about amassing easy treasure.

"Go, marn," said Littlejohn. "But fus' give me tobacco."

Desmond fumbled for his last tobacco scrap. It would never have occurred to him to keep it for himself.

"No more be vex by that damn' arse," he said thickly, referring to Sweet'n-Sour. "No more work for make people down there fat." Doubtless he spoke of the merchants who paid him pennies for his rum. "Goin' Ninglarn onna big boat, marn." He appeared to be resentful that Littlejohn remained so unimpressed.

"Is never mind," said his brother expansively, "if you go all a way to Trinidad. Long as you come back by…by Fridee evenin'." Fermenting of the mash would take that long, and Desmond would be needed to help with the distilling. Desmond sucked his teeth impatiently, his attitude implying that no one could make a fool like Littlejohn understand about these things.

"Don' humbug me, marn," he pleaded. "Goin' take one full week before that boat fin' Ninglarn. And ain't comin' back to this small island, finish with it now."

Littlejohn scratched himself, and made his cigarette.

"Island big enough," he said. This was, as I learnt, portion of the pattern of their lives. It was time for Desmond to go down to the big town, to roister in the taverns and tumble a girl or two. "You got money?"

"T'ree dahlar."

Sufficient at least for rum, at forty cents a quart, even if he did not take his own.

"Bring me back tobacco," Littlejohn instructed him, and Desmond assumed a grieved air.

"Goin' Ninglarn," he muttered, "an' he aks me bring back tobacco. Oh, marn!"

As if to cement the occasion we all shared a cup of rum, and then another, and Desmond set out for Basseterre. I decided to go with him as far as the house, and off we stumbled down the trail with Desmond lurching in the lead, cursing stones which struck at him and branches which moved cunningly to hinder his way. Supported by his vision of fame and wealth to be discovered in far England, he blundered down among the hills without bothering to rest, and in the course of time we arrived at the house. Dogs streamed out to greet us. As drunk with anticipation as with rum, his bold decision fostering a fine sense of importance, he advanced upon the house and brushed Jacqueline aside when the girl ran out to meet us.

"Make way, marn!" he announced with a touch of arrogance. "You see a person on his way goin' Ninglarn."

"Oh, glory be!" cried Jacqueline, and gave me an inquiring stare. Grandpa poked his head out of a window, and from within the house Bibby roared with laughter.

"Ho-ho, Desmond dear goin' Ninglarn, be goin' paddle one raft with he harns!"

"Drunken fool," said Olive derisively, replacing Grandpa at the window. "Bottle talkin'."

Grandpa came to the door and eyed Desmond curiously. Desmond paused just outside and stared back, hands akimbo and gently swaying.

"Better nobardy vex me," he drawled, shifting his gaze to Olive. He was feeling weary, but as strong as three white mules. "Ah said, Ah goin' Ninglarn. You see me goin' now. Ah come for me dancin' clothes. And don't nobardy give me any shit!"

A muffled squeal of laughter issued from the shack, and Olive sniggered. Desmond subdued her with a lusty epithet.

"Ah think you can go, son," said Grandpa thoughtfully, moving aside to let us enter. "Ef you got the right feelin' at jus' the right time, jus' the right amount of rum and the big boat waitin' there, Ah think you can go. Pay these quackin' women no heed, son. They don't none of 'em unnerstarn a marn's business." And turning to me, "'Evenin', Mistah Peter, you goin' Ninglarn too?"

"No, Grandpa," I said. "That place too far for me. Maybe I'll go back in the morning and give Littlejohn a hand. He wants tobacco."

"Well," the old man said uneasily, "Ah dunno, Ah jus' dunno at arl."

Alexander nodded as I entered the room, but his glance fell away as I smiled, and Bibby's greeting seemed a little strained. Was something wrong, I wondered? Could something be amiss? Pussy waddled fatly towards Desmond, stumbled and fell on the floor, decided not to cry and expectantly looked to him to pick her up. He seized her gladly and swung her high, then rested her astride her hip.

"You comin' too, chile? Comin' Ninglarn with me?"

He held her for a moment and then set her down, and went into the other room to find the orange crate where be stored his dancing clothes. They consisted of a pair of good plum-coloured shoes and a turquoise shirt, finery for festivals and trips to Basseterre.

"White marn bring police!" Olive purled triumphantly, and a hush fell on the room. I looked around at Grandpa, Bibby, Alexander, but they dropped their eyes and looked elsewhere.

"Alexander, did police come here?"

He wriggled with embarrassment, staring out the window.

"Policeman come," chimed Olive. "Come to the door for aks where white marn be, and why."

Ah, so soon, it was unexpected. Had someone seen me come here? But, if they had, surely no one would bother reporting to police. There would be no point. But Desmond now stood at the door of the second room, scowling ferociously.

"Damn' bastard Judas man Benjamin!" he cried. "That marn done make harm for we, tell it damn' policeman."

"Like I said would happen," Olive intoned righteously.

"Shut a mouth!" Grandpa shouted.

"And comin' back inna marnin'," she went on.

"Shut, shut!" the old fellow howled, launching himself towards her. "Shut a mouth woman, or I cut he tongue for feed a dog! Guest in my house be welcome!" He struck feebly at her, but she ducked and moved away at once fearful and exultant.

"Calm, calm," said Bibby anxiously. "Keep God's peace. Mis' Peter know what he goin' do."

Why yes, there was only one thing to do. To keep God's peace in the house, and policemen away from the door, I would have to go away. The very thing which Alexander feared had come to pass. I had already brought embarrassment, and if I stayed I might well invite disaster.

The matter was discussed as we all sat at supper. Desmond forgot to go to England and fell asleep at table, Grandpa was reluctant to admit that I must leave, Bibby wept a little, and Alexander glumly kept surveillance on Jacqueline's tender gestures of distress. That night I slept in the house again.

At first light, before the others were awake, I quietly rose and went down to Basseterre to take the ferry on to Nevis Island.

2

NEVIS ISLAND

The Weak Degenerate

THE great chain of islands swinging east and south from Puerto Rico to the coast of Venezuela forms a quadrant of vestigial colonies peopled largely by the heirs of Negro slaves. The white man's commerce is maintained by a seasoning of professional expatriates; but a piquant spice is added, from the tropical Left Bank of St Thomas to the slums of Trinidad, by a soupçon of social deviates from North America and Europe.

Some are refugees from police, or wives, or other forms of organized oppression; others there are who escape from urban obscurity to strut in the flickering candlelight of pale-skin prestige. Some delude themselves in search for the golden beach: others deceive the world at large to feed on the generosity of fools. Visionaries, sensualists, fugitives and seekers—essentially individualists warring with some aspect of convention or craving the distant lotus, they are characterized by forms of odd behaviour the more easily practised among tolerant Caribbeans.

Odd indeed was the quaint quartet who discovered me on Nevis.

A lone white man stood at the head of the jetty, lean and blond, perhaps thirty, and as the throng of arriving passengers poured forth from the ferry burdened with merchandise from the markets of Basseterre I was aware of his careful scrutiny. Not an unusual thing. I was the only European who arrived, my luggage was stowed in a striped sack and slung across my shoulder, and one hand gripped a vicious-looking speargun; but there was thoughtful speculation in his gaze which suggested he might soon find some excuse to ask me questions.

A familiar figure, I decided; the ardent exile who eats loneliness, ever ready to snatch the stranger to his bosom and suck his heart for the sweetness of admiring sympathy. Ah, but was he? No rigid formula could anticipate the pattern of such folk; and I wondered who he was.

But walking resolutely I passed by, for ahead in the lane which led to the village centre I had glimpsed a brief vision, a flash of blue and ruby-gold, a gay blue dress sheathing supple curves and crowned with a disciplined wealth of hair sunfired to citrine copper. And during that first brief moment when a traveller arrives in a new place he has the unquestioned privilege to address whom he pleases. But even as I boldly moved towards her she entered a car, glanced back once, and drove away.

An unfamiliar figure, I decided ruefully, and wondered who she was. But it seemed impossible that she could hide for long in a village of this size.

The faded elegance of Charlestown remembers with regret the days when this small, but charming village was a centre for the socially *élite*, a health resort for wealthy West Indies colonists who came to the tiny island to bathe in thermal spas and take the cure. The once fashionable houses lining the single street have been transformed to humble stores and beerhouses, stuffed to overflowing with modest vendors and their kin. Hemmed in by brush and by palm-fringed beaches either side, the shabby little dowager crowds close to the jetty as if about to embark, like the whites who abandoned her, and sail away.

The original capital had been Jamestown, but it was submerged in a tidal wave three centuries before and slid down under the sea with all the inhabitants.

Since Nevis was regarded as a province of St Kitts, neither immigration nor police were crouched in ambush, and having left my chattels in a tavern I hopefully walked forth to expose myself to such as might happen to one here. No matter where one goes there is something waiting there, strange new fellowships or unpredictable adventures which for ever remain unknown and untasted unless one takes the trouble to arrive.

The blond, young man was waiting just along the waterfront. The knee-sprung corduroy trousers and demoralized tennis shoes offered little cause for comment, but the sweat-sucked nylon shirt, socks and even wool-string tie were of an identical saffron shade suggesting careful effort to impress. His bleached Zapata moustache and uncut hair appeared as a studied attempt to be mistaken for some despairing left-wing intellectual with a pocketful of unsold tracts, enthroned on top of the usual mushroom cloud.

"I say," he said, "did you see the seven virgins when you were in Basseterre?"

I was frankly surprised. It seemed a tall order for a town like Basseterre. Even in the Virgin Islands the definition of a virgin was a three-year-old girl who could outrun her four-year-old brother.

"No," I said, haltingly. "I don't think so."

"Pity." By his tone and manner he was obviously English. "But perhaps we'll be lucky, the odd one comes here."

A valuable discovery.

"The odd virgin?" He seemed passing odd himself, but quite friendly.

"No no, the odd film. *The Seven Virgins*. My brother has a part in it, Paul Selwyn. Oh, pardon me, my name's Geoffry."

We introduced ourselves, and commenced to stroll through the village discussing unimportant things.

"I've been here six weeks now," he confided after some minutes, "and you've no idea what an incredible collection of snobs live here in Charlestown. Of course the Europeans were top dogs before, but when they left their status was taken over by their bastards, locals with high colour. And they've invented degrees of caste and breeding to the nth degree. All a matter of light colour and straight hair. High colour being those with more than half European blood, down through second-class high colour to proud low colour, second-class low colour and low-minded low colour with kinky hair and just a touch of white. They look such easygoing blighters, but their passion for precedence and social climbing is unbelievable. Colonials, y'know. No bigger snob than a colonial. Of course the black Negroes don't have to worry, they're right at the bottom of the ladder anyway." He patted his hair affectionately and added, with a smile of satisfaction, "I must say I don't have to worry either. We whites are right at the top of the scale. With my fair hair and fine fair skin I'm practically a peer of the realm."

And the greatest snob of all, apparently.

"You're American, of course?" he inquired; and not wishing to jeopardize my new-found status by admitting I was merely a "colonial" myself, and an Australian one at that, my silence allowed him to assume that he was right. Several varied years spent between the Arctic and the Panama Canal had lent an American accent to my speech: life is sometimes easier if one adopts the protective colouring of one's daily environment.

"I'm quite fond of some Americans," he admitted thoughtfully.

"As a matter of fact there's one here. You'll meet her soon enough.

Complete phoney, but quite pleasant in her own way. She thinks I'm a phoney too; but, of course, that's inevitable."

He observed me suspiciously for a moment.

"I wouldn't judge you," he said cautiously, "to be a very, er…a very close follower of conventional morality?"

"No, I suppose not." A camp-follower, perhaps, at best.

"Good. Moral laws are only expedient inventions to regulate the functions of a society, anyway. The individual is supposed to contribute to his society: I don't contribute, so, they call me a phoney. I've been called a phoney for as long as I can remember. I'm not. I'm a thinker. But I'm damned if I'll do other people's thinking for them."

He challenged me with a distraught frown. Possibly he was confusing moral and positive law, but even moral law appears imperfectly contrived, changing shape as intellect evolves, so I merely nodded.

"I don't know what you are," he went on with gathering intensity, "and it's no concern of mine. But I know what I am—I'm a thinker. An esoteric thinker. To think in abstract beauty is the ultimate value of the greatest forms of art."

He observed me for a moment to see how I was bearing up.

"To write poetry is nothing, you merely prostitute inspiration and the intellectual spectrum to a hopelessly limited form of communication. A form of communication limited by statutes governing public acceptance." He beat one fist rhythmically on the palm of his hand. "I am not interested in reason. I am not a logician. I am only interested in the essences of beauty. I am an artist," he enthused, "but I paint without colours. I translate impressions into ecstasies. My brain is an alchemist, it is a powerhouse. Matter is gross, and only the abstract has infinite beauty."

He dwelt at length on abstruse matters and I politely listened, wondering if the moderate brain of man was really an adequate vehicle for analysing absolutes. Was he happy, this Englishman, locked up on an island for which he seemed to have no love? We passed by a grizzled Negro selling sweetmeats from a gaily painted little barrow: he wore a floppy, old straw hat, tattered singlet, and pink pyjama trousers which threatened to slide down from his hips; and his barrow, with its three brass bells, was entitled "Reviving Texas". He favoured us with an easy grin, and I replied in kind as we sauntered by. Was he less happy in his humble way of life than the Geoffries who scourged themselves with visions of serenity?

Visions…the vision in blue and gold was coming down the stairs from lawyer Walwyn's office, and I was strongly aware of her. Would Geoffry know her? Or how could I address her?

He paused in his soliloquy and nudged me.

"That's her. The American type I mentioned. Not quite my cup of tea, really. Claims she's a Hollywood movie producer. Bloody rot. Runs around with an expensive movie camera, with no film in it, pretending to take pictures."

As she smiled and came to meet us, one could see she was in her early thirties, but maturity had lent her gracious carriage and trained her in convivial acquaintance. Her face suggested gentleness clothing sudden spirit, and the sprinkling of freckles only served to accent the natural vigour of the upswept incandescence of her hair.

"Geoffry! You've been avoiding me. I called to you this morning and you pretended not to hear." He opened his mouth irresolutely, but she turned to me smiling. "How are you? I saw you arrive this morning, but I had to rush away to see my lawyer." She laughed softly, and my heart twitched as she went on. "I knew you couldn't hide for long in a little place like this, anyway. Geoffry, aren't you going to introduce us?"

" Uh…."

"My name's Lee," she went on. We introduced ourselves, while Geoffry stood limply at our side. One gained the impression that she scarcely admired him—or, womanlike, was she determined to provoke him, to see how much he cared?

"Well, I'm off," he said abruptly. "I've got some things to do."

"Wait! Have you seen Pearl?"

"No, and I don't particularly wish to. She's a raving lunatic. Bye."

We began walking slowly, Lee and I, back towards the centre of the town, with Geoffry grimly stalking off ahead. He had soon disappeared.

"A nice boy, Geoffry," she remarked, "but trying so hard to be theatrically effete. Did he tell you he was an esoteric thinker?"

"Yes."

"He carries a knife at his own throat. And you—you carry the oddest-looking luggage I've ever seen. Even the darkies were staring at you, and grinning. Didn't you notice?"

"It's a mistake to carry luggage at all. When you arrive somewhere, you have to find a place to put it, and then keep coming back to it like a yo-yo."

"You're not American, are you? You talk a little like one. I'm from Los Angeles myself, home and husband in Beverly Hills. I've been down here six months now working on the story and groundwork for a film; but I'm not going to bring my crew down until after the hurricane season. What are you doing here?"

"Drifting down-island."

"Where to?"

"Oh, South America finally, I think."

"Lucky you, then. I'm beginning to feel as if I'm in a prison. My God, I've been having a difficult time."

Five months of malicious gossip within the confines of a closed community had, she revealed, almost driven her into the ground. Strikingly attractive, socially gifted, radiating a curiously feminine appeal designed to unsettle husbands and infuriate their women, she provided an exquisite contrast and bitter threat to, local planters' prissy wives whose worn and ragged charms had become too slack to support the further attentions of their men. Scissoring tongues had done their best to shame, humiliate, slander and destroy her; and at times, almost friendless amid hostility, her courage had barely controlled her urge to flee. Her critics sought to prove that she was not from Hollywood, had no company, was not and never had been in films, was not and never would be a producer.

"But I'm almost ready now," she confided. For a little way we walked in silence, until abruptly she turned to me with a searching stare, examining my face, and said quite unexpectedly, "I think I want you. Come on, let's go down to the beach. There won't be anybody there."

Ghost of a flippant turtle, I thought happily, here is a woman of decision. One might hardly expect a lady of her calibre to proposition a total stranger on such slight provocation. The beach, then? We passed through a narrow lane and came out on grassy ground leading to the beach and its secluded ranks of palms: and her obvious impatience infused me with both wonder and desire. But when we reached a sheltered place far from prying eyes she motioned me to sit with her.

"Let me tell you part of the story," she said. "There are five minor leads. One of them concerns a Nevis Island planter, a white man, who is utterly degenerate. He not only souses himself in rum, but also cheats and lies, abuses his Negro slaves, and uses the prettiest girls absolutely as he pleases. Generally, he's a drunken profligate. But he takes ship to England, and there he marries one of London's most desirable debs. He's a *poseur*, you see. He can be quite charming when he wants to. Follow me? Then he returns to Nevis ahead of her, and she's to come out on the next boat. But as soon as he gets home he reverts to his old ways, and of course she arrives a little later to discover she's married to a drunken profligate. A weak degenerate."

An appalling specimen indeed, I decided, impatient to receive her promised favours.

"You'd fit that role like a glove," she fervently announced.

"Role?"

"The part of the weak degenerate, in my film. Capable of a certain amount of charm, but absolutely without morals. A sly, dissolute villain."

Dogs' codpieces, what was happening? Her words rang in my ears like cracked cathedral bells. Dissolute villain? Weak degenerate? Even if there had been anything to say I could not have trusted myself to speak. Rarely had my pride been so professionally trounced.

"It's in your face," she went on without mercy. "Just the right touch of make-up, and you'd be absolutely perfect."

What was wrong with my face, so suddenly? It was commonly accepted as an ordinary face, passing without comment. Never had it been insulted with such devastating sincerity.

"How interesting," I murmured huskily, but the comment came forth like the sound of a seal clearing its throat. Desire had fled, supplanted by an urgency to hide.

"Would you agree to accept the role, if tests turn out all right?"

"Oh, but of course," I rasped mockingly. But I mocked myself—I, who had assumed with such incredible presumption that she wanted me. Why, if I so much as dabbed her bosom with holy oil, she would flinch away in horror.

Weak degenerate, indeed!

As she chattered on about her plans to use other local people, and her ambition to be Hollywood's first female movie producer, I brooded darkly on certain recent events which seemed to prove no woman is ever what at first she appears to be, that none of them can ever be possessed or really trusted. Even the sensitive man must finally revert to the ancient formula: treat a whore like a lady, and a lady like a whore—never be the lover, but contrive to be the loved.

Finally she rose and we walked back to the village, and hardly were we there than a second woman darted out from ambush. A thin and angular European of middle age, robed in long white gown caught at the waist by a heavy tasselled cord. Her lank hair was dishevelled and a hint of persecution lurked in her dark eyes; she might have been some pagan priestess escaped from a plundered tomb.

"Harlot!" she cried, dramatically flinging a rigid arm and finger out at Lee.

"Oh, Pearl. Be good, dear. This is—"

"On the beach, together! In broad daylight. Oh, thou shameful woman!" But as suddenly she relaxed and smiled, and giving Lee a little hug she turned to me. "I'm just practising. I have a part in the film. Where did you find him, Lee? On the beach? Sleeping under a tree?"

Perhaps I should have practised for my part as well, alone with her on the lonely beach. If she consorted with degenerates, what else could she expect?

Lee turned to me, saying kindly, "Pearl is something of a mystic. In fact she knows more about the black arts, and putting spells on people's doorsteps, than is good for her. She spent a few months in the hills of Haiti." She gave me a quick, significant wink as if to suggest "she's not all there, be kind to her". "Pearl's looking after me. Aren't you, dear?"

"Lee, my lovely, you know you're the only real friend I have in all the planets. I don't ask you to believe yet, but you will."

We seemed to have come to the end of our walk.

"Where are you staying?" Lee asked. "At Mrs. Pea's?"

"I don't know yet."

"That's the best place; everyone stays there. Funny old house cluttered up with hideous elegance like a Victorian museum, but she feeds us well."

"She might object to a—er—profligate scoundrel."

"Oh, I don't think she'd mind. She takes all kinds of weird people, as long as they aren't any greyer than she is. Well, see you later then."

Deep in thought I wandered on, alone, reflecting with some amusement on the paradox called woman. Her ways were devious, her heart was false, her tongue a sugared serpent, her face was masked, and her body absurd magic causing men's emotions to vibrate like forked tines.

Weak degenerate! Had she been a man, her blood would have spilt out on the sand: and yet, remembering her magic, I was obliged to admit my pleasure that she was woman, and not man. Later, when I returned to the tavern by the pier, Geoffry sat at table with a darkly handsome youth called Wiseman, and introduced me. Wiseman was a Pole, by way of the British Isles and the seaports of the world, an unsmiling and intense young churl whose mane of thick black locks hung in close confusion to almost hide his brow. The table was bare, so I ordered beer.

"So Lee gave you the beach treatment," said Geoffry. "Did she get to the part about the weak degenerate?"

I blinked my astonishment. "Why yes. Yes, she did."

He chuckled cynically. "Routine performance for all arriving males between twenty-one and forty. But wait till she gets to the part about shaving off your hair to look as if you're in the last stage of syphilis. You know, there was one idiot of a tourist who actually shaved off all his hair? Can you imagine it? All within forty-eight hours he fell in love with her, shaved his hair off, fell out of love, got a blistering scarlet sunburn, and rushed off on the ferry again like a lobster escaping from a pot."

I burst forth in a happy belly-laugh. Oh, it had not been so bad after all. At least I was only one of many victims. Ho-ho, and one had shaved his head? At least he was a greater fool than I, and that was consolation. What a fine court jester she would make, until some maddened king cut off her head! I looked kindly on the Englishman; he had salvaged the day from despair and heartquake.

"I'm glad to know I'm not the only one. She had me worried. I wanted to crawl under a stone and hide."

"What's with the speargun?" Wiseman asked suddenly. But his question was a challenge, and unfriendly. "What you t'ink you gonna catch with that? You a tourist?"

But I was in no mood to quarrel, so I shrugged.

"Fish, sometimes. I'm travelling." I had to admit to myself the spear had not been used since leaving *Zara*.

"Where you travelled?" His sardonic tone was undisguisedly discourteous.

"Here and there."

"Europe? Asia?"

"Yes."

He grunted disapprovingly. "Africa? You been to Lagos? Algiers? Mozambique?"

I nodded, familiar with the form of inquisition and its aim. He would be one of those who travelled in order to have travelled, a name-dropper whose persistent social trick was to litanize the names of distant places he had—or had not—seen. His suitcase, if he had one, would be swarming with a salad of bright labels.

"Bangkok? 'Frisco? Sydney?"

"Sydney?" Sydney, Nova Scotia, I had never seen. Sydney, Australia, was my home.

"Ah," he said, content at last, "you shoulda been to Sydney. You missed out, boy, that's the best city in the southern hemisphere. Cheese, the women there go crazy for a seaman, they never see foreigners down there, hardly. Crazy Aussies. Half-castes, most of 'em, but willing? Cheese!"

"Half-castes?"

"Yeah, all mixed up with the natives. Half Polynesian. Grass skirts, and nothing underneath. They come out to the ship in big canoes to trade. I been there lotsa times. Cheese, but they give us a royal time."

Well, things must have changed a little since I was last there. I tried to imagine my doughty maiden aunt standing in a canoe trading coconuts for glass beads; and electric trains crowded with chic stenographers clad in simple grass skirts, bereft of any top covering and with flowers tucked behind their ears. Mentally I swept the harbour clear of the bustling green ferries and substituted sampans and canoes. And what of the bridge, and the thrusting skyline of neon lights and ferro-concrete?

"They've got a native brew down there sends 'em all mad," he added happily. "Cheese, but strong!"

So, at least that part had not changed.

"I seen a tribal fight, too. All mad on this brew and beltin' each other up. Hell, you shoulda been there. You ain't seen nothin' yet!"

A Sydney versus Melbourne football match: perhaps things were much the same, after all. He seemed more kindly disposed to me, and filled my glass with beer.

"Staying long on Nevis?" he asked pleasantly.

"Oh, I don't know. I'm looking for a—"

"Better stay at Mrs. Pea's," Geoffry suggested. "There's no other place in Charlestown fit for a white, anyway. Lee stays there too, and an idiot called Pearl." He smiled a strange, shy smile and added eagerly, "You could share my room."

Wiseman snorted and reached for his glass.

"It's quite a lovely room," Geoffry went on. "You'd like it. And sometimes during the night, if it's hot, we can all go down to the beach and cavort in the raw."

What was this?

"All?"

"Well, you and I and Wiseman. He and I often do."

"Cheese!" Wiseman muttered miserably. The situation was saved by the arrival of a grey-skinned woman of sagging flesh, who entered from the sunlit street and trundled towards a nearby table. But at once she caught sight of us, since we were the only customers, and Geoffry called out gladly.

"Oh, Mrs. Pea I say, do come and sit with us? I want to introduce you to someone who's just arrived. He's looking for refined accommodation."

She smiled on him maternally, and he and I rose as introductions were effected. Seated once more, with Mrs. Pea ignoring Wiseman to beam on Geoffry and me, the Englishman said casually, "I thought he might share my room, you know. If you've no objections."

She hesitated. "Well, there's a spare—"

"Of course, you would still charge the same rent for me and additional rent for him. And it would be rather fun to have some company."

She was immediately mollified. "Of course, Geoffry dear. You know I always try to please everyone. If the gentleman agrees, then it's settled." She looked at me expectantly, and I poured her a glass of beer.

"Fine," said Geoffry. "I'll move some of my things."

She looked as if she had powdered her face with Portland cement.

"Actually," she said smugly, "there's nowhere else in Charlestown you could go. There are one or two other places, but they're only for low people." She dismissed the Bibbies and Grandpas and Alexanders with a disdainful motion of one hand and began to mould the doughy flesh of her neck. "I keep a respectable place."

At that moment excited shouts came to our ears, as of some woman in distress or ecstasy, and Pearl burst in from the street wild-eyed and gibbering.

"The drums!" she shouted. "Hear the drums! The drums!"

"Really, Pearl!" Mrs. Pea objected sharply. "Control yourself, for heaven's sake! You can't—"

"Boom—boom—boom!" She, gripped my, shoulder with a bony claw, trembling with excitement. "Listen, listen!"

We all listened. Indeed, there was a slow, rhythmic beat somewhere outside. Through the open door we could see the jetty, in process of extension and a Samos piledriver was ponderously punching a wooden pile into the sea-floor.

"But Pearl," Mrs. Pea complained in dismay, "it's only the—"

She was talking to the air. Pearl had wheeled and fled as rapidly as she came, gown and tassels streaming out behind her.

"Really," Mrs. Pea declared with embarrassment, "she's quite impossible. Quite, quite impossible. I don't know what to do. She's of European blood, you know, like us, I can't turn her out." She kneaded her neck with ancillary satisfaction, and I was sad for this Caucasian-Negro who shrank in distaste from her own rich heritage. "And may I inquire," addressing me, "what is your mission here on Nevis?"

Mission?

"I have none," I confessed. Except to discover Tic-Tac, and this hardly seemed the moment.

"Oh. Then you're a tourist?"

"H'm, not exactly. I'm just travelling."

She eyed me with the beginnings of suspicion.

"But, I mean, you're not just a beachcomber, of course. Or a vagabond, or anything like that."

She looked at me expectantly, but I sipped my beer in silence. I had no great taste for such egregious inquisition; let her feed upon her own imagination.

"I keep a respectable house," she said finally, ruffling her feathers, "and I like to know a little of my guests. You must excuse me for being cautious. Believe me, some very strange people come to these parts."

Aye, one could easily believe that.

"Only the other week," she went on, "we had a young French girl who absolutely scandalized the place. She had no luggage of any significance, she—"

"What?" I cried delightedly. "Here?"

"...was grossly impertinent, and really, the only clothes she had were tiny wisps of things I wouldn't care to wear in my own bedroom. And dancing a polka on a beerhouse table!"

"Tic-Tac? Madamoiselle Toe, is she still here? Where is she? Is she staying with you?"

By the gods, here was luck indeed! It could be no one else. The description fitted perfectly. But Mrs. Pea had drawn herself up to observe me with congealing hostility.

"You know her?" Her tone was scathing. "She...she is a friend of yours?"

"Friend?" I laughed happily. "I should hope so! But she is here?"

Her face was cemented with an expression of pained distaste.

"She is certainly not here! I was obliged to instruct her to leave my premises. I believe she left the island and I don't know, and have no wish to know, where she might have gone." She composed her expression to prim disapproval. "You must understand we have no use for such people here. They are not welcome in my house. Perhaps, if you are a friend of hers, you might prefer to stay somewhere else?"

She shafted a challenging stare at me, but I shrugged. It seemed a matter of too little importance to debate. Where the devil had Tic-Tac gone to now?

"She actually, actually, passed her last night on the beach. A white girl, of good European stock presumably, and she slept on the beach like any nigger. Incredible!"

So she might have. I had told her about the beach.

"On Pinney's Beach?" I prompted.

"Why yes, on Pin—" She broke off, suddenly suspicious, and plucked vigorously at her neck while an expression of concern crossed her face. "But…your name is Pinney too?"

"Yes."

"Could…I mean, were they any relation to you, the Pinneys who lived here?"

"Yes, same family." Or at least a close branch of it. "I thought I might visit the old estate while I'm here."

It had been the second largest estate on the island, and included four miles of beach known then and now as Pinney's Beach, but when the island was devastated by volcanic gas the family fled to North America.

"But I didn't know." She breathed, eyes wide with crisis. "My God, I never thought—"

"Of course."

"Oh, my dear gentleman, you must forgive me I never suspected for a moment. Oh, Geoffry, why didn't you tell me?"

"Because I didn't know." He was plainly enjoying her discomfort.

"Oh, but I'll make you so welcome!" she cried, regaining her composure. "You'll have the finest room, the best my house can offer. Oh yes, we'll arrange a party too." Anticipation cleansed her face with joy. "You'll be able to meet all the best people. Everyone will come. And where is your family now? Where did they go from Nevis?"

"North America, and then Australia. My home is in Sydney, Australia."

Wiseman chirruped like a plundered squirrel.

"Sydney?"

"Aye. We wear grass skirts and paddle canoes, you might remember. Perhaps you saw me there."

"Uh…yeah, well…."

"Excuse me," I said standing up.

"Of course." Perhaps they thought I wished to use the toilet, but I walked right out of the door and into the street, leaving them with the privilege of paying for three beers; and, though Geoffry came to the door and called after me, I walked on without caring to look back.

Among the taverns of the town I found ready company, dark and courteous folk whose easy conversation reflected freedom from the contagions of snobbery, ambitions, and neuroses. Later, in the dusk, emerging from some humble restaurant, a man who sat in a doorway called to me.

"Hey, mistah, you lak buy one buppy?"

Shades of Alexander, were dogs to pursue me through these isles? I went to him, and he was the grizzled Negro with the floppy hat who had been selling sweetmeats from a barrow. The puppy lay asleep at his feet, an off-white mutt in the last hour of life, it seemed, long of tooth and short of hair and abounding with quick fleas. Squatting on my haunches, I gravely looked it over.

"A fine puppy," I admitted. The old man had the grace to look astonished, but was quickly master of himself.

"Oh yes, my own buppy six month ole, but he lak travel. Hang around a jetty all a time." He shrugged with crafty nonchalance. "Is good buppy, Ah lak him too much, but you can buy him."

"H'm. Does he have a pedigree?"

"What's dat, bedigree?"

I tried to explain, and it sounded passing strange in a land where children rarely knew who their fathers were.

"O.K., Ah unnerstarn," he said at length. "You got one shit of pepper?"

A shit of…?

"Oh. No." If I had had a sheet of paper, he would have written out a pedigree then and there. He offered me tea, I invited him to rum, and together we talked with folk who knew a little of the old estate. His son was absent fishing, so I passed the night on a wooden bench, with a pillow made from an old sack stuffed with paper.

In early morning I walked north from the village on a winding gravel road, through an avenue of poinsettia and sabre-thorn, flame trees and wild plum. Fields and palms and cottages were suffused in soft new light, the risen sun was hidden by the towering volcano. Country folk walking to the village bearing produce greeted me with friendly curiosity, for white men rarely fared afoot on Nevis, and girls giggled their pleasure when I ventured some brave remark.

Gentle people, living gentle lives.

The island is an old volcano thrusting upwards from the sea, and Columbus named it Nieves for the white clouds which, formed by condensation of moist air rising up its flanks, stream out like snowy pennants from its peak. The dark greens of the upper slopes melt into softer pastel lowlands patched with sugar-cane and cotton, and fringed with cocos palms.

At little more than a mile was the entrance of the estate, and a roughly contrived notice said, "Entry Forbidden. Except for Buying Shells, or on Special Business." The way led in through groves of coconut and bananas and clammy-cherry-trees to a scraggle of shacks set amid the stone ruins and tamarind-trees of what had once been a great estate. John Wade, the current owner, was a stalwart young Negro who lived in one of the shacks with his wife and a chuckle of small infants. I told him who I was, and why I came: at first he was ill at ease, doubtless wondering if I hoped to claim the place, but soon regained his confidence and proudly told me what he knew. The first Pinney to come here had originally been imprisoned as a rebel and banished after Monmouth's defeat at Sedgemoor, but secured these lands and prospered with coffee, sugar-cane, and copra. He and his descendants held the land for a hundred and sixty years, but history's only comments were chiselled on a scattering of graves.

"Once ago it was a big, big place," said John. "It had a sugarmill, and hundred acres' coconuts, and arl. Two Englishmen called Bone and Walwyn had it once, and then two Syrian rascals called Carvarjo, and then my father bought it. Mostly we makes copra—" pointing to crude drying sheds—"and sells the shells for fuel. We used to lease some land for people to grow sugar-cane, and cotton, but they never pay no rent, so now we put cattle there to graze."

"No old books or anything left, I suppose? No records?"

"No records. We done forget those people now."

As well, perhaps. The lot of the Negro slave had not been pretty. I put my hand on his shoulder and he grinned with embarrassment, and the thought came to me that here was the scion of Negro slaves in proud command of property once owned by whites who whipped his forebears; and here was the son of those distant whites, a landless stranger come to visit the grey ruins. What price the fleeting arrogance of those who held the lash? The conquerors were conquered, the Negroes had endured. He had paraphrased the history of my clan, We done forget those people now.

"Up there," he said, pointing farther up the slopes, "is the ruins of the big house. Montravers House they call it now. Not much lef'. My dad took arl the timbers and tiles and a lot of the stone, and statues, and sold it. Now he's sold arl that part up there to Judge Allen. The judge figures to rebuild, make it a hotel. Gonna make a golf-course an' arl, I hear tell."

He took me to his house and gave me breakfast, and I walked on alone towards the big house some distance up the slope. The lush soil and fecund growth of the alluvial coastal strip quickly changed to leached clay and dry thornbush; but even farther up, where men had never ravaged the good earth, the heights were dark with jungle.

The big house "once ago" must have been quite a formidable mansion, a two-storied building of cut stone looking down on Charlestown and the verdant coastal belt dark against the Caribbean Sea. Starlings nested in the creviced walls and plants grew in damp crannies, the interior was thick with seeds and brush. Attending the large building were quarters where slaves had slept; there was a curious hexagonal kitchen, with underneath a grim little dungeon where unruly slaves were chained. At a distance were the stables, where camels had been kept; one could see four mangers like iron baskets set high in the stone walls. Aye, camels, John had said. Where had they come from? From the far Sahara? Or were they, perchance, a few beasts salvaged from the unsuccessful camel corps imported by America for use in desert areas during the Civil War?

Had they been happy here, those English exiles? They had prospered in this alien place, with their slaves and cane and camels. Here they had wed and banqueted and died. But in the isolation of this once splendid house, bearing the white man's burden on the backs of Negro slaves and overshadowed by the mighty volcano, had they known peace?

The place was consumed by silence, no ghosts appeared, the stones which knew the answers would not speak.

We done forget those people now.

Far below the big house where the old estate came down to the sea I lay at ease on the long white beach, in the warmth of the westering sun. The leaning ranks of coconut palms marched to the edge of the sand, and indeed a number of palms had fallen victim to erosion by the sea. With every storm the sea crept farther in and a few more palms were lost; but they were rotten with neglect, cancerous with boring worms and termites, and for all their beauty as they overleant the beach they could not last for more than a few short years. No effort was being made to salvage or replace them; soon they would lie in rottenness among the flowering vines infesting the approaches to the beach.

Behind the beach, among the palms, was a small lagoon where cattle wandered: the haunt of wading birds and frogs, of fingerlings and tadpoles; water-lilies were white on the pond and yellow pea-flowers grew around. A peaceful place. During the day I had bathed in the sea, and discovered fallen coconuts not yet destroyed by rats; and passing folk, who used the beach as a coastal path, discovered me. A man who cast his net in the sea presented me with fish, refusing payment; from market women I bought plantain, to be roasted, and a gourd of some sweet fermented drink. I would leave the gourd by a certain tree, and the owner would retrieve it in the morning.

More than a hundred years ago this beauteous, abandoned beach had been the resort of wealthy Europeans; more recently, the boudoir of a mischievous nymph called Tic-Tac. But now a single European called for wide-eyed comment: some islanders avoided me, hushing their voices and walking among the palms, others smiled and saluted me and passed a little time in conversation. But this was a sunset shore and therefore sandflies came at dusk; I built a fire of smouldering husks to fend them off. Later I would use a bed of coals to roast my fish and plantain, but meanwhile the rich brew in the gourd would serve me well.

A soft voice near at hand challenged me.

"White marn!"

I swivelled quickly. He had approached without a sound, and stood not ten feet distant. In the twilight his features could not be clearly seen, but he was young, well muscled, clad only in loose trousers held up by a rope. Such quiet approach at dusk is rarely friendly. He glanced up and down the beach as if to assure himself that no one else was near.

"What you doin' here, white marn?"

His tone was insolent, yet wary: a meeting ill begun in the gathering night. I lit a cigarette with a chunk of smouldering husk, and casually kept the husk in my hand.

"Sitting," I said curtly. "So?"

Again he glanced along the beach. He squinted out at the dark sea in search of a possible boat, peered into the thick gloom among the coconut-trees as if they might hide some vehicle.

"You alone?"

"No."

"Somebardy wit' you?"

"Yes. One damn' fool with a mouthful of questions. He can go away."

He sneered damply. "I don' got fear for you, white marn."

There was silence for a time, and as I stirred the fire I wondered what villainy was poisoning the air. There was rustling among the fallen fronds behind me, and I listened: it was only rats, coming out to feed.

"No good you sit here, white marn. Might be bad bipple come. Maybe duppies. You no got fear for duppies?"

Had I misjudged him? Was he merely solicitous?

"I don't fear bad people, friend," I said more kindly. "Or duppies. Cigarette?"

He accepted a cigarette and lit it from my brand.

"You no got woman?"

"Not here."

"You goin' slip here?"

"Maybe." But I would sleep with a wakeful ear.

"Few nights back one white woman been slip here," he said, grinning. "I bin slip wit' her. Eh, she bin like one young tiger."

Wishful fool! He had seen Tic-Tac here, and sought to boost his ego with a tale. I grimaced sourly. No profit could be had by upbraiding such an oaf.

"She gone Antigua, she say. But I pretty good for her that night, so she give me somet'ing. See."

He took a silver object from his pocket, and my heart lurched with dismay. It was a small silver Buddha she had worn at her throat. It had been my gift to her.

"You bastard!" I cried scrambling to my feet. "How the hell did you get that?"

He backed away as I advanced, pocketing the bauble, and flicked his cigarette away as if prepared to fight. Had he robbed her? Had she left it on the sand, so that he found it?

"That white lady give it me," he protested.

Had he...assaulted her? But she would have ripped his face with her nails. She could fight like seven hellcats. What happened? How had he taken possession of that keepsake?

"Get out!" I said harshly, advancing with the burning piece of husk. "Beat it, before I stuff this down your throat!"

He backed away at first, then walked off slowly, often looking back, and when at a safe distance he paused to shout.

"She bin willin'! She say, O.K.!"

Sickened, lonely, fearful of what might have happened to her, I went back to the fire. But he might be close by, and there could be harm to come. As the shadows deepened I left the fire, left the fish and plantains too, and crept off with the gourd like some miserable fugitive to lie down in lonely darkness with mosquitoes, rats, and giant crabs.

Four days later I returned to Charlestown, having slowly made my way around the island. It had only been a matter of some twenty-five miles, with ample time to search for such shards of family history as remained. I would never return, I knew, and felt obliged to see what could be found.

The day was far advanced, so I rode the last few miles aboard a truck chartered by a church, at thirty cents per passenger. The vehicle was jammed to tight capacity with churchly folk clashing tambourines and triangles and trumpeting forth hymns, and as finally they scrambled forth I was almost borne into the Pilgrim Holiness Church. Clutching at a gatepost for an anchor, I held on grimly till they passed, and went along the road to the Rookery Nook where a Syrian and his daughter served cold beer.

Where could I go from Nevis? It seemed that one could only return to Basseterre.

"We have no planes calling here," said the Syrian.

"There's only the ferry, the *Island Queen*. It goes to Basseterre," Irene, his daughter, chimed in.

"No other boats? Not even to Guadeloupe?"

She was working her way south, and she was French. Why should she have gone to British Antigua? More likely to Guadeloupe, a French possession south and east, if transport went that way.

"Nothing to Guadeloupe."

Well, I could catch the evening ferry, if there was nothing else. But I knew that Tic-Tac would have found a way; she would never have turned back. I drank my beer and left, walking along the street to inquire here and there for news of onward transport: there was none. There was only the ferry, and it went to Basseterre. Why should anyone want to go elsewhere?

As I neared the waterfront I met Geoffry, doubtless waiting around to see if any whites came on the ferry.

"I say!" he cried. "Where the deuce have you been? But you disappeared into thin air, what happened to you? We waited for hours and hours, Mrs. Pea was terribly upset."

"I was here and there."

"We even asked the police. They said you'd been seen on the other side of the island. Did you go on safari, or something? Your things are still in the restaurant. Someone swore you'd been seen mending nets."

"No, a man was teaching me, that's all."

He eyed me curiously. "So you've turned up, at last. What are your plans now?"

"I suppose I'm going to Basseterre, on the ferry."

But I had caught sight of two small vessels near the jetty, native trading craft, and leaving him I walked out to hail the nearest; the second was far out. Three men were aboard.

"Where are you bound?" I cried.

"Montserrat!"

Montserrat? That was the next island downhill, on the way to Guadeloupe. Why, that might do very well. From there I could find some craft to take me farther. Far better than returning to Basseterre.

"Can I go with you?" I demanded.

"See the captain," came the answer. "He be at Port Office now for fix it papers. Ef you want come, must hurry."

Turning on my heel, I strode off the jetty towards the village centre. But now here was Lee, in turn demanding to know where I had been.

"Tour of the island," I said, anxious to hurry on.

"And now you're leaving?"

"Yes. Before someone shaves my hair off."

"It fits in," she mused. "The godless sinner who—"

"I went to church yesterday." I grinned, and she scanned my face.

"It doesn't show. Where are you off to?"

"Montserrat. But please excuse me, I must hurry."

But at the Port Office, when I inquired for the captain, he said he was certainly not going to Montserrat.

"But your crew," I protested, "they told me you were."

"No, dat's the *Diane*. The little sloop, I t'ink she goin' Montserrat. My schooner be big one far out, de *Yvonne Marie*. But she goin' Dominica."

Devil's eyes, here was luck. Dominica was even farther than Guadeloupe.

"Will you be calling at Guadeloupe?"

"No fear, we got no paper for dat French place."

So. But doubtless something could be arranged.

"Then could you take me to Dominica?"

He avoided my eyes, discomfited, and then said apologetically, "That be almost thirty-hour journey, sir. We no fixed for good accommodation."

I laughed. "I'm a seaman, friend. Sleep on deck, no trouble. How much money?"

He scratched his chin, frowning.

"Wal, I got to fix it on a paper, your name and that. Cost you...cost you eight dahlar for de trip."

"All right. Four now, four when we get there." I paid him four West Indies dollars, or one pound. "When are you sailing?"

"In one hour, I t'ink. Arrive Dominica tomorrow night. O.K., gimme your name, passport number, I fix it on a paper wit' the marn here."

Light of heart I left the office and marched back down the street, and entered the tavern to claim my luggage there. But I was assailed by exclamations from three people: Geoffry was there, and Lee, and Mrs. Pea.

"But you're leaving us?" cried Mrs. Pea. "Oh, my dear, I'm so very disappointed. I had such plans! I would have given you such a pleasant time, you would have met all the best people. And where are you off to, may I ask?"

"Basseterre," said Geoffry.

"Montserrat," Lee declared.

"Guadeloupe," I corrected them.

"But you said—"

"Changed my mind."

"My dear," breathed Mrs. Pea, "this is all too swift for me. But what happened to you? Where did you go, that afternoon? Where did you sleep?"

"At the barrowman's hut, I forget his name."

"Barrowman?"

"The one with the little street-barrow called 'Reviving Texas'. He gave me a bench to sleep on."

"Oh, my God!" she shrilled, plucking briskly at her neck. "But you're joking?"

"Not at all. The second night I slept on the beach, and the third in that funny little Santa Maria Bar at Newcastle. I'd better not tell you about the fourth, it was rather improper. And now—"

"But those low people!" she cried in mounting horror. "Oh, no one could…no white gentleman could…oh, they're such low people!"

I chuckled richly. "Then we're lower still, for they're better people than any of us."

I shouldered my sack and took up my speargun, nodded briefly and walked outside. A man was fortunate indeed to be able to quit such company at will. The spear I gave to my friend the barrowman, whose son was a fisherman, and then I went out on the jetty to join *Yvonne Marie*.

My last glimpse of Charlestown showed Geoffry standing there, waiting for the ferry to come in.

3

SCHOONER "YVONNE MARIE"

Seven Days to Mutiny

THE Negro is a deft freshwater boatman, and captured slaves
transferred their skills from the Congo and the Niger to mastery
of various new forms of rivercraft from the Mississippi to the
Chattahoochee River. But he is not a deep-sea man; unlike the
Polynesian, he has never been the master of salt water. After several
centuries of slavery and upwards of a hundred years of freedom the
Caribbean Negro still sails point to point, requiring daily landfalls, and
creeping close to shore: and the cresting sea, like a nervous horse, seems
to sense the unskilled hand and fearful heart.

Yvonne Marie was an average island schooner, a sixty-three-
foot vessel constructed with rough grace from broadleaf, pine, and
greenheart; an old vessel with splintered planking and strained
timbers, as such freighting schooners often are. Her home port was at
Kingstown, at the island of St Vincent. She carried a crew of four, and
her captain was an anxious Negro gentleman by the name of Conrad
Adams.

"Ah hope that ocean don't rough," Conrad confided as we prepared
to put to sea. The ancient longboat, patched with flattened cans and
scraps of boxwood, had been hauled aboard and wedged amidships, and
attempts were being made to start the engine. The vessel was almost
flush-decked, with a sentinel-box of a galley lashed to the forward mast,
and an odd little kennel set astern to house the captain's bed.

"Eustace, make it that damn' motor go!" He peered down the
narrow companionway as if to listen for some reply, but there was only
muttered cursing and the clink of tools, and the black abyss of the
engine-room might have been some cavern with Moloch and his priests
devising evil. Mysterious rites were being carried out down there by
three black men with candles, ministering to an ancient one-lung Lister
diesel. The breeze was freshening, but the sails would not be used.

"Eh," Conrad lamented, straightening, "one day I goin' get one
proper motor. This one humbug all a time. You brung food wit'you?"

"Bread, sardines, bananas."

"Never can tell, sometimes voyage take a little long."

How right he was. The thirty-hour journey was to take us almost
seven days with mutiny, hunger, thirst, and a fine attempt at shipwreck

thrown in.

"Pray to Gard," he murmured, "that ocean don't rough bad."

Suddenly a backflash seared the engine-room with flame, and the diesel started.

Whoof! Putt-putt. Whoof! Putt-putt....

A tin can covering the exhaust outlet flew high in the air and bounced from the mainmast into the sea, and such dense clouds of blue-white smoke issued forth from both exhaust and engine-room as obscured the aft deck from the sight of man and bird. Conrad and I groped our way forward to clearer air, seconds ahead of the gasping engineer. The deck trembled, the rigging shook, and every loose object in sight jumped in unison each time the engine whoofed. Smoke billowed astern on the breeze and the crew of *Diane* shouted ribald comments, people on the jetty stared with interest. As the engine heated, the smoke began to clear.

"Yes, harl up a ancha-a-ar," Conrad shouted.

He went aft to the helm and engaged the gears to slow-ahead, while three of the crew, as the mate stood by, hauled in chain and manhandled the heavy anchor on board. As we moved out from the lee of land, the schooner began to plunge, scooping spray, heading directly into the south-east trades.

Aye, but it was a happy thing to be travelling through the night to Guadeloupe. Rigging slatted in the breeze, the rays of the seting sun fanned out to blaze on serried clouds, and their shadows streaked the furnaced sky with violet. The breeze was constant now, the tired old diesel had settled down to give a whoof at every second lamp-post. In the morning there would be time to talk of Guadeloupe.

Conrad insisted that I bed inside his kennel, that he had another place, so I slept in a wooden box six feet long and two feet wide, with a tiny sliding door, bouncing loosely on the deck with the jolt of each new wave.

During the night the engine stopped. One minute it was firing normally, the next it coughed, sighed once or twice, and died. I was instantly awake, listening. There was no sound of movement, all was silent except for the swishing of the sea and the soughing of the breeze in the rigging. Several minutes passed, and I opened my kennel door:

the helmsman had left the tiller to sit on the engine-room housing, comfortably scratching his groin and gazing dreamily out to sea. The vessel began to wallow and roll as she fell beam-on to the waves.

Conrad appeared from some secret niche.

"Alltok, wha' harpen, marn?"

"Wha' harpen? What you mean, wha' harpen? Bloody motor finish, that's wha' harpen!"

Conrad rubbed his jaw and peered down at the black silence of the engine-room. Then he gazed up at the night sky, and the distant bulk of Montserrat, and sucked his teeth in irritation.

"Wha' harpen de motor?" he asked uncertainly, but the helmsman cursed him with quick passion.

"How Ah know what harpen wit' bloody motor, you damn' ole fool? Not bloody engineer, marn. Go call it engineer, aks wha' harpen!"

Alltok: I made a mental note of the name. Not a man to cross, it would seem. Conrad groped his way forward and shouted down the forecastle hatch until the engineer reluctantly appeared, towelling his face and torso with a rag.

"Go fix it motor, Eustace," Conrad demanded. "We driffin'."

Eustace purged his nose with his fingers and wiped them on the rag. He was a thin, drooping individual with a face too large for his head and bones too large for his carelessly draped flesh.

"Done tole you plenty times, ole marn, dat motor no damn' good."

"Good motor, marn. Go fix it."

"How fix it? How I find it in a dark? Wit' candle?" He kicked at a flying-fish stranded on the deck.

"Lend my flashlight, fix a motor."

"Eh! Maybe fix it in a marnin', when got daylight."

Eustace went below again. Conrad braced himself against the comfortless roll of the ship, and stared unhappily about the deck. Essentially a good and kindly man, his tendency to add self-pity to recurrent indecision left him ill equipped to deal with small emergencies at sea. He finally prevailed upon his crew to come on deck and raise the sails, and thereafter through the night the vessel ploughed on slowly to the sounds of rigging working, and the creaking throat of the ponderous mainsail boom.

The motor was dead, and no one ever managed to bring it back to life.

The morning meal was half a mug of sweetened coffee, white bread, and a banana; I had thrown my rations in with those of the crew.

The breeze was light, the vessel sluggish, the sails were poorly trimmed and, as we ate, we kept glancing at nearby Montserrat hoping to gauge evidence of progress. The current was against us, and we were making little more than two knots. The distant bulk of Guadeloupe was fine on the port bow and every inch of fifty miles away: tomorrow, with good luck, we might arrive there.

But Conrad, who had been silently observing Guadeloupe as he sipped his coffee, said, "That island be Antigua, I think. But where be Guadeloupe?"

I looked at him in surprise. How could anyone mistake the formidable lump of Guadeloupe for the smaller and low-lying island of Antigua?

"That place you lookin' at be Guadeloupe," said Tobago. Tobago was the mate. A dour and colourless intravert of musky odour and scaly skin, his sole distinction lay in hailing from far Tobago. Alltok turned on him.

"Talk shit, marn! Be Antigua, Guadeloupe far off. See Guadeloupe tonight, maybe."

I could only stare, from Alltok to Conrad to Guadeloupe. Antigua was far to the north-east, on the other side of Montserrat and quite obscured from view; the island ahead was undoubtedly Guadeloupe. The shape was unmistakable.

"Better we come more right," said Conrad, and Thomas the cook brought *Yvonne Marie* broadside to the breeze.

"Hold it so," said Conrad contentedly, not bothering to reset the sails to reach. "Keep Antigua on the lef', and Guadeloupe must be straight ahead."

Hell's tits, but it was Guadeloupe he was keeping on the left. We were headed for Curaçao, Columbia, the Panama Canal—deliberately avoiding the very destination we desired. Should I say something? But I was a passenger, a guest, it was not my place to try and run the ship.

The Yvonne Marie arriving at Roseau, Dominica

Captain Conrad Adams of the schooner, Yvonne Marie

Author and crewman on Zara, previous to Yvonne Marie

Festival time on the Papeete waterfront, Tahiti

"Do you have a chart?" I asked. As soon as they looked at the chart they would see at once what the situation was.

"No chart," said Conrad. "We familiar with these places, we don't need no chart."

A matter of opinion, perhaps. Five hundred miles of open sea lay ahead of us, if we held our present course: and not so much as a shilling atlas for a chart! Well, this suggested a most promising adventure—Caracas, Maracaibo, Curaçao. We might end up anywhere.

If we survived.

Tobago scowled and sucked his teeth, murmured a violent curse and went off to the peak to sulk alone. He aired his temper and disgust with a stream of profanity largely lost in the sigh of the south-east breeze. Alltok drank the remains of Tobago's coffee and scowled at me from under lowered brows. He was less dark than the others, rangy and lean, a man of prolonged silences broken by explosive bursts of passion. The spareness of his frame revealed the strength of tendon, bone and sinew, rippling under his smooth brown skin with fluid power.

"What you t'inkin' about, white marn?"

It was at once a query and a challenge, and I thought of the rogue I had encountered back at Nevis. Conrad moved uneasily, watching us.

"I was wondering," I said carefully, "if Thomas the cook has a big, big pot."

"Big pot? What for you wanna big pot?"

"Because I think maybe we're going to have to carve you up and eat you. And you look too damn' tough to eat raw."

His eyes bulged.

"Eat me?" Dramatically he laid one bony hand across his heart, leaning forward on his haunches to stare in utter surprise. "Me?"

I stifled a grin, saying, "Because, if we keep on our present course, we're going to be at sea a long time. So I figure we'll run out of food. We can eat the captain first, because he's fat; and then we'll eat you."

Slowly, quite slowly, a grin of understanding spread throughout his face, and he sat back on his heels and laughed.

"Ho, bloody white marn carnibal, gonna eat a black marn! Ho-ho, eat a captain fus', because he fat." He stabbed a finger at Conrad. "You fus' inna pot, captain. Ha-ha!"

Had I offered him mere courtesy, he would probably have scorned me. But he had a sense of humour, and the risk had been worth while.

"Too tough!" he chuckled happily. "Yeah, marn, I pretty tough. More better eat the captain fus', he sof' and fat. Hey, white marn, you like more coffee?"

"Thanks. But I'd like it even better if we went to Guadeloupe, instead of South America."

He laughed softly, pouring me the last of the coffee.

"Yeah, O.K., we do that. I know is Guadeloupe, that island. But I say is Antigua, jus' for vex Tobago."

"What you talk, marn?" Conrad frowned. "That place I say Antigua, you say is Guadeloupe?"

"Yeah, ole marn. Be Guadeloupe for true. More better we go that way."

So we turned away from South America, and went back on course for Guadeloupe.

Conrad was a thick-set man of middle age, heavy jowled, with a splendid swollen blue-black hide, which glistened and shone in the sun like well-oiled gun metal. His coarse, blunt features were redeemed by his companionable smile and large, gentle eyes which, though shot with veins, suggested inherent kindliness and an attitude of constant childlike wonder. He had married well; his wife was owner of a hotel-grocery business in St Vincent; two years ago he had purchased *Yvonne Marie*, and sailed forth as her captain to enter inter-island trade.

He had never owned a boat before, had never been to sea, and for months his hopes for commercial gain took sorry second place to sheer survival. The boat was old and strained, the engine obsolete, the sails were rotten and the rigging patched with bits of fencing wire. Generous, weak, pursued by real and imagined fears, her captain lacked the drive to coerce his ineffectual crew into carrying out any but the most rudimentary duties. Giving orders to other people carried the risk of giving offence, and much of the time he scarcely knew what orders he should give. There was no organized watch on board, and only bitter dispute could persuade anyone but Alltok to take the wheel at night. The deck was persistently a shambles. Lines sprawled anywhere in hopeless tangles, rope ends frayed like ponytails, objects tumbled loose about the deck for hours; canvas rotted and rigging rusted as it willed. To use the toilet one chose some spot anywhere along the lee rail, or astern. The boat sank, and was salvaged; it ran aground on rocks, and was repaired. He lost his way when trying to find Barbados, ran out of fuel, and the trade winds blew him to Martinique. He sailed for Trinidad and ended up instead in Venezuela, with his ship seized by customs and his crew all clapped in prison until suitable fines were paid. His vessel had no chart—he could not read them—dead reckoning was a foreign word, and a sextant might have been some form of amorous pursuit; the taffrail log was a fishing-line baited with yellow cloth, and the only navigational aid *Yvonne Marie* possessed was a bruised and sticky compass almost drained of all its fluid.

Somewhere, then, Conrad Adams had great courage. Few white men would have cared or dared to daily trust their lives to such a craft. His only solace while at sea was the bottle of strong rum concealed within his kennel, and which I found.

To Conrad I confided my hopes of being set ashore at Guadeloupe. We sat aft on the gunnels, with Alltok at the tiller, while the rest of the crew sprawled out asleep on deck.

He regarded me inquiringly.

"Dat French place? You want go there?"

"Yes."

"No, marn, we can't go there. No got it paper for dat place. Go Dominica."

"But, look, couldn't you just put me ashore in the longboat? Anywhere, I'd be all right."

"Oh no, marn," he said wide-eyed. He seemed offended. "Somebardy see us, we got big trouble. Police come, an' arl."

"But supposing we edged in close tonight," I parried persuasively, "you could set me ashore in the dark, at some quiet place. I'll pay you, of course. I'll pay you twenty dollars for your trouble."

"Wal, Ah dunno." He was obviously distressed so I raised the offer.

"Twenty-five dollars then. And I'll still pay the other half of my fare too, the other four dollars. Twenty-nine dollars in all. Make it a round figure, say thirty."

But I had misjudged him. He was not so much concerned with money. His embarrassment stemmed from fear of offending me if he refused, and fear of discovery by police if he agreed.

"Keep it dahlars, marn," he said unhappily. "Ah don't fret for dem. Ef Ah help you, Ah does it for a fren'."

I lowered my eyes to the deck in shame. Here, it seemed, was a man whose heart was beyond the reach of silver.

"Wha' for you want go dat French place?" he asked, solemnly regarding me. For a moment I was tempted to contrive some cunning lie, some urgent tale of life-or-death importance. But he shamed me. I would not be further shamed.

"For my woman," I said simply. "I think she's there."

"Ah-h."

He was silent, and I could not know his thoughts. Here was a stranger asking him to risk seizure of his vessel, merely because a woman might be on Guadeloupe. A futile proposition; the risks all to him and the reward, if there was one, all to me. Well, I would go, to Dominica, and from there perhaps I would find a boat to Guadeloupe. But he stroked his jaw a moment.

"We can try, then," he said. "Pray Gard we don' find trouble. French bipple put we prison."

A trickle of anxiety passed through me. Prison? But, no, he would be safe; there would be little danger in landing a single man in the dark of night. Great tracts of the island's coast were quite deserted. It was I who might go to prison, for landing without a permit, but some suitable form of story could be manufactured to meet the occasion.

That evening we closed with Guadeloupe, standing out to sea until dusk had fallen. But during the night, as we edged towards the island, looming mountain masses blocked out the south-east trades, and the vessel barely kept sufficient way to hold her course. The foresail slatted idly, and the mainsail boom groaned and creaked as it slowly swung in the roll of an easy swell. The hours passed, midnight came and went, and not until early morning did we feel the rhythmic surge of shorebound waves lifting our starboard quarter.

The sea was quiet. It would be an easy landing. We scanned the coast, and not a light or any building could be seen; the navigation lights had been doused, and the longboat already trailed astern. A haze of light cloud obscured the stars, and the shore two hundred yards away seemed free of any hazards.

"Better you go now," Conrad said. "We driffin', better not go more close inshore."

I thanked him warmly for his trouble, knowing it was unlikely we would ever meet again. He shook my hand and wished God's peace upon me.

The longboat was pulled alongside, Alltok scrambled down and I followed with my sack. Thomas and the engineer offered their farewells, Tobago glowered, and as Alltok took the oars I started bailing: the bilge was awash, water was pouring in through cracks and dried-out seams. The shore was a hundred and fifty yards away when Conrad gave the order to come about. There was plenty of room, with deep water in to the very shore, and slowly the schooner turned into the gentle breeze.

I wondered where this place might be, if there would be a road. A track at least, I might have to walk along the coast for miles. To the right, where the lights of a distant township had been visible when we were out at sea; there I would find a bus, perhaps, to carry me on to the central town of Point-à-Pitre. The longboat yawed on a cresting swell and straightened up. Alltok gazed astern, gauging the waves as they assumed authority; breakers ahead were swishing up an escarpment of smooth, round stones.

"Eh!" he murmured suddenly, ceasing his labour to stare back at the schooner. I turned. *Yvonne Marie* had fallen off, she had refused to come about. Pudding-bellied, sluggish with marine growth, she did not have enough way on for her bow to pass through the eye of the breeze and come around on the other tack.

"Let her run, marn!" Tobago shouted. "Let she get way on!"

She nosed back on her inshore course, drawing closer to us, beginning to pitch sharply as she was shouldered by steepening waves. But the closer inshore the weaker the breeze became, blanketed by hills and thrusting headlands. Alltok slowly resumed his rowing as the schooner drew nigh: the waves were not large, but they were steep and sudden, and the landing would require a certain skill.

"Come aba-a-aht!" came Conrad's anxious cry. Again we watched.

Tobago slacked the foresail, Conrad leant hard on the tiller, Eustace and Thomas held the mainsail towards the breeze to coax the stern around. Slowly the schooner turned, but almost immediately lost way, broadside to the urgent waves, helpless, wildly rolling in the steep swell. The heavy mainsail boom racked violently back and forth, loose impedimenta were flung across the deck, the captain's kennel skittered to and fro like a loose pea. Only sixty yards from shore—there was not a chance for her making another run to come about.

The longboat lurched drunkenly, shipping water as she slewed in a breaking wave, and Alltok fought to swing her before the following wave could catch her broadside.

"Put out a ancha-a-ar!" Conrad cried in anguish. But just at that moment the foresail boom went wild, fetched the mate a mighty wallop, and he disappeared from sight. A cresting wave hit the vessel's underbelly on the inshore roll and she heeled awkwardly, hard over and skidding on her port beam, ten yards closer to the shore.

"O, Gard, we done wreck!"

Thomas and the engineer scurried out of range of the threshing mainsail boom. Thin cries for help could be heard. There was no time to be lost. There was just one chance of saving her from being washed ashore. Alltok backed towards her, cursing profanely as he strained at the oars, and I shouted to Conrad to pass us down a rope.

"Tobago dead!" he shouted in distress. "We los' Tobago, he done drown. Oh Gard, oh Gard!"

"Give it rope, bloody fool!" demanded Alltok as we swung to *Yvonne Marie*'s bow. "Rope, rope, rope!"

Thomas scampered to the bow and threw down a line, and as I secured it Alltok manoeuvred the longboat to rescue the foundering Tobago. Sick, wretched, waterlogged, he was dragged aboard and dropped in the bilge, and Alltok braced his feet against the mate's buttocks as he strained anew at the oars.

The rope we had proved to be the jib halyard. As Alltok rowed, the sail went up. Finally Thomas secured the line around the sampson post, and the longboat was tugged this way and that by the frantic movement of the schooner's bows.

It was too much for one man, to pull that hulking vessel around.

With the bilge bailed almost dry, I took one oar beside him, planted one foot on Tobago's shoulder, and mightily we strained to drag *Yvonne Marie's* nose back towards the sea. She was stubborn as any woman, and we could not gain an inch. Nothing. Sweat, strain, swish of spray, schooner plunging and longboat lurching every time the towline was drawn taut. Pull man, pull! Tobago vomited in the slopping bilge and Alltok cursed him.

For all of five minutes we fought, every ounce of our strength flung on the creaking oars, sweating, swearing, gritting our teeth till chips flew. The schooner drifted closer inshore, the longboat was steadily sinking as the bilge rose. Then slowly, slowly, half a degree at a time, Yvonne Marie began to come around. After a little while the light airs began to help. Conrad and the engineer had secured the mainsail boom, Thomas backed the foresail; in another few minutes the schooner picked up way, sluggishly moving seawards, and we rested at the oars.

Alltok bowed forward as if in prayer, letting his armpits hold his oar. His chest heaved in unison with mine, and wearily he spat on Tobago's outstretched hand.

"Damn' rubbidge boat!" he said bitterly. "Who want be bloody seaman?" Guiltily I held my peace, perspiration trickling down my face and oozing from my body like warm soda, and began to bail again. For my own selfish ends I had almost brought destruction to the schooner. *Yvonne Marie* was under way, the longboat was bumping against her bull.

"De mate livin'?" Conrad asked, peering down at us. Light was filtering into the sky, and it would soon be dawn.

"Aks him," said Alltok curtly. He kicked Tobago's rump. "Giddup, ef you livin'! Damn' humbug, fallin' in a water. Giddup, Ah say! Useless damn' fool, floatin' about in a sea!"

The mate was still alive. As he was hauled aboard he vomited on both of us, provoking a litany of furious oaths from Alltok; then we took the longboat in and swung the schooner around on course again. Out to sea this time, on the port tack.

"Eh," said Alltok, when Conrad passed rum around, "eh, but Ah laugh for see Tobago. Big marn, know everyt'ing, full up wit' big talk,

and when trouble come and everyt'ing mash up and de vessel wreckin',
Tobago go swimmin' in a sea."

He gulped his rum and squinted maliciously at the mate, wretchedly
hunched against the waterbarrel with bile still dribbling from his
mouth. There seemed to be a standing feud between Alltok and the
mate.

"And then when we done save he useless life," he continued as if in
surprise, glancing around at Conrad, Thomas and myself, "then he sick
on a marn's haid! Eh? Tobago, you damn' goat, why you done sick on
my haid? White marn help save you, you sick on his haid too!"

"Eh, praise Gard we all still livin'," said Conrad piously. "You two
done save de schooner," looking from Alltok to me. How like him, this
generous Conrad, to overlook so much and offer gratitude instead of
angry curses.

The new day came, *Yvonne Marie* moved on slowly south towards
Dominica. Everything I owned was soaked, but at least nobody had
actually died, the schooner had not actually been wrecked.

Thomas the cook was a devilish-looking rascal with a sinister little beard
lending a hint of purposeful evil to his pockmarked, pixie face. He
might have been Mephistopheles' disciple at work on some fiendish task
as he crouched beside the cooking fire at night, the flickering flames
varnishing his face and naked torso with tongues of moving light. But
he was not yet twenty-one. Bravado and insolence had not yet hardened
into profane self-assurance.

There was a time, in North America, when I had received the
equivalent of ten Australian pounds each day for cooking for five men.
Thomas cooked for five men, in his fashion, and received a shilling if he
was lucky.

Tobago customarily sat in isolation on the peak, or lay at ease
on the canvas of the jib, which had rotted beyond repair; Thomas
stationed himself near by at the galley, or sprawled on deck by the two
tarred water casks. The galley resembled a small country convenience
haphazardly built from discarded old fence palings, lashed to the
foremast, and the stove was nothing more than an open fire just
outside, exposed to all weather, insulated from the deck by a few inches

of sand in the sawn-off bottom of a fuel drum; firewood was split on a
chopping-block with an axe. Rations were meagre and poorly cooked,
and often as not included some bug or roach; stores were locked below
deck under a small aft hatch where rats and roaches could feed on them
undisturbed, and consisted of salt fish, rice, sugar, flour and bread.
Specials, including coffee and cocoa and sweet condensed milk, were
kept in special places by the captain: there was nothing else. Breakfast
was of coffee and bread, the noonday meal was a plate of verminous
rice topped by a one-ounce cube of salted fish, supper was dry bread
and cocoa. When bread gave out, Thomas subjected us to gobbets of
yeastless dough scorched black on a sprinkling of salt in an ungreased
pan.

The vessel had been provisioned for three days. When the fifth day
came, there was nothing to eat but flour; some cocoa and condensed
milk still remained. Tobacco and cigarettes were completely gone. One
freshwater barrel had been empty when the voyage began; the second,
scummed with bitter tar oils, had a maximum of four gallons left.
On the previous day we had hailed a passing motorboat, and though
somewhat timid of our ragtime crew her captain tossed us half a pack
of cheap cigarettes, and four garfish to be used as trolling bait. The line
which we trailed, with its lure of yellow cloth, had caught us nothing;
a garfish was now fixed to it, and likewise caught nothing. The three
other garfish mysteriously disappeared during the night.

Thomas became the target of the increasingly ill temper of the crew,
manifested in both violence and bitter monologues. When the last of
the wood fuel had been used, and he split the chopping-block to burn,
Tobago cuffed his ears for sinking the blade of the axe deep in the
deck. As he lay asleep in the longboat, Conrad rudely jerked him forth,
declaring the rotten craft too frail to be used as a daytime couch by lazy
cooks.

But it was Alltok who launched the most determined assault on
Thomas, thereby becoming involved in mutiny.

It is the habit of these islanders to suck their teeth when vexed, and
to direct long, muttered monologues at the cause of their vexation.
Forward, in the bow, Tobago exploded at timed intervals in the manner
of a geyser, violently upbraiding everyone by innuendo, lapsing into

silence rendered scarcely less eloquent by expressive gesturing. The darkling sloth called Eustace sat staring out to sea, from time to time indulging in rich curses to include old schooners, obsolete motors, dirty fuel, lice, bad candles and worse women. Conrad persisted in sucking his teeth in self-righteous soliloquy.

Alltok, who during the day spent much of his time at the tiller, was the most vociferous of all.

Possibly this mannerism of muttered communication derived from a type of clandestine expression by an enslaved and lonely people, becoming stylized in time to folk-art form. A combination of miming, rhetoric and digital dance: it is intended to be overheard, understood, even acted on. No one would ever laugh at or otherwise deride a muttering person, but rather would observe him secretly with serious and even worried glances. One man would find an excuse to move closer, a second would lift his head the better to hear. A mere recitation of curses was apt to be ignored, but a man who spoke of actual grievances would always be assured of a captive and attentive audience and enjoyed, as it were, a sort of inviolate rostrum from which he might preach as he willed.

On this particular afternoon Alltok, lounging at the tiller in his dirty, ragged shorts which displayed a pair of pendulous black testicles to almost any view, held forth in anger at the cook. It was his habit to conduct both sides of an imagined conversation, as if arguing with himself.

"Grarb your arse outa here, marn!"

"Who you aksin'?"

"Not aksin', marn. Fuggin' dry rice dry rice like marn be goddarm dog, eat live like ani-mal." (Suck.)

"Uncle say fish all finish." (Suck.)

"Catch fresh fish, we eat fresh fish. Fix good bait onna line strong hook goin' catch fresh fish for eat, but useless damn' cook teef baitfish lyin' on a deck in a sun all day. Haul-haul-haul, put fish on a deck make cut it, cook it, boil it wit' salt, got good fish for eat. Damn' cook teef all a baitfish, no can catch fish now. I got shillun' on a land goin' eat fish wit' sausage an' potato."

"No sausage in a sea here marn." (Suck.)

"Damn' teefin' cook eat all a food, burn food black, spile everyt'ing, put bugs in a food, Ah eat his arse. Ship sail this way, that way, this way, that way, no fuggin' wind, drinkin' water finish. We in a serious position. No damn' cig'rette (suck), las' voyage I makin' on this ship, call hisself damn' cook, eat my arse, this way that way shit boat drif', drif'. Dog can't eat cook's food...." (Suck.)

I sat on the gunnels watching as his flow of bitterness poured forth. Everyone was listening, Thomas himself was slouching on the edge of the engine-room housing twenty feet away. But presently he turned, threw Alltok an envenomed glance, and with pure insolence raised his head and deliberately directed a thin jet of spittle into the air towards him.

Alltok went wild. Abandoning the tiller, he seized a bottle of kerosene and hurled it at the cook's head. It missed by several feet and whizzed into the sea. As Thomas dived for the axe, another bottle exploded against the foremast by his head. The engineer ducked for cover, Tobago scrambled to his feet. Glaring distractedly about him, Alltok wrenched the long tiller handle free and sprang forward to meet Thomas and his axe. The violence of murder was berserk on deck.

Conrad plunged into action. With surprising agility he leapt on Alltok's back, and bore him to the deck with a rousing crash. As Thomas moved towards them with the axe, Tobago seized it from behind and found himself involved in furious struggle with the cook. Alltok and the captain threshed about on deck, the captain grunting heavily and Alltok squealing with utter rage. Legs flailed, elbows pumped like pistons, bodies heaved back and forth as hands clutched and clawed and smote. Tobago and the cook wrestled wildly amid the excitement of clattering pots and scattering pans, threatening with each moment to sever each other's head, and obscenities and howls of passion filled the air.

Into the midst of the mêlée came the engineer, moving on tiptoe with exaggerated care, wary of any menace to his person, and bearing a ball hammer in his hand. Balancing with the light uncertain rhythm of a mantis, wide eyes intense with fearful purpose, he advanced along the low housing to crouch by the writhing figures of Tobago and the cook. I watched, fascinated, from my discreet refuge behind the captain's kennel. The engineer held his hammer out, poised a moment to await the proper timing, and soundly rapped the mate on the back of his head.

The mate relaxed, sagged, and Thomas was immediately astride him. The engineer rapped Thomas on the head. The cook fell sideways, stunned, and lay on the deck with his head on a saucepan lid.

Eustace now moved towards the remainder of the fight, stalking Alltok and the captain. But now Conrad had the better of his man; Alltok was half throttled by a powerful arm locked about his throat, and Conrad's knee pressed powerfully at his spine. His eyes bulged, he rasped for air: then abruptly Conrad released him, rising to his feet, and stood above him breathing heavily.

The engineer caressed his hammer thoughtfully, and Conrad glanced suspiciously from him to the mate and the cook. The cook's eyes were open but still dazed, Tobago was propped up on his elbow as he whimpered and rubbed his head. The mutiny was definitely over.

"Wha' harpen those two?" asked Conrad.

"Sleepin'," said the engineer, poker-faced, and let the hammer drop down the engine-room companionway. "Fightin', done bump they haids, now sleepin'."

Alltok sat up and studied Conrad's legs, then suddenly looked towards me with a grin.

"Fat captain," he said. "Fall on top a marn, like to kill he daid." He handed the tiller handle to Conrad. "Go steer a boat, marn. We go Dominica."

Then he also rose, and with magnificent insolence went to the specials locker, wrenched it open, casually stole the last half can of sweet condensed milk, drank it, and happily spooned the sticky dregs out with his fingers.

On the sixth day the water proved virtually undrinkable. Only dregs were left in the barrel, sloshing about in the vessel's movement with a slime of curdled tar oils: no one had even pretended to wash since leaving Charlestown. We were close to Dominica now, but the port of Roseau was still distant and elusive. Although we were constantly beating against the trades, the sails were set for a close reach and the lazy schooner tacked at sixty degrees to the breeze. She was short of headsails, her canvas quite unbalanced, and the tiller was kept hard over to prevent her luffing and pitching to a halt "in irons", sails racking idly.

There were no more matches, so a fire could not be lit even if some sort of fuel was found. We had sailed the night before without any navigation lights, for the two bottles Alltok hurled at Thomas contained the last of the kerosene. The compass was no longer visible at night and the helmsman steered according to the wind, when there was wind. But this was less important than it seemed, for the metal hurricane lantern normally set beside it deflected the needle a full ten degrees, and anyway no one paid it much attention.

Evening fell in an atmosphere charged with apathy and ill temper, sibilant with the sounds of six men sucking teeth. During the afternoon, as I dozed in Conrad's kennel, Alltok had let the vessel luff so that the big main boom swung to and fro across the deck. The topping lift was slack, and caught one end of the kennel as the boom swung across. The world was suddenly upside-down as the kennel was violently wrenched on its beam ends and flung on its roof across the gunnels, teetering there as if deciding whether or not to fall in the sea. Even as it was in flight I was clawing my way free, and tumbled out on deck in sleepy panic to be met by roars of laughter from the crew.

A little later I found myself, like them, muttering dark comments and sucking at my teeth, while they politely listened.

Conrad was depressed this night, although the lights of Roseau could be seen five miles away. "Eh, everyt'ing go bad," he confided to me. "Ef Ah don't watch out, maybe we have another *Santa Maria* thing."

He referred to a large Portuguese liner, which had been seized the year before in the Caribbean by political adventurers. His fears included riot, mutiny, murder, starvation and thirst, as well as the normal risks of shipwreck, fire, and drowning. He brooded on the gunnels in his customary place, anxiously observing his supperless and scowling crew, sucked his teeth and sadly muttered.

"No bardy is con-sarned. No bardy care. They only interes' to loaf. Somet'ing mash up, somet'ing los', no bardy is con-sarned. How must Ah exist under these con-dishuns? (Suck.) Bipple fight, throw 'way pariffin, take axe for cut a haid off. Everyt'ing go wrong. A marn obliged to struggle against life wit' the tools he has, and always somebardy come an' try defeat he pupposes. (Suck.) Ship don't sail good, wrong wind blow, bipple waste all a matses, waste water, brek de motor, can't steer good, steal a food, this must be all my fault? Not my fault, marn. Captain give direk-shuns but a crew no good, no expreence enough to carry out a order. No bardy is con-sarned. No bardy care." (Suck.)

His audience sat listening in the dark for some fifteen minutes, until finally he went to ground in the aft trunk housing. But he passed an uneasy time there: tickled by roaches, nipped by fleas, itched by bugs, he grunted and grumbled and his rest was frequently broken by intensive searching of his cubby-hole with a torch. At last he lay down with the torch on, its light perceptibly fading as time passed.

Alltok thumped at the trunk with his foot.

"Put out a light marn, it die soon. Forget de bug marn, go slip."

Thump. "Put out de light, I say. Light don' help, no good for you to show a bug where he can bite you. Got no sidelights, if steamer come how we goin' to show him light, if you kill it helpin' bugs to come an' bite you?" Thump, thump.

The breeze fell off, the schooner drifted idly. Conrad went to sleep with the dim orange glow of the torch beside him, and Alltok sprawled out to snore on the trunk housing. The other three had gone to bed in the damp and smelly confines of the forecastle.

At dawn on the seventh day we woke to find *Yvonne Marie* adrift in gentle airs half a mile offshore from Roseau.

4

DOMINICA ISLAND

Beware the Honest Man

WHEN Queen Isabella of Spain asked Columbus to describe the island of Dominica, the great navigator crumpled a piece of paper in his fist and set it on the table: this, he declared, would provide Her Majesty with some idea of the incredibly rugged nature of the island. From Mad Mountain in the south to Devil's Mountain in the north, Dominica is a monstrous confusion of thrusting peaks and magnificent labyrinthine gorges.

But during his bold quest among these islands Columbus failed to discover that the brooding, thunder-pulsing savagery of this splendid volcanic citadel was more than matched by the corrosive violence of its people: and he died without ever knowing that the collision of Spain's gallants with the Dominican Caribs would erupt in all the bloody, suicidal fury of the invincible locked in mortal combat with the unyielding.

The Caribs had originally come to these islands in canoes. They had brown skins, straight black hair, the flat noses and high cheekbones and other characteristics of Mongoloids, but their origins are a matter for speculation by wise men. The Arawaks, Warraus, and Wapsiani were relatively peaceful; the Caribs hunted them for their flesh much as a man today might hunt wild cattle. As Vikings of the Caribbean they spread terror and desolation, raiding and slaughtering as they willed: they killed the males and ate them, and emasculated boys to keep as slaves. Female captives they systematically raped, and fattened their male children to be eaten at celebrations. It is said they preferred the flesh of Arawaks; but, when the Europeans came, they changed their preference to Spaniards.

As elsewhere in the Indies, the overseas armadas of France and Spain and Britain fought among themselves for possession of the island, and the Dominican Caribs fought them all. The European marines and colonists were backed by princes, piety, piratical greed and guns: the Caribs were backed by primitive savagery, indominatable courage, and a homicidal urge for self-survival.

History has rarely seen such dreadful fighting and racial heroism as took place on Dominica and adjacent islands. An expedition under Juan Ponce de Leon, sent specifically to exterminate the natives, was ambushed by an avalanche of screaming savages: the Dons were slaughtered to the last man, their Spanish women were ravished and enslaved. King Ferdinand ordered that every Carib captive should be branded to distinguish them from the less warlike Arawaks and Warraus. This excited the Caribs to such extreme fury that there followed the bloodiest, most merciless battles the Caribbean has ever seen. Wise in bushcraft, impregnable in the hills, invisible in the jungles, they bitterly contested every attempt the white man made to extend his sphere of influence. Heedless of volleys of musket-fire and the cannon's lethal roar, they swarmed in attack to overwhelm Spanish strongholds and carried prisoners off to devour. Settlers came to regard them as fiends incarnate, to be treated like wild beasts and shot on sight.

The very word cannibal derives from a Spanish corruption of the original Caribal, or Carib.

Gradually the Caribs were forced back: reprisals against them grew in frequency and force. Increasing numbers were captured, but stoically refused the role of slaves. The English governor of Montserrat, finding a batch of Caribs purchased from Dominica refused to work at all, loaded them with chains to teach them discipline. They dragged themselves to the sea, and were forcibly restrained from suicide. Enraged, the governor had their eyes put out, but they still preferred death in grief and hunger than life as captive slaves.

James Rodney wrote, in his *History of the West Indies*, "Hundreds died of starvation; thousands committed suicide; many jumped from precipices. They hanged, they stabbed and they drowned, they poisoned themselves. Mothers destroyed their babies to save them from the misery of living. If caught in such attempts they were flogged. They had boiling water and molten lead poured over them and were otherwise tortured to death, until death came to their relief."

Christian piety and European commerce had come to the Caribbean.

But there was more, much more. European settlers imported Negro slaves, and the Negroes brought their knowledge of occult lore. Voodoo, obeah, black magic: the name is unimportant. On many islands the forbidden science suffered severe restraint from Christianizing influences, but flourished in Haiti and Dominica. Until quite recently, there was a clause in the Haitian Code penalizing those who used zombies, or the walking dead, as labourers in the fields. Possibly identifying Dominica's brooding mountains with Africa's Guinea coast, sensitive to real or imagined emanations from a wilderness reeking with the blood of a slaughtered race, the Yoruba and Ibo slaves were in any case successful in establishing here the vigorous practice of black magic. Obeah is a power on the island, a fear in its people's hearts.

On Dominica the cult largely draws its strength from the law of contact or contagion, which assumes that a person may be victimized by expert misuse of his hair-clippings, nail-parings, excreta, or even articles such as clothing which have come in contact with his body sweat. Savants of obeah are in demand by those who wish to ensure success in a love or business affair, safety in travel, the happiness of a new house; or to guarantee the failure of a rival, to throw "tying magic" on a straying wife or husband, or to bring confusion, even death, to an enemy.

If the matter is sufficiently important and good money can be paid, a séance is held in some sequestered place. Even the rites of the infamous black mass have been imported, the impious Mass of St Sécaire with the profane sixth and seventh books of Moses. Obscure vegetable poisons, and bamboo dust which punctures the stomach's walls, ensure the strange success of voodoo spells.

"Eh-eh, fi' cent," she sang, a happy smile creasing her fat face. I hid my delight, pretending to examine the huge mango with the critical air of a connoisseur. Five cents only, and already reduced from seven, for this sumptuous golden fruit? Why, it must weigh at least two pounds.

"Three cents," I said, observing her severely. I would have gladly paid her ten, but toyed with the occasion in order to watch her quick expressive face. The market was vociferous with hucksters bargaining, and furnished to overflowing with every form of comestible Dominica produced.

"Arright, special-special price for you," she relented, and laughed. "Four cent. Las' price, four cent."

How could a woman be so fat and her smile so beautiful, I

wondered. Immense arms, breasts like great balloons, and the belly of a dropsical ox: lumpy black face with twinkling eyes, and a smile to tickle the heart of a drowning toad.

She confided something in a whisper to the woman at her side, and giggled.

"*Cadeau*," she announced suddenly, beaming. "One present for you, I give. For *casse-croûte*. No money."

I chuckled, wondering who had won the best of the bargaining.

"All right, I take it. And for you—" placing seven cents in her basket—"I give *cadeau*. For buy cigar."

She burst into peals of laughter which trembled through her frame in liquid ripples, and I turned away grinning with the mango in my hand. The market people were best of all, I decided.

The market was set at the edge of the sea on the southern edge of Roseau, below Fort Young, a concentration of shouting vendors and haggling wives, truckers and girls and barrowmen, fishermen and farmers and itinerants selling trinkets. Heaps and piles of produce as if spilt from some magical cornucopia: reds of tomatoes and chillies, yellows of mangoes and limes and papaya, greens of avocados and plantains; heaped bananas, stacked pineapples, sugar-cane and candles, fish and flesh and coconuts, frogs and flowers and gugu worms, seeds and leaves and bark to cure the ills of the infirm. Many folk there spoke the creole patois in use between Martinique and Guadeloupe.

Only one other European was in the market, a thin young man of sallow cast who slowly stalked about with a sombre and disapproving air; once our glances met, but he turned away as if the person whom he saw was patently unworthy of a nod. Sometimes white folk scurried into town from distant haunts, hurried through their small affairs, then hurtled off in their cars again as if contagions were snapping at their wheels. But the delicate conviction of their social prestige would rarely let them mingle with the rabble of market folk. Cooks or maids were employed for such errands.

Only three hundred yards to sea *Yvonne Marie* was anchored; one could make out Alltok busy with a mallet of some sort. The stem of the longboat had pulled from the planking to expose rows of rotten copper nails like barracuda's teeth, so that Conrad and I had been obliged to borrow a skiff from a sloop near by; now Alltok was at work hammering. Perhaps, I reflected with a smile, the ball hammer the engineer had used to flatten Thomas and Tobago.

Clutching a hand of sweet bananas and the mango, I walked along the waterfront and sat on the broken seawall in the sun, and broke my fast: and fast indeed it had been these past few days. Begrimed, unshaven, a solitary figure in soiled jeans, I was the subject of curious glances from people who passed by. Immigration had impounded my passports, and only let me through when I insisted I had scurvy and the fare to Guadeloupe. There had been an hour of questions spiked with all the thinly controlled distress of West Indian officials when unexpectedly confronted by an English evangelist, Barbados red-leg, or other species of professional Poor White. Austere, unsmiling, of high colour, the chief had European blood obviously promoting an esteem for protocol: and who was this oddment of a white man in paint-spotted trousers, thong sandals, and a shirt whose sleeves had been torn off roughly at shoulders?

"You are not a credit to your country, sah," he had said resentfully, and was plainly shocked when I laughed. Customs had retained my sack "for inspection". It would be delivered, they assured me when I booked at a hotel.

What would happen in Roseau? There were no boats to Guadeloupe just now. Would I meet another Alexander, or a Geoffry, or some lady? It seemed a quaint and old-fashioned town, stained with age and neglect, but splashed with the ochre and white and red of bright new buildings; not so large as Basseterre, but more robust than Charlestown, with a snarl of congested central lanes fanning out to shabby suburbs with wide streets. Something would happen, doubtless, while I waited for a boat. But in order to encourage Fortune's pleasure I would surely have to shave, and wash my face and clothes.

To the north the town was bounded by a sun-glittering stream, which chuckled out of the sudden lumpy hills and tunnelling ravines, swirled lazily over a wide bed of smooth boulders and bubbled into the sea. Two bridges crossed to the northern suburb, and up the farther bank of the stream there wound a trail leading to a verdant shelf of river-flat luxuriant with papaya and banana plants, breadfruit-trees and sugar-cane, maize and sweet potato. Above the bridges the stream was a woman's place, where girls and women came to bathe, and draw water, and wash their clothes by pounding them on the pleasing smoothness of great boulders; coveys of children splashed about in shallows.

The advent of a white man along the river trail was cause for secret tittering; dresses which were hitched up to the waist were lowered to conceal plump black buttocks, and bosoms which had flopped from open blouses were stuffed back out of sight. But when this casual intruder paused on the riverbank and methodically began to shed his clothes, ripples of alarm sped to and fro and people on the bridge paused to stare. Who was this white fool? Where had he suddenly come from? Was he about to rush naked through the stream, pursuing women?

Modestly attired in swimming tights, worn beneath my jeans for such occasions, I carefully made my way to a vacant space and rolled with satisfaction in the water. It was cool, fresh, as sweetly smelling as a mountain nymph's boudoir. For a full minute I lay face-down, in the manner of one drowned, then raised my head to meet the gaze of a gaggle of anxious women, squirted a jet of water at them, and deliberately turned away. They whispered among themselves, laughing, and one by one resumed their labours. He might be mad, this stranger, but his madness seemed quite safe.

Children gradually came close, tinkling with shy laughter, asking who and why and from what place; a group of youths came down from the bridge prepared for easy mischief, but sat down as I shaved, and talked of comparative education in the British and French islands. A tourist couple came with cameras, and with formal courtesy took photos; an elderly Negro lady sought employment as a cook and offered me God's blessings before she went away. Why, one could make fifty friends in Roseau before nightfall! Who had said this was a friendless town?

Small adventures occupied the day, and in late afternoon I walked south from the town past the Fort. The scent of oleanders hung in the evening air, and folk in doorways nodded as I passed. Somewhere in the suburb to the south, strung out along the edge of the sea, I would find a place to dine and then walk back to town to rendezvous with a Swedish journalist.

A car pulled up beside me.

"Lift?"

The driver was the pockmarked European I had seen in the market-place; beside him sat a smugly prosperous Negro, who observed me with quizzical concern. I thanked them, taking my place beside them, and the pockmarked one drove on. He was American, his name was Myers; the Negro was introduced as Hunter, a visiting solicitor from Castries in St Lucia.

"Where you walking to?" Myers demanded brusquely.

"Nowhere in particular. Just looking."

"Wasting your time. Nothing to look at down this way."

The authority of his tone was as final as the slamming of a door. I shrugged, and dismissed him in favour of the view.

"But you are not English?" Hunter queried in a high-pitched quaver. "Someone told me you were English."

Someone? What someone?

"Betcha sweet life he's not English," Myers interjected scathingly. "You owe me ten biwi, Hunter."

"But from where do you come?" the solicitor persisted.

"Australia."

"Ah, ah!" The satisfaction in his voice suggested that he should have known this all along. "Australia of course." He rubbed his hands, staring straight ahead. "And what of Communism in Australia?"

"It exists," I said indifferently. The car was turning left, along a road which ascended steeply inland. Should I alight? But Hunter began to speak.

"Exactly. It exists. And you people do not care, you do nothing, you are too busy with your sports. Cricket is more important. Is that right?"

His manner nettled me. Damn this popinjay, I would nettle him.

"Exactly!" I mocked him. "We don't let politics interfere with our pleasure. Whoever heard of a senator running a four-minute mile?'

Myers grinned broadly, but Hunter fluffed his plumage with righteous indignation.

"Precisely as I thought. You are lazy people who play games, while the Communists work wickedness among you. Oh, yes, I know all about it; my nephew went to the Olympic games in Melbourne. He told me all about you. Lazy, lazy people!"

"Worse than St Lucians, even?"

"My deah!" He turned on me. "No one can call us lazy in St Lucia. The city of Castries totally destroyed by fire: what did we do? Play games? No, sir. We laboured with our bare hands in the sun and built a fine new city."

His hands were soft as butter and the nails daintily manicured: difficult to imagine this overnourished epicure toting bricks and sweating with a shovel.

"Relaxation is a virtue," I suggested. "And we are virtuous people."

"Oh!" he cried in pain. "I cannot hear you say that. You in Australia—" wagging a plump finger—"are so…so smug. You are snobs. Oh yes, you are known as snobs. An empty country full of snobs, and you will lose it, I say. They will take it from you, while you play games. Look at yourself: casual, debonair, you don't care. You came here when—today? And don't think people aren't already talking of you. Lounging about on the seawall eating fruits, washing trousers in the river where no respectable person ever goes. Drinking liquor in low places, riding on a donkey cart with a porter, in Federation Avenue! Australian: oh, I should have known."

He produced ten biwi dollars from his wallet and stuffed them in the glovebox.

"You win, Myers. He is not an Englishman. He could not be an Englishman in a thousand years. He is an Australian, exactly."

Well, now I had upset him. Should I leave the car? Where were we all going? But Myers chuckled sardonically.

"You're a sucker for a slow curve, Hunter," he said. "One day you'll grow up."

As we climbed to the heights of Mount Bruce, among attractive villas flanked by frangipani and hibiscus, we caught glimpses of the township down below. It appeared as a wedge of russet and yellow, lead and magenta between the river and the slopes of Consecution Hill, crowding to the water's edge and giving way on the inland side to splendid botanical gardens. The gardens spread to the foot of the

Mount Bruce precipice, luxurious greens framed by the sudden flare of flamboyants, tulip-trees, and flowering cedars.

And inland, mountain peaks were pushed against the sky like the nipples of a nubile land.

Hunter alighted at the top and haughtily huffed off without a word or glance. And I wondered if I should also leave, and walk back down to town.

"Stay," said Myers. "No sense in going back. Nothing there." His house was a mile or two farther on, a rambling wooden structure set on a mountain slope, its veranda overlooking a jungled valley. The main room, which we entered, was a large and sparsely furnished lounge which, though meagre in its appointments, contrived to appear as the haunt of some ascetic, but pixilated scribe. A typewriter sat on a table, crowded to the edge by a scattering of unwashed plates and cups, the floor was strewn with paper clippings and manuscripts and various reference books. Copies of the *Christian Science Monitor* competed with scientific journals and a fletch of dried tobacco leaves for possession of a sadly sprung old sofa; other books and magazines were stacked roughly in odd corners, for the room lacked any shelves which might have held them. One side of the room gave onto the veranda, drawing in the valley's wondrous view; a corridor led off to other rooms.

Myers dumped his load of market purchases on the floor, and the parcels I carried for him followed suit. As I strolled across the room to admire the valley, he barked abruptly, "You a writer?"

Sometimes, I reflected, but to name oneself a writer is to inter one's self, in people's minds, in a familiar and constraining pigeonhole.

"No."

"I am."

"I wish you the luck of it," I offered.

"Why should you? Matter of work. No luck needed." He turned his head and shouted, "Trudy!", and took up a calabash gourd to pour measures of dark liquor into two unclean tumblers. "Hunter's a typical product of the British colonies," he went on, passing one of the glasses. "A greengrocer with a bowtie. Parrot in peacock's feathers. Goddam little *poseur* trying to pretend he's the king's uncle, scared someone'll look inside his skull and find there's nothing there except a ball and chain. You should have told him you were a Communist. I hoped you would."

As I sipped my rum, I noticed that the room bore marks of violence. A coffee table in flight had scarred the panel of one wall and lay upside-down with two legs broken. A window was smashed, another fractured, and the fragments of a white china jug had been swept into the company of books and magazines. Other scars and scratches on the walls invited one to wonder at the cause.

Myers turned his head to the corridor and yelled again for Trudy. Doubtless the Negro cook, who would be waiting for the stores that he had brought.

"So," he said at length, his pale eyes fixed on mine, "you wonder why I brought you here. Eh?"

"H'm. Yes and no."

"I pick you up in town and shanghai you out into the jungle. So what happens now? You think I might be desperate for company. Or I might be a queer. Or after your dough. You're sitting there waiting to see what gives. You're expectant, nervous, hopeful, curious. And right now, at this moment, you're getting embarrassed as all hell by what I'm saying."

"I don't embarrass easily," I said.

"And already you're wondering how the hell you can get away from this scabfaced idiot, who says he's a writer. You feel insulted, but you won't admit it. You feel you're losing control of the situation. You've suddenly got an unfamiliar problem on your hands, and you don't know what to say. Eh?"

There seemed to be more nuts running around loose on these islands than there were growing on trees, I reflected.

"Not at all," I protested politely. What the devil was I doing here? He might be mad. I must take care, lest I provoke him.

He nodded with satisfaction, and grinned.

"You're a liar," he said flatly. "Three questions, three false answers. Cock's crowed three times, and you've denied yourself three times. Why? Because you're a hypocrite. 'Humbug all a time,' as they say down here. You couldn't tell the stark truth, even if you were whispering to a stone. Why? Because you're scared. You've no damned idea who you are, what kind of a person you are, and you're scared someone else'll find out."

There came the sound of someone padding lightly up the corridor, and a growing flare of light among the shadows announced the approach of someone bearing a lamp.

"People can only afford to be honest," he continued, "when in complete control of a situation. If they aren't in control, they have to resort to stratagems. Any sort of rivalry, political or otherwise, breeds...."

But he was talking to himself. Into the room, carrying a hissing pressure lamp, came an unexpected figure in a blue satin slip. A white girl, lightly tanned, her lank tawny hair falling past her shoulders in mild disarray, her face dull and gentle, but her body exquisitely proportioned. The satin slip outlined her modest bosom and sheathed her cunning flanks with an artistry of libertine suggestion; she walked barefoot, and I studied her as she set the lamp near by. Passing me with the merest glance, she sat on the floor at Myers' feet, leaning back on his chair and resting her head against his knee.

"...but we've evolved beyond that animal state, and survival itself has evolved to a matter of resisting vicious social pressures. No longer animal, not yet divine; somewhere in between, still subject to the constant law of change, still in love with genocide. And in our present state we can only be controlled by fear. It's not important whether Russia or the West is in control, but there must be that control. Communism will almost certainly win that control, with ethnic groups divided into cells: then it will fragmentate, the whole structure will collapse, and...."

I had met her many times, in many places, but she had never been my woman. Artist's model in Chelsea or Copenhagen, "hostess" in Hamburg's Reeperbahn, Parisian waif, and chicknik for San Francisco's beats: physically alluring, mentally a wasteland studded with purple peaks of unsanctified emotion. Too unimaginative to absorb even the patter of *avant-garde* cults, she would drift among the chosen as a sort of built-in fringe benefit for nature-loving males. Too lost to be discovered, too sensuous to be ignored, men mistook her silence for detachment and her boudoir nonchalance as evidence of sex sophistication.

"...eh? Do you agree?" he was asking. Agree? Agree with what?

"Of course."

"Oh God! Don't be so damn' egalitarian. Even if a human brain functions perfectly, one hundred per cent instead of about sixteen, it'd still be a primitive instrument subject to limitations. It couldn't cope with cosmic consciousness. It's only designed, at this stage, to cope with a specialized environment...."

He was off again. For more than an hour he talked. Myers intense, the girl mute, myself becoming anxious about supper. Twice she rose to pump the lamp, and when she did I tried to ignore the perfect silhouette detailed by strong lamplight flaring through her slip. She obviously wore nothing underneath. Once Myers stroked her hair, so that she stirred with gratitude, but persisted in his vigorous discussion of some emasculate philosophy which seemed to be a formula guaranteeing universal fear, intellectual thrombosis, and perpetual misery for at least a million years.

After half a dozen rums he relieved himself from the veranda, piddling on the heads of startled chickens down below, and as he returned to his chair there was a voice at the door.

"Myers? You are there?"

Myers grinned happily. "Jacob! Come in, don't stand there like a black goddam turnip."

A tall, smiling Negro entered, handsomely clad in a light suit and pronouncing his delight to see us all. His manners were precise, his diction academic, and in general his bearing was suggestive of scholarly diplomas and close association with elegance in living.

"Picked up this bum on the waterfront today," Myers explained to him as he sat. "Been giving him the usual verbal vaccination. Not exactly a genius, but at least he hasn't thumped me in the teeth." He smiled at me thinly. "That was a Canadian music-man I brought here last month. He couldn't take it." He squinted over his rum, and added maliciously, "You're an Aussie. You don't let coloured people into your country. They wouldn't accept Jake, he's too black, the customs wouldn't let him through. You have any colour prejudice yourself?"

Jacob met my glance levelly.

"That depends," I said cautiously, "if—"

"Oh goddam!" He sighed explosively. "Do you, or don't you?"

"Not in general. Some of my best friends are white."

They both laughed.

"You like black women?" Myers persisted.

"Sure. There was a huge mountain of a woman in the market this morning who—"

"To sleep with I mean, idiot!"

"Not particularly. I prefer white meat to dark meat in fish, turkey, and women. But this is a preference, not a prejudice."

"What do you prefer, Jake?" He laughed evilly. "As if I didn't damn' well know. What do you think of this bum I picked up, anyway?"

Jacob gazed at me reflectively as if seeking substance for some firm opinion, studying my clothes and face as he pondered his reply.

"Well, I do not know yet," he said. "In his appearance I feel he is not bothering to try and impress anybody. But I do suspect he is still trying to be correct, and saying what be thinks will be, ah, acceptable to us. I don't think he is honest. I do not feel I can trust him."

Shades of Satan, I was being sniped from both sides!

"Jake's a disciple of mine," said Myers cheerfully. "When I first met him he wouldn't say crap to a chicken, but I've got him in training. Never met so much fear in one man in all my life. Eh, Jake? Fear of being black, fear of white snobs, fear of the slave stigma, fear of obeah: all these on top of the kinds of fear you've got. But he's easy to deal with. His fears have the direct, open quality of the uncluttered primitive. The Negro derives ecstasy from fear, it's the quality of fear that provokes fanatics to invent new and terrible gods, and sacrifice young virgins."

He noticed Jacob eyeing the girl covertly, and a sly expression crossed his face. He patted his thigh with one hand.

"Trudy. Come."

The girl obediently rose and sat on his lap with one slender arm draped about his neck. He stroked her thigh, and she smiled vacantly.

"Trudy's nearly honest," he said, "but on the animal level. A mass of unreasoning reflex. She responds predictably to given stimuli. If I touch her here, she'll kiss me."

He passed his hand across her breast, and she kissed his ear.

"If I touch her there, she'll bite my neck."

He touched her there, and with a sigh she lowered her head to bury her face between his head and shoulder. He glanced mischievously at Jacob.

"You want her?" he asked me.

Want her? Was be offering her to me?

"No. No, I don't."

He chuckled, patting her rump.

"You're a liar. And you're mentally preparing to dodge out of sight behind a smokescreen of lies, because that's how you've been trained. Right?"

Devil take the fool: how much must a man endure in order to be fed? Were we, indeed, to be fed at all? There were no sounds coming from any kitchen.

I shrugged, and he spoke to her.

"Trudy. Stand up." She slowly uncoiled herself and stood before him, her slight but regal figure marred only by the coarsely sculpted profile of her obtuse young face.

"Take off your slip."

"Uh?"

"Take it off."

For the space of several seconds she just stood looking down at him, vaguely sad, then gracefully shrugged the straps free from her shoulders and let the slip whisper down her body and tumble to the floor about her feet. In nakedness she stood there, arms by her sides, looking down at him in melancholy silence. Jacob stared wide-eyed, his hungry gaze licking over her, and Myers threw his head back and laughed.

What in sweet eternity was he hoping to prove? What prompted him to stage this exhibition? Was he completely abandoned by good taste? I disciplined myself to disregard her, if I could, not so much from any sense of chivalry as resentment at being a guineapig for Myers to torment.

"You still don't want her?" he demanded craftily.

I rubbed a hand across my face, wondering how best to put an end to this. What other parlour tricks might he devise? I was his guest, and in his house. But had be not forfeited his immunity as host? No wonder the Canadian had struck him.

"She's available," he prompted, mocking me.

"You must pardon me," I said coldly, "my appetite is concerned with food. Dinner. I never make love on an empty stomach." Or an empty heart, for that matter.

"Aha! I suppose she doesn't even attract you? Aussie, you've got so many lies in your mouth, it's a wonder you don't choke to death. You're scandalized by a new experience. You feel you're losing control of the situation again. Trudy, do you want him?"

"No," she murmured, not even glancing at me.

"Do you want Jacob?"

She turned her head slightly to glance furtively at Jacob, and when she saw his fever of lust she shivered, and looked away. What kind of a life did she lead in this place, I wondered. Was she his wife, his plaything, what? Was she merely a white rabbit to pull out of a hat, to astonished guests?

With a brusque wave of his hand he dismissed her, and she padded softly out of the room leaving the satin slip on the floor where it had fallen.

"You're a phoney, Myers," I observed, and he looked at me alertly.

"So? Enlarge."

"You're still adolescent, you haven't grown up. That's the kind of stunt schoolkids pull in the coal cellar. A stag-party trick for frustrated old men. You're all front and façade, Myers, with nothing but a spoonful of poison slopping around in your skull."

He grinned delightedly. "Now we're getting somewhere, at last." He chuckled. "That's probably the first flash of honesty you've had since you came in the room."

"Still putting on the backroom act, trying to prove things to yourself. Do you bite beer-bottle caps off too? Why don't you learn card tricks, or palmistry? And fix a big spotlight to shine on you? Or, if you really want to impress people so much, why don't you just try being pleasant? Carnegie-style, tell them nice things about themselves. Believe me, it fascinates them. It works. And you don't have to keep morons like Trudy to help you do it."

He was shaking with mirth as I spoke, mocking my anger with small, expressive gestures of glee, and now he burst forth in merry laughter.

"Oh, you're beautiful, Aussie! You're trying so hard. Goddam, it's wonderful. Provoke a human being enough, and eventually he starts being honest. It's like lowering a pail into a stagnant well and bringing up a bucket of champagne."

Jacob rose, murmuring excuses, possibly disturbed to see his idol so profaned, and went off.

"You're merely searching for an excuse to revel in licence, Myers," I gritted. "But why did you have to come all this way? Harlem would have done just as well, or Little Sur, or New Orleans. You'd find lots of sick minds to keep you company, and a bigger audience. And apparently that's what you crave, an audience. Or are you scared? Scared to have more than an audience of one, stuck away in a mountain hideout?"

"The audience is necessary, sometimes," he admitted with a smile. "I bring someone up when I feel the need." He re-filled our glasses from the calabash gourd, and went on, "I've got pretty deep into this thing, with my writing, but sometimes I have to drag myself back from the theory to the practice, and re-establish contact with the fundamental theme."

Obviously, I decided, his mind was polarized by this quasi-intellectual infection which magnetized his ego. He talked on, and I was silent. I could walk back, if need be, to the town.

But not many minutes had passed when suddenly the girl screamed from somewhere in the house. I stiffened. He ceased his dissertation, but sat quietly in his chair. The silence of the night was now broken only by the hiss of the power lamp. And then her cries rang through the house.

"Oh God...oh God...oh God...No-no...no-no...."

"What the hell?" I burst forth, standing. "What's...go to her, you blasted fool! She's in trouble."

A curious expression of near ecstasy crossed his face. His jaws worked and twitched, but he made no move.

"Yes!" she screamed. "Yes-yes! Yes-yes!" And then a long-drawn, trembling quaver, "Oh-h hell, that's wonderful!"

Myers rose from his chair quivering with excitement, his fingers flexing and face twitching, and gazed at me eagerly.

"Want to watch them? Come on, it's all right. Goddam, he's magnificent to watch!"

I stared at him aghast as I realized what he meant, and what the screams had meant. But surely he was mad, insane! He tugged at my wrist.

"Come on! Watch! They like it. I often do. I want you to see. Damn it, he's the most—"

But I had jerked my wrist free, and swiftly drawing back my hand I struck him violently across the mouth with the back of it. He staggered backwards, arms flailing, tumbled over a cane chair and crashed to the floor. But as I turned towards the door, picking my, way among the market purchases in the lamp's uncertain light, he laughed.

"You're wonderful, Aussie." He was sitting on the floor, and wiped a hand across his mouth. "Goddamit, I could love you!"

I paused to stare at him. What manner of man was he? What conceivable reply could he expect? I could have happily pitched him into the nearest open grave.

"God help you," I said huskily. "I doubt if there's anyone else who can."

He slowly shook his head, smiling. "I don't need help, Aussie. But if you stayed here with me a month or two…ah!"

At that moment Jacob hurried out of a nearby room, from which there issued a soft glow of light; his loins were wrapped in a coloured towel.

"What?" he cried, seeing Myers on the floor. "What? What?" He glared at me. "You bus' him?" he cried excitedly, advancing. The towel fell away. Myers remained on the floor, watching with interest, and I caught a glimpse of the girl emerging from the room.

"You bus' my fren'?" Jacob demanded, enraged. "Marn, Ah goin' bus' your haid for true!"

He was too big, he could kill me. I seized a basket of vegetables and flung it at his head. He parried it with a powerful forearm and vegetables scattered through the room. But even as I fled through the door he was in vigorous pursuit, and bore me to the ground within ten paces. A vicious blow jarred my head, and a hand strongly pinioned my left arm. Twisting and writhing under his weight, I fought to free myself, gouging at his eyes as he grunted purposefully and sought to pulverize me with one great flailing fist. Somewhere near by the girl shrilled with pleasure, and I was vaguely aware of Myers calling Jacob. For perhaps half a minute we engaged in rapid struggle: but then, as he finally bestrode me, one fist now pinning my throat and the other drawing back for a mighty blow, I brought my knee up powerfully to punch him in his unprotected groin.

The ancient, classic last resort of assaulted women, cowards, and desperate men.

He howled with pain and clutched himself, rolling on the ground, and I was running before I even gained my feet. Plunging through the darkness, I burst through shrubs and bushes, grazing unseen trees, making in the general direction of the road. After perhaps two hundred yards I stopped to listen; he had quickly recovered, it seemed, and I could hear him casting about in the thickets of brush behind me, growling curses. If he thought of it, he could head me off: could race ahead, and hide in ambush by the road.

I hurried on, bruised and dirty, scratched by unseen hazards, perspiring freely. What evil star had sucked the richness from this day of social pleasance? How had I come to be here, a nervous fugitive hastening through the dark?

And then, scrambling around rocks and past a confusion of thick shrubs, I suddenly stepped forward into space.

Falling, falling....

Billowing grey mists were drifting past a disembodied blaze of pulsing yellow. A dark grey monotone, slow and uniform, moving steadily across a throbbing furnace colour which rhythmically receded and advanced. There came the anguished cries of people helpless, terrified, about to be consumed by some fiery phenomena....

As I opened my eyes a little, on the edge of consciousness, the furnace blaze diminished and the grey was streaked with thin, dark lines; the shouting of the people persisted, but no longer in terror and distress. I tried to move, but at once gave up, for my body felt like shattered glass gripped in bands of iron. The thin dark lines of greyness became the bare old weatherboards of some construction, perhaps a wall. My head buzzed and throbbed, and somewhere in the distance people were still shouting.

Where was I? What had happened? I could remember nothing. There was daylight somewhere, and I lay on an unyielding sort of platform, on my side. How had I come to be here? What country was I in?

From some dimness my mind picked up a vagrant thread of memory. Cuba. A country lock-up, the bare wooden cell. They had just seized the A.C.S. sugar-mill and thought I was some agent bent on sabotage...but no. Not Cuba. The memory thread developed, wandered farther. The hot wooden box of a room at Port Royal in Jamaica, with the jukebox pumping dissonance up from the bar below...no. Not Jamaica either. There was more. Tortola Island? The house we shared in Road Town, the bare wooden walls we tried to hide with travel posters, the grey fatigue of slaving at the printing press, the dark room, editing and publishing the *Times*...but no again. Not there.

Myers! I groaned softly. Lucifer's apostle: why did he have to happen to me? Jacob, raining blows on my body. But how had I fallen? Down, down...I had impacted with shocking force on some kind of gravel surface. There had been a moment of consciousness when I had called out weakly, and then nothing more. The rest was blank.

Then where was I now?

Gently I began to move. My legs responded, but something in my rib-cage grated harshly and I gasped. My right arm was bloody from some extensive, shallow abrasion, clotted with black earth; my left wrist was swollen to three times its normal size. The watch, which had been there, was missing. There was a great lump on my forehead, and other minor cuts and bruises; otherwise, I was still alive.

So much for the evening's revels, I decided bitterly. Why in the name of the devil had he picked on me? Because I was a stranger, and would not stay to carry tales? Jacob, one could easily forgive, and the girl was nothing other than pathetic. But Myers! There was something of psychopathic evil in that man.

Carefully looking around, I saw that I was in a room, a bare room littered with secondary debris, unswept, the door fallen on its side, the windows gone. Where? Painfully I eased to my knees: and, on a thought, felt at my hip pocket. My wallet was still there, and the razor. I could look down on the ocean; it was less than thirty yards away and a little below. And there was *Yvonne Marie*! That shouting I could hear, that would be the morning market. Why, I had somehow found my way back to Roseau, too late to find a hotel, and like some wounded animal had crawled in here to sleep.

Well, conscious or not, that showed some spark of common sense.

Grimly I rose to my feet, and although one knee was stiff I could hobble well enough. Limping through the door, I found myself in a large, neglected courtyard surrounded by a clutter of weatherboard rooms, which seemed to be abandoned. I was inside the Fort, the seaward gate was open, and another gate led inland to the street. I must find a hotel, a bath, some sort of food. But, as I made my way towards the gate, I heard voices in the nearby guardroom. Three constables were there, one of them holding a conversation on a telephone. I walked straight on through the gate; no one saw me, and not until I had passed under the stone arch and entered the street was I discovered by a sentry stationed there.

Stab me softly, this must be some kind of police outpost. And I had slept there? I must have been mad. But no, I would have entered from the seaward side and dropped down in the first room I found—the sentry at this gate would not have let me past. He studied me curiously as I walked by. Soiled and bloody, nursing my left wrist, my clothes and hair dishevelled and my face bruised and scratched, I mustered such aplomb as I could and limped past.

"Sir?" he called inquiringly. I ignored him and walked on.

"Excuse me, sir."

Let him call. Nothing more could happen. I would tell them I had been tossed from a flying saucer.

"Please, sir!" He called to his confrères, asking them if they had seen the thing which had walked out of the Fort. There was a chattering of voices, but no sounds of pursuit.

Past the market I limped, wishing fervently the fat woman there could tend my wounds. She would have sensitive hands and the power of healing men. Pedestrians in the street paused to stare, so that my passage was marked by a trickle of inquiry in my wake: and suddenly Alltok was beside me reasty with the smell of rum, slightly drunk. He weaved a little as if the street were slowly rocking to and fro, and his attempts to see from under drooping eyelids lent him the expression of a suddenly wakened owl.

"Hey, wha' harpen you?" he asked anxiously. "You been fightin' too?"

It was obvious that his night had also included various adventures.

"Aye, fighting," I said. "I met an honest man."

He blinked heavily, peering closer. "An' he beat you up?"

I nodded, smiling. Here, at least, was contact with a world I understood.

"Damn' flurrum bastard!" he cursed. "Black marn beat you up? Take me dere, Ah tear he belly out for feed a crabs!"

Even sober, I felt, he would offer to do that, for in his casual way he accepted me as a friend. Dirty, drunk, violent, profligate rascal and penniless sea-tramp with a thousand homes and none, he was my friend too. God's gift to the Caribbean, I reflected, is the Negro without a colour bar.

"Not a black man," I said kindly. And, indeed, it was Myers who kindled all the mischief. "A fouled-up white man with a sick brain, Alltok. And listen—" I gripped his shoulder with my good hand— "you're a liar and a thief and a villain and you couldn't tell the truth if you tried, and I love you for it. If you ever meet an honest man, beat the hell out of him for me!"

Sheer surprise lifted his drooping lids, and his eyes were fixed on me in wonder as I walked away. Near by at the Federal Hotel I requested a room, assuring the solicitous patron—his name was Clive Jacobs, no relation—that all I required, after having fallen down a well and spent the night there, was a bath, some food, and a bed.

For the following seven days I was the constant companion of that bed.

5

GUADELOUPE

"Women are Fantastique"

THE French *gendarme* is a *poseur* with an opportunist's flair for sensing drama, where another might consider no drama could exist. He is an artiste inclined to dapper elegance, with a peacock's sensitivity to attitude and posture, and in seeking his own reflection in the eyes of other folk his agile brain, tutored to suspicion, is apt to interpret the merest glance as marking the hunted evasion of the guilty. Where the British constable has all the calculated prudence of a well-sited fort, the gendarme is a plumed cavalier questing far afield astride his own romantic fancy.

One might assume there would be gendarmes on the wharf at Point-à-Pitre, and my passport lacked a visa for entry to Guadeloupe. There had been no French consul on Dominica, and little need for one, for not only could islanders travel to and fro with few formalities, but even Englishmen required no special permit. Australians, it seemed, were somewhat different. They are not particularly beloved of the French, who still recall their indiscretions during the First World War and regard them as exuberant, unruly, and intolerant of government controls. Years before when in Athens, applying for a visa to enter French Tunisia, I had observed the *sous-consul* leafing through a large black tome, wherein he discovered a page describing conditions of entry to French colonies for Afghans, Australians, and Somalilanders.

Perhaps, if one could enter Point-à-Pitre without having been discovered, the end result would be the best for both the French and me: any expressed desire to enter without a visa might be scornfully dismissed, but surely one's wish to leave would be received with interested, and even excited, consideration. A chartered vessel called *Delgres* had carried one hundred and sixty people from Guadeloupe over to Dominica for a grand May Day ball: I had boarded the vessel with them when the time came to return, and it seemed reasonable to assume that one might swarm ashore in their midst at the French port without detection.

Delgres had left Roseau at midnight with a host of hilariously happy whites and blacks wearing flowers and waving bottles, dancing merry reels on the foredeck and bawling lusty songs in the saloon, a foment of laughter and revelling delight. She arrived at Point-à-Pitre at seven in the morning, and spawned forth a suffering disorder of wretched miseries red of eye and weary, seasick, scragglehaired and drooping with depression, pathetic refugees from what might have been three days of continuous disaster. Dragging their possessions, they shambled along the wharf, inclining bodies slightly so that feet would shuffle forward questing balance, and with barely a muttered curse moved out of the dock gates and into the street. Half supporting some dull-eyed creole, I moved with them, and my condition was even worse than most: my left wrist and two ribs were strapped in plaster, my tender spine recalled the violent ministrations of a Negro chiropractor, and massed scabs of gravelrash infested my right arm.

Two police were at the gate, and a customs officer. Immigration officials were on hand, but if anyone observed me my gaze was not on them, and they assumed I was merely another victim of May Day merry-making. We moved past them into the street, and as the throng dispersed I left the creole to stagger off wherever he wished to go, and marched off up the street with more purpose.

A gendarme was standing not twenty feet away. *Bon Dieu*, but he was stationed there to look for such as I! My glance barely grazed him, no expression crossed my face, but his quick intelligence reached out with the inquiry of invisible antennae.

"Monsieur?"

Eyes of a throttled fox, I was discovered! To walk on would only excite increased suspicion. I greeted him with a brevity designed to hide my accent, but he said, *"Anglais?"*

English: yes, of course, I must be English. As such I would require no entry permit.

"Yes, monsieur."

He smiled politely, and indicated the immigration office back inside the gate.

"But it is necessary for you to report. You must have your passport stamped."

I nodded, and leadenly turned back towards the gate. So clever I had been, I reflected caustically. Now I was exposed to all the critical suspicion directed by authority at those who employed transparent subterfuge to avoid due process of the law. What would they do? They could not send me back on the boat, for the boat stayed here. But whatever punishment they might devise would interfere with my chances of finding out if Tic-Tac was here.

The officer behind the immigration counter thoughtfully stroked his throat as I appeared, and his appraising gaze swiftly flickered over me with professional interest. He was my own age, but paler and dark-haired, the hand caressing his throat was prettily manicured, and with his uniform he wore an air of casual confidence.

"Excuse me, monsieur," I began, "may I have my passport stamped?"

He ignored the volume of passports which I laid before him on the counter, and silently considered me. His disciplined moustache, impeccably pruned and waxed to upswept horns, competed with a shoal of little pimples for possession of his cheeks. His brows were oiled and brushed, his marcelled hair gleamed in smooth waves, and the collar of his uniform betrayed small signs of talc. A sartorial epicure, then: what shivers of delight must accompany his private contemplation of the mirror! How he must frown upon the pustules which disfigured the clinical perfection of his face!

"I've just come from Dominica on the *Delgres*," I said, to break this uncomfortable pause.

"And you left the docks without reporting?"

His tone suggested an irate parent rolling up his sleeves. I sighed heavily, making a droll face.

"I am almost dead, monsieur. I was at Dominica, everything was very quiet, and then suddenly a boatload of your people arrived, and the whole town went mad with festival. Dancing through the streets, singing, laughing, all day and all night for three days. *Dieu*, but you French are incredible! I am exhausted, I could not keep up with them. This morning I could walk through the gates of Heaven and Hell and never even realize I was on my feet."

"Ah so," he said with satisfaction. He seemed to be somewhat mollified, and even gave a tight little smile.

"Your girls have such life, such a joy of living," I continued. "And your men: but they are *formidable*, they never tire, they had everyone in Roseau dancing in the streets."

He nodded, grinning, and glanced at my wrist.

"But you broke your wrist?"

"Oh, three young Frenchmen and I went at night to put the tricolour above the town hall, and I fell from the edge of the roof to a balcony below. Fractured a bone."

"The tricolour? You went with them to help put the tricolour." He looked down at my passport and fingered it thoughtfully. He would be wondering why I, by accent American or British, should replace the federation flag with that of France. The old green leather cover which contained my six passports was printed with the legend, "*Protectorat de la République Française au Maroc, Gouvernement Chérifien.*"

"*Maroc?*" he inquired, arching his brows.

"Just a souvenir," I admitted agreeably. "I was there. A magnificent colony, before its independence. A credit to France. Ah, you should see those half-French dancing girls at Meknès, they wear no—"

"Ah so?" he interrupted joyfully. "I was there for three years. Meknès, Fez, Marrakesh. I was with the Makhzen."

The Makhzen! Aye, I had met them in the alleys of Marrakesh. We had hurled bottles of soda-water at them from rooves above, exploding like glass bombs; and, when they searched a man, they thrust long fingers where no man should ever search.

"The Garden of Roses," I said cunningly, "by the Djaama el Fra. The White Russian they called Zapote, she—"

"The Garden?" He laughed, delighted, touching his moustache as he observed me with new interest. "Oho, they know me there. And Casablanca's Busbiah, full of man women who—"

"They ripped the shirt off my back and sewed it back on, without charge," I remembered. I had been wearing a beard at the time, which was later distinguished by being removed by a barber in Seville. "And the Maison Blanche, in Fez? Did you ever go—"

"*Meutre!*" he cried. "La Maison Blanche, the little Chinese-Armenian nautch-dancer who used to oil herself and defy any man to—"

"And they'd lower her down from the ceiling in a basket."

We burst out laughing at memory of the incredible can-can, which featured the girl in the basket and the frustrated dwarf who had no arms. Chuckling to himself, he glanced at the cover of the first passport, and threw me a friendly glance.

120

"British, yes? *Anglais?*"

"Oh yes." The cover bore the bold statement "British Passport", with underneath in smaller print Commonwealth of Australia; but, if he saw the smaller print, he made no comment.

"*D'accord...*" He entered my name and passport number in a ledger, recorded "*Anglais*" after them, stamped a vacant page and returned my volume to me with a smile.

"They have a little place here," he confided, "called Du Chat qui Pelote. They have cockfights, and then they put the monkey with the rooster, you know? Ah, you'll find things to do. And if in any way I may be of service...."

A Makhzen man, I reflected. But he was not such a villain, surely. With the stroke of a pen he had admitted an impostor to the French overseas territory of Guadeloupe. I was now *en règle*, to a large degree. No more embarrassing questions would be asked: indeed, I could even ask my own.

"Do you happen to know if a young French lady by the name of Toe—they call her Tic-Tac Toe—recently entered Guadeloupe?" I tucked my passports out of sight and he was thoughtful, considering the name.

"H'm. Toe....H'm, no, I don't recall the name. Of a certain species?" he inquired, describing curves in the air with his hands.

"Of exactly that species," I agreed, smiling. He nodded approvingly, crossed to the telephone and rang *Sûreté Nationale*: and after questions had been asked, and a certain time had passed, his eyebrows signalled me a measure of success.

"When?" he demanded over the phone. "And where is she staying? Oh. Yes. Not at all."

He replaced the instrument and grinned. "She has arrived. Ten days ago. By aeroplane, from Antigua."

Tic-Tac, *chérie*. She was actually here, in the same city, perhaps less than a thousand yards away!

"Where?"

"Ah, I cannot say. She has no registered address. She must be at some private address. She's not staying at any hotel or the *Sûreté* would know; the hotels have to send in a *fiche* for every guest. But she's still here, at least. They have no record of her leaving."

Anticipation effervesced through my veins. She was here, this wonderful Tic-Tac, I had found her! Sooner or later our trails would have crossed, but now we would re-join and life would again assume a spirited pattern of high colour. She passed through life like a feminine whirlwind, stirring the dead leaves and tossing her skirts, whipping dull normalcy to feverish agitation. Ah, but life was good! The day was bright, here was a fine new city, and somewhere I would find her and we would dance a merry roundelay before astonished strangers, and skip from island to island down to South America.

"I thank you," I said warmly to the gendarme. "If my uncle was here, he'd thank you too. I've been looking for her everywhere."

"I hope she's a trifle fat," he confided drolly. "Thin women think too much, and thinking makes them vicious." He sighed happily. "Ah, women. They are *fantastique, non?*"

I chuckled, realizing just what he meant, and even shook his hand, then marched out through the gate. To the gendarme standing there I threw a gay salute and briskly walked towards the city centre. Here was a new metropolis and the freedom to move about as one might wish, with laughter and the flavour of excitement in the air. And a handsome city too: the docks important with transatlantic shipping, the seaward phalanx of weathered ferro-concrete offices steeped in the commerce of *outre-mer*. Here was the sturdy fruit of hard-headed Gallic enterprise: the buzzing streets were flanked by the diligence of merchants striving to reproduce the pattern of French life, and a sprinkling of splendid modern buildings emphasized the colony's ambition.

Smiling faces, black and cinnamon and white: extravagant courtesies, quick anger, sudden giggles and excited argument. Where would she be, this girl of mine? How could one find her amid this seething thrust and parry of swarming city life? She must know I would come, she would expect me: what sort of signal might she leave to mark her trail? She could walk forth from a shop at any moment, or appear beside me in a sudden rush of joy...and awareness of her raced in my blood as I envisioned how we would meet.

There was a likeness of her in the Prado, in Madrid, which I had seen. In Hans Memling's "Adoration of the Magi" there was the figure of a green angel in the left-hand panel, the clear intent girl-face suggesting virtuous confidence edged with frustrated carnal curiosity. Tic-Tac was neither virtuous nor frustrated, but the stranger might have reckoned her naïve, angelic in synthetic innocence and frugal with her gifts.

The market-place was superbly Negro, a whispering swirl of brilliant cottons infesting a giant palette daubed with fruity colours, and an acre or two of the Champs-Elysées had been transplanted to Place de la Victoire. The air was of sudden perfumes, spiced cooking, and aggressive drains: coloured and caste girls tinkled and flashed with costume jewellery, skirts and bodices flamboyant with bold designs, needle-point shoes squeezed their toes and thin stiletto heels pocked the torrid bitumen with a rash of tiny craters—in the British islands they would have been draped in Mother Hubbards, shuffling in flat slippers which never left the ground. Dainty French ladies minced from shop to shop, eyes heavily painted under upswept hair bouffant, lips of fashionable pastels to reflect the Parisian trend, and gay frocks seasonally cut to show their knees. When the English woman dresses in the colonies, she appears as if about to visit clergy: these French, one suspected might all be *en route* to cocktails at the house of Madeleine Chic Décor.

Several men were squatting on the sidewalk drinking thirstily from green coconuts, and I joined them. The vendor deftly sliced the top from one and passed it to me with a straw, and as I drank I covertly observed my fellows. White men, black men, mulattos: business men, coolies, they squatted side by side without distinction and too casually correct to merit comment, quaffing the cool juice and scooping out the soft meat with chips of husk. Had I, then, finally discovered a colony where democracy's fine phrases had reached down from rarified air to embrace the lowly, and the poor? An integrated island, perhaps: a city of champagne, surely, bearing the label of *vin ordinaire*?

At intersections I would pause, scanning the four streets: would she have left a note with the British consulate? But I went there, she had left no message. The post-office? But they had nothing either, and even *Sûreté* did not know where she was. Then how would she let me find her? What should I do?

Inland from the city centre the streets lost confidence, the shops were narrow booths of tawdry merchandise, from which the vendors peered like birds of prey. Here was the grotesque commerce of petty bazaars and mansard rooves, avenues of small, dark cells crammed with trinkets and used tyres, essences and ear-rings, shop-soiled clothes and slightly damaged silks, elixirs in bright bottles and every type of shiny bauble to entice pennies from Poverty's slim purse.

"Monsieur, I make you happy." Three brown wenches giggled from a doorway, and I frowned in mock severity as I passed. Their laughter followed.

"Hey, monsieur, come see." A dark little gnome of a man beckoned urgently from tumbling, old premises, which threatened to fall about his head. But I winked and walked on, and never discovered what it was he wished me to inspect.

"You like white girl, meestair?" a stripling asked in English. "Chinese schoolteacher?"

I grinned. "No thanks."

"My seester? She sixty-nine."

"Too old, man."

"No no, she sixty-nine for you, she make love dat way for you."

"Spanish fly, monsieur? Regard...."

"Meestair, you like see white girl flog black man?"

"You sell something? Benzedrine?"

"*Capot* anglais?"

"My seester...?"

"Kif?"

After perhaps eight blocks the city dropped all pretence, and beyond a skirmishing throb of restive buses even the shabby bric-à-brac shops refused to venture. The pavements broke up and disappeared, sloughs of mud and clay appeared, the ancient wooden buildings with their wrought-iron grilles gave way to a festering slum of ragged hovels built of hessian bags, flattened tins and scraps of broken wood, and rotten mats of thatch. One might have wondered if someone had reduced a giant rubbish-tip to a series of small mounds. Pigs rooted in sewage and foul drains and wallowed in pools of filth beside the road, children played in ulcerous little swamps of stinking refuse. The floors of the huts were of moist black earth, sodden from recent rain, and bags or perished canvas spread on rancid grass were beds for impoverished Negro families, who collected these shards of rubbish and pretended it was home.

Here and there old people sat by the wayside with pitiful displays of oddments which someone, if he was mad, might chance to buy. Huddled in misery, defeated, dull eyed: nothing more could happen to them. Squalor and misfortune had dragged them down so far that only death came next, and they had neither the strength, the knowledge, the ambition, nor sufficient time remaining, to set out on the long, upward struggle towards life.

Abandon hope, all ye who enter here.

Pausing by one old crone, I inspected the things she had for sale, spread out in orderly array before her. One half of a pair of scissors, three metal strings from a piano, a hinge broken at one corner, candle-stubs and empty bottles, a small pile of smooth black pebbles, another small pile of used and rusty nails, assorted seeds and pods, the nickle-plated case of a cheap alarm-clock, several ends from burnt-out welding rods, a short length of toilet chain, pieces of bone and hair and unnamed things, and a hopelessly broken automatic office calendar. Not far away an aged man sat by a hovel in the sun, loose and scaly folds of dry grey skin sagging about his wasted frame, stranded by the tide of years on the bleak shores of loneliness: one scabby leg was swollen with elephantiasis to the thickness of his waist.

The old woman's gaze travelled slowly from my sandals up my jeans, but halted at my knees as if she knew too well they supported nothing of great worth, and fell away. What road had brought her here? She had once been a girl, pretty perhaps, laughing with other girls: did she remember that? Her fingers were twisted, her skull was mossed with scattered tufts of short white hair. And the children playing in the mud, what would their fate be?

"Go!" she rasped suddenly. "Go, go, go, go!"

Leaving a small gift beside her, I walked on. A girl child, half white, naked, observed me with one bright wondering eye and solemnly picked her nose. The other eye was clogged with matter, which had oozed forth from it and dried to a matted scab, clustered now with busy flies; and suppurating sores, some scratched and bleeding, could be seen amid the grime which soiled her legs and arms. As I dawdled past, too conscious of the white man's guilty burden, she found something in her nose and put it in her mouth.

Less than half a mile away there loomed a great new building, and someone told me this was a modern hospital—white and blue and shining splendidly above the foetid encrustation of sickness and defeat. I wondered who might be there, tucked in beds with clean white sheets, cared for by white doctors wearing starched white coats.

Blackness: the white man's symbol of despair. Even when he vomited with social guilt he achieved little more, sometimes, than the sliming of his sharkskin coat. A city of champagne, still? More like the union of a barren philosophy with a castrate land.

And farther, where the road branched west, there was a grotto in the side of an embankment; a natural hole it seemed, some four feet high and two feet deep, blackened by the smoke of innumerable candles, the bottom ranged in rough ledges and coated with wax from candle-stubs. A sinister sight: for set within were several score of idols, images, figurines, crosses, holy pictures—each of them headless, broken, split or torn. Arms and legs were missing, broken torsos piled on one another. Shattered images of saints, decapitated Virgins, dismembered Christs, ravaged dolls: a shrine to the snake god, someone said, and indeed it may have been. Why not?

The island had known terror enough, even apart from the destruction of the Caribs by the whites. One and a half centuries before, for example, during the rule of the ferocious Victor Hugues, the French defeated and captured a British force of three hundred. They guillotined twenty-five in Point-à-Pitre and marched the remainder out to Morne Savon. The prisoners were forced to dig a common grave, then stood beside it and fell in as they were shot. Owing to poor marksmanship, some were only wounded, but the living were buried with the dead just the same, along with the heads of the other twenty-five.

Alone throughout the day, and lonely still at dusk with no trace of the French girl to be found, I sat at the arcade beside Place de la Victoire to drink *bière Lorraine*. Here one could watch the well-fed matrons walk with dignity, and clean white children, among the

mango- and flame-trees, and towering emperor palms. With dark the
city closes as if afraid of shadows: and the wretchedly poor then come
to hunt like ferrets through the Place, gleaning edible garbage from the
trash-cans and snatching fallen mangoes from the lawns.

Champagne? There was no pattern of human love in this congestion
of strange contrast: all was façade, pretence, there was no common *joie
de vivre*. It was like the marriage of a eunuch to a whore. It swallowed
light, and laughter was lost in the hungry solitude of night. And so at
last, to a man alone, it became a city of *vin ordinaire* masquerading as…
vin ordinaire.

Three days passed, money exchanged hands, a whisper went forth
from the bazaar. A white girl, but definitely French, of such and such
appearance and mode of dress; her hair was dark and short, she might
or might not wear a wide gold wedding band. A white man sought
her, and would surrender the other halves of this torn paper money
whenever she was found.

She might be anywhere within the city of Point-à-Pitre. Paper boys
watched for her, two youths roamed the shops, an old man stationed
with his barrow by the market entrance in Schoelcher Street called her
name when any likely girl passed him by.

And still I searched.

But where could she be? Her skin was like honey, and her heart a
pagan flame. She was here, she would not hide. Did illness confine
her to her bed? Was she eating loneliness? Life was a feast at which she
danced a gay fandango, despair was a hungry presence lurking beyond
the circle of the banquet's blazing lights. One could sometimes sense
a nervous urgency, a desperation in her when the feast grew drowsy
and the lights burned low, and her dance would grow wild and wilder
yet with the panic of the extrovert attacked by loneliness. In dreams
she had seen aloneness as an enormous cockroach feeding in the dark
solitary places of her mind: her own fearful sobs would waken her to
hurl herself from bed and turn on lights, radio, record player, anything
to push back the loathsome presences. She refused to notice unpleasant
things until they were forced upon her, resulting in much happiness
pierced by sudden invasions of distress. Emotional, impulsive and

frankly passionate, she may have been true to her own self, but her loyalty to others was a matter of sophistical expedience.

The Manhattan, the Oasis, Café de la Rive Gauche, La Sport, The Piddling Cat: she had been seen at none of these, or so they said.

Then, on the fourth day, an uncertain message came. She had been seen, almost surely it was she, entering a house near Quai de Lessups, a stone's throw from the dock where I had landed. A boy had called her name and she turned, gave him a startled glance, and disappeared at once inside the house. A white girl, but definitely French, of such and such an appearance and manner of dress; her hair was dark and short, and she wore a wide gold wedding band.

The lad took me there, and waited while I went inside. There was an office of some sort, a corridor, and stairs. Where would she be? There were too many doors. I could challenge them one by one if it came to that, but surely there must be some other way. A shabby place it was, with cracked wooden walls and scuffed lino on the floor...and so close to the docks, would not the ground floor be used for storing goods? Quietly I mounted the stairs, as a cat which stalked its prey. If it was really Tic-Tac which my scout had found, why had she turned away as if in flight? She would never flee from anyone, except herself.

Eight doors lined the corridor upstairs, four on either side, and led to the balcony which overlooked the street. One was wide open, another slightly so, and brief inspection reassured me that neither one held her. Six doors left: from one of them there issued the sounds of two men discussing quarry prices for rough stone: she would hardly be in there. Five doors, five silent doors. But why did I fear to call to her, or knock? Why did I move with the stealth of a thief? Peering through a keyhole, nervously alert lest someone find me, I saw portion of an empty room with a bed which had no mattress. Empty, unoccupied. The next room had its key in the lock, blocking any vision: its occupant must therefore be inside. My heart was drubbing in my chest, my throat was dry. I knocked softly.

"Tic-Tac?"

A rustle of movement, a moment's silence, and then she opened the door. She was clad for the boudoir, her eyes were wide with wonder, and I drew my breath in sharply as I saw once more her beauty.

128

"Peter! Oh, sweet God, I didn't want you to…to…"

As we embraced, I kicked the door shut with my heel, pressing her to me, burying my face in her richness.

"I've searched for you, searched for you."

Her fingernails bit into my flesh as we kissed, then she wrenched her face away and shook her head.

"I didn't want you to find me. Oh, why did you let me go away? I didn't want to. Why did you let me leave?"

But I gazed at her in wonder, for her eyes were shining with tears. I touched her cheek, searching now to find if joy or distress provoked her tears. She was thinner, her face was peaked, the pallor of her skin betrayed fatigue.

"But you were hiding? You were hiding from me?"

She nodded, brushing at her tears with one hand.

"But why, *chérie?* You must have known that I'd find you?"

"Yes. I saw you once. By the Credit Bank, yesterday evening; you were watching all the office girls go home. I wanted you…and I turned and ran away. Please, why did you ever let me go?"

What foolishness was this? We were lovers: why would she fear to meet me? Why would she avoid me, to hide like a hunted animal in its lair?

Suddenly she seized me in embrace, so that I winced from the pain of my fractured ribs, desperately kissing my throat, lips, eyes.

" Oh, I love you so much, " she whispered. "So much!"

Later, when an hour or more had passed, I sat to pillow her head on my lap as she lay on the divan, and told her of the honest man I met on Dominica, tenderly observing the delicate nuances of alarm and humour which sparkled in her eyes and tugged the corners of her mouth.

"And then this local witch-doctor, he weighed about a hundred and fifty kilos, would make me lie on my stomach while he felt up and down my spine with his fingertips. His fingertips were sand-papered to make them more sensitive, and it felt like a spider waltzing back and forth on tiptoe. Then he'd tell me to breathe out, empty my lungs, and suddenly, Wham! he'd give a little jump and come down with all his weight on the heels of his hands in one place, beside a vertabra. Crunch-crack, and another one would go back into place, and my two ribs felt as if they were stabbing right through my lungs. The cure was worse than the illness was."

"But now you're mending."

"Aye, all I need is the proper exercise." I kissed her nose. "But you…you look pale. You've lost weight. Have you been ill?"

She shrugged evasively. "Nothing, really. And now? What will you do now?"

"Oh, I don't know." We could wander down-island to Trinidad, and Venezuela. "South America," I suggested. "We seem to be headed south."

She said nothing, but lay there staring at the ceiling deep in thought.

"We could do something there," I went on. "Work in Rio for a while, maybe. Carnivals, dancing, new people. Did a red-headed woman in Nevis offer you a part in a film?"

She shook her head. Did something trouble her? She was not her usual self, something had dimmed her customary fire. Gently I ran one finger up her arm and caressed the smoothness of her throat…and abruptly a cold flame burned within my stomach.

"The silver Buddha. You lost it."

"Yes." She began to say something, then seemed to change her mind. "The sink," she said. "It fell down the sink, the drain. There was no bend in the pipe, and it fell right down. Oh, I could have wept. I was so lonely for you, and when that went I felt it was an omen."

"The sink? Where?"

"Here. In the ladies' closet."

The cold flame was a sickness, a fevered constriction flaring through my bowels. Lies, Tic-Tac, lies! A Negro has your Buddha back on Nevis. I closed my eyes and lay back, and the vision was a sunset beach where a strong, young buck without a face was shouting, "She bin willin'."

A flood of hot resentment swarmed through my brain, pursued by a chill rush of bitter logic. She lay with him that night: she gave herself to him. But what did that mean? Does it prove anything you didn't know before? She lay with another man. Why not? You weren't the first. Why shouldn't she lie with another man, as long as you don't know? A black man…is it that which fills you with a rage of jealousy? His blackness, and her fair whiteness: is it that which stabs your bowels with the poisonous lance of hate? Laugh at yourself, you and your fine ideals—black man, white woman, your woman, and theory dissolves to a bellyful of gall.

Tic-Tac my loved one, why? Why?

For a long time I sat there, waiting for the fury of jealousy and hate to cease washing through my brain in bitter fire. Accept, accept! She was free, free. No human can possess another human, no one can hope to understand the obscure electric impulse which causes the human pendulum to swing this way and that.

But, by the bones of a sacred turtle, she even gave him the silver Buddha! How many ways could a woman devise to make a man a fool? She was remote and unknown as the mist on mountain peaks. The fault was mine, I should not have let her go, I should have bound her to me with a cord of living steel. But how to bind the wild goose? She was a wanderling, a waif adrift among the shipping-lanes of life and fearful of the solitude she found. Perhaps she had not been willing? And he had stolen the Buddha from her? Visions of that night hurled themselves unbidden through my mind. Tic-Tac and the Negro clasped in embrace on the beach…the trinket in his hand…his strong, heavy features devilish with red light as he lit his cigarette from the smouldering piece of husk.

"She bin willin'."

Footsteps sounded in the corridor Tic-Tac gasped, and sat bolt upright on the divan.

"No!" she whispered tensely. "Oh no, please no!"

The door was not locked, and a thin, young white man entered the room smiling. He froze to instant rigidity when he saw us. One hand grasped the door-knob, the other held a batch of documents, or papers. Devil's tits, but who was this? Some lover? Who else would boldly enter without knocking?

"Michael!" she cried shrilly. "I…he…"

"Wha-what—"

A passion of berserk fury engulfed me in red waves.

"Bastard!" I shouted, and leapt from the bed. As I lunged towards him, he stood there speechless, frail and white, clear young eyes clouded with the pain of stark despair. Tic-Tac screamed as my fist shot out and cannoned on his jaw. He fell back like a wooden doll, and crumpled in a heap outside the door.

"No, no, no!" She rushed to kneel beside him. Doors were popping open along the corridor. "Michael, Michael! Please, oh please, Michael!"

She turned on me with blazing eyes. "You fool! You dog's urine! He's my husband. We were married here a week ago, you swine, you filthy swine!"

The walls of the room were reeling, the floor seemed to sway beneath my feet. A dizzy stupor fogged my head, and I rested one hand against the door for support. Husband? Married? Tic-Tac, and this pale imbecile?

The world was a madhouse, there was no logic any more, my skull was stuffed with cotton. What was happening?

Folk were gathering in the corridor and murmuring inquiries. She was joking. Married, just like that? Impossible. But who was he? What rights did he possess? She couldn't have married a sickly, pale young apronstrings like that!

Someone helped her pull the body inside the room, and then she closed the door. Muttering and argument sounded loudly just outside.

"Married?" I whispered, incredulous.

"Yes, married," she flamed. "Or maybe you don't think I'm fit for anyone to marry? He's English and I met him in St Kitts, and we met again in Antigua and then came here, and we were married last week and please I never ever want to see you again. He's good and kind and gentle, and he needs me and he has a regular job and we're going to settle here. He's lost without me, he's a child, he can't do a thing without me and I'm going to look after him for the rest of my life. And now you can go and never come back. Go to South America and keep on going and never stop, because you never will stop and I'm damn', damn' sorry for any damn' fool female who ever falls in love with you, because you'll drag her around the world until she dies of sheer exhaustion."

She paused for breath, her bosom heaving.

"Please," she entreated tearfully, "please go away!"

It was the end, the finish, there was nothing left. Go? Where was there to go? It was the end of the road, there was nothing more. Married? She married him? But in heaven's name why? In her hands he would be nothing but a toy: and I felt a brief twinge of sadness for this toy that she would use. He was the lover, she the loved: Lord in Heaven help him, for she would cause him pain.

There was nothing more to say, the end was here in this room, at this moment. Poor, weak English fool! A regular job, but unexpected luck had brought him home in the middle of the day to find his week-old bride with some berserk stranger.

As I moved towards the door, I saw a sheaf of currency lying on the floor among spilt papers. French francs, a goodly sum. Suddenly there came a thought that good might come of this, and I stooped to pick them up. I would give them to the gaunt old crone who sold piano wires and rubbish while she waited patiently for death. This day was doubly cursed, and it needed someone's blessing.

Tic-Tac gasped and rose to her feet, eyes wide with horror. Despair possessed her face.

"No, no, don't take it! Oh please I need it, I need it!"

Why, she was in a panic of distress—she, who cared so little about money, acting as if it grew on trees, or could be picked up by the roadside like dead leaves. How could any woman change so much?

"Please, give it back." She moved towards me with her hand outstretched, and her face was pinched with fear.

"There's plenty more in the street," I said cruelly. "I've got a use for this."

"No, no, please, I'll do anything!" She touched my arm, and I flinched as from fire. "I really need it desperately."

"No. Let him pay for you. You're sold, Tic-Tac. He's bought the rights."

I moved towards the door, but she tugged at my wrist.

"Listen," she pleaded, glancing back at Michael's prone figure. "Listen, I'll do anything you want. Anything. I'll go with you. I'll go away with you anywhere, if you look after me. I need-"

"Look after you?"

"Oh, please!" She pressed her head to my shoulder. "You know I love you. You know that? Take me with you and…and…"

"But you're married to him! Aren't you? Isn't he your husband?"

"Yes. I had no one. I had to have help. But, *bon Dieu*, I need that money. Please?"

"No."

"Then take me with you? Let me go with you?"

I pushed her gently from me, bewildered, and scanned her face. She looked pale and exhausted, a shadow of the Tic-Tac I had known.

"What help? What do you need the money for?"

She hesitated, embarrassed, and a numbness crept through me, rejecting all emotion as absurd. Emotion was obsolete, it was exhausted, it could not keep the pace.

"You're married," I said thickly. "Then have his child. Stay with him. Be good to him, sometimes. Have his child."

"But I don't know if…if…"

Bones of a buttered toad!

"If it's his?"

"No. Oh, dear mother, I don't know, I don't know."

Woodenly I held out the money, and she clutched it to her face, sobbing brokenly. Turning from her, I opened the door, but as I entered the corridor something struck me violently on the side of my head and once again I was falling…falling…

He sighed deeply, hands clasped on one knee as he sat on the edge of a table and stared down at the office floor. The rest of the *Sûreté* staff had long since gone, the evening was late, and the lights of the docks could be seen through the tall glass windows. The tip of his tongue licked back and forth on his bottom lip, his carefully pruned moustache curving up in horns among the little pimples which peppered his pale face.

"It is a story," he said simply. "A man can never see beyond a woman's face."

I said nothing, slouching in defeat on the hard wooden chair. My head still throbbed, my wrist had swollen to press against its bindings. Who would have thought my only friend in all this city would be an immigration man, and my refuge his office in the dockside *Sûreté*?

"I once helped a woman find her man," he went on, "and he committed suicide the same night. Sometimes when a woman comes to me seeking information of her man, I see only spite and trouble in a skirt, but still I have to help her if I can." He wagged his head, pondering the problems of mankind.

A good man, I reflected soberly. A professional inquisitor in gendarme's clothing, and yet I liked him. I had been dragged here half conscious by a pair of angry fools, who swore I had been assaulting wives and damaging their husbands, but when he learnt I was the victim of a woman's thorny wiles he had ordered them away, and brought me wine. I told him little, but it was enough.

"What will you do now?" he asked. "Will you stay here? If you wish, I can—"

"No. No. I won't stay."

"Will you go back to, ah, England?"

I glanced at him quickly. "It's too early. I don't know. Somewhere. Anywhere, so long as it isn't Guadeloupe or Dominica."

Dominica! Twice, within such a short time, an unsheathed female had stabbed me through with torment and hurled me down an abyss of despair. A pox on them all, I decided savagely: henceforth a life without them would be a life well lived.

"South America," I said. "I'll go to South America, up into the mountains. Women can't live above fifteen thousand feet. There's not enough air to support their lies."

"Ah, South America," he echoed approvingly. "I would like to go there. They say the women there are—"

"The same as women elsewhere," I snapped. "Faithless, lying, deceitful, predatory…*arrrgh!*" Words failed me. Women? The world would be well without them. Give me a few dishonest men, a handful of happy rogues and an unfrocked priest or two, and a rousing song with a mug of rum could damn all the women to Hell. "How can I get the devil out of Guadeloupe?"

He pursed his lips, and fingered his moustache.

"Well, there's Air France tomorrow, you could go as far as—"

"Tonight. What's leaving tonight?"

"But nothing," he said, concerned. "Not until tomorrow. Air

France—"

"No boats? No island craft?"

He gave his moustache a twirl and grinned wryly. "Well, *La Vierge de la Mer*, but that's only a native schooner."

Ah, there'd be some companionable scoundrels aboard her!

"Where to? Where does she go?"

"Martinique, I think. Yes." He was worried, eyeing me askance. "But these island boats, they aren't...comfortable. And the crews, they're a rough lot. I don't think you'd—"

"When does she sail?" Martinique was south, on the down-island run to Trinidad.

"Er, midnight. Or soon after. But it's too late. I completed their papers for them this afternoon."

"There's still over three hours. Could you fix it for me?"

He hesitated, ill at ease. It was long past his time to go home for he had delayed several hours to bring me wine and food and sympathetic conversation.

"Let me get off this accursed island," I pleaded. "I don't want to spend a night here by myself, with her and that Englishman a block or two away. I'll get drunk, I'll get into trouble, I'll do something I'll regret, anything can happen. Let me get on that boat and go."

"I suppose—" he began uncertainly—"it's irregular, but I suppose I can do it. We wouldn't want you to get into more trouble, would we?"

"My troubles are over," I said sadly. "Women don't exist any more, from this day on."

He smiled, his eyes slightly glazed with imagination.

"Ah, women, women. But they are *fantastique, non?*"

6

MARTINIQUE

Anatomy of a Crime

LA MARTINIQUE—Queen of France's Caribbean colonies!

The seaward slopes of the soaring Pitons du Carbet were yet stained with the purples and blacks of night as the schooner powered steadily towards port, and the dragon-toothed ranges of the island's silhouette bared their dark fangs to the dawn-bright sky beyond. Here and there the new day stroked the soft, round buttock of a green hill with light, and pink young clouds laughed down on the sleeping land. We had come upon the island before it was awake, still lying tousle-haired in her silken disarray of damask mists, and as the schooner motored in to Fort de France we watched the dawn's warm light spill in splendour on her peaks.

An elderly mulatto, sitting by me, said with drowsy content, "This de bes' place in de whole wide world. I bin everywhere, Trinidad and Grenada and Barbados and St Croix, and there ain't no other place like Martinique." He spoke with the quiet intensity of one who uttered sacred words, and I was silent. He nodded towards the pink and white and yellow city swarming the coastal slopes either side of a great fort on a thrusting headland, and went on, "And that de bes' town in de whole wide world. Fort de France. I don't born dere, but it be my home until I die."

"Better than Point-à-Pitre?" But he scowled, and spat aft towards the way from which we came.

"You see me spit?"

I also turned and spat. Never again would I go to Point-à-Pitre.

"Dey say, if any marn slip one night on La Martinique," he murmured dreamily, "she steal your heart an' keep it in a pot on top of Pelée Mountain. Then if you go some other place, you must only find disappointment dere. You must come back to her."

The fair city of Fort de France was almost pushed into the sea by the ponderous weight of the mountains beyond; two days and nights at sea had cleansed away a little of the phlegm which clogged my brain, and furtively I wondered what substance this dark man's words might have. I would leave the Caribbean, I would find a ship and go: but, again, what has travel across the face of the world to do with escape from grief? A bird which flies through the air must carry its lice wherever it goes. The heart is not rested by running fast: if I gave my heart to La Martinique, to be kept in a pot on a mountain top, might it not be protected from poisoned hatpins and long nails?

Fifteen years of travel through a hundred different lands—there was a weariness within me, an unfamiliar longing for some form of spiritual peace. Neither gods nor riches had I found, no stirring doctrine or pansophy had disciplined my quest across the earth. I had come into the world as nothing, and nothing I remained. There was an aching deep within me, a yearning, some urgent sort of void: and suddenly I wondered if here, on Martinique, I would stay.

Passing close to the crumbling immensity of Fort St Louis' walls, we came into the Baie du Carénage, and tied up at the small-craft dock with other sloops and schooners of our kind. Listed on the manifest as English, I was again received as such, and wandered forth from the docks towards the city. The day was young, the streets already clamorous with traffic, shops and eating-houses quickening to the business of the day. In a nameless, old wooden hotel I found a room, where Rue Bouillé considers entrance to a large bayside park called La Savanne. Monsieur *le patron* was a gentle Negro elder, who received me with anxious courtesy and followed me upstairs.

"You want something else too?" he asked anxiously. It was a large, airy room with two beds, a chair and washstand, and a broken slab of mirror nailed beside a window which overlooked the street. The floor was of sagging wooden boards, which creaked inquiring chords as one walked, spider-webs on the walls were hung with lifeless shards of moths and roaches. A lizard eyed us from the windowsill and darted out of sight.

"A towel," I said. "Are there lice?"

He hesitated, avoiding my eye, so I turned back the covers of one bed, to see if there were any little bloodstains where the last occupant might have moved in sleep to crush the swollen bodies of feasting bugs.

"You want company?" he asked.

"Girls, you mean?" So near to the docks one might be expected to have girls.

"If monsieur wishes, there are two—"

"If you send a girl up here, I'll slit her from her guzzle to her gutch!"

I snarled ungraciously, and his eyes popped in alarm. "All I want is a towel, fairly clean, and a bath. Nothing else."

He hurried away and returned with a towel. The bathroom was on a balcony above a central courtyard, and had surely not been used in several months. It was locked, and there was much shouting between balcony and courtyard before a young Negress appeared with the bent handle of a fork.

"Monsieur?"

She smiled invitingly, and rubbed her bust against me as she brushed by to joggle the implement in the lock. I pierced her with a hostile stare, and she sneered damply. I would be a *fouf,* she was thinking, a man of doubtful sex. Aye, well let them think what pleased them, so long as they kept away.

Various unlikely objects were discovered in the bath: a chamberpot with holes in it, a dead bird, the broken handle of a broom, a crumpled length of rusty chicken-wire; half an inch of dry ashes suggested the place was never used. When *patron* had discreetly vanished and the girl had flounced off with the rubbish, I found the tap of the bath was not connected, and waited for some time while the drunken shower rinsed itself with spasms of indigestion and rusty water. After being thoroughly kicked and shaken, at last clean water came.

Gratefully I sluiced away the grime of *Vierge de la Mer,* the dust of Guadeloupe. And if a tear mingled with the water, to the memory of a vision corrupted by the flesh, no one would ever know. What did it matter? A man's life, one brief gasp in eternity. What was this adolescent urgency, so prettily labelled Love, but a primate's instinctive coupling, a swollen gland, an invasion of the intellect by hormones? There was an armour of bitterness about me, which water could never wash away.

As I soaped and washed my hair, I became aware of maledictions and cries of alarm arising from the courtyard below, and idly wondered at their cause. Muffled shouts, the scraping of chairs on concrete: were people fighting? But as I swept the hair back from my face and thought to peer outside, the door was opened suddenly and the Negress stood there again.

Devil rot the wench! She stared at my nakedness.

"Monsieur, if you—"

Splat! The soap I flung at her head hurtled past her ear, ricocheted from the door and disappeared. She fled, slamming the door. Could a man not be free of the vixens even in the privacy of his bath? Blood-rich with indignation I quit the shower, towelled myself and dressed: and on walking outside observed the cause of the commotion. The shower water, running from the bathtub and failing to find any sort of outlet in the bathroom floor, had flooded in tide under the door and across the balcony, and onto the heads of persons at food in the courtyard below.

We walked at leisure amid the evening quiet, of Place Clemenceau.

"But there's nothing difficult about it," he argued persuasively. "All you have to do with the dame is cut her in half and—"

"No."

"...let the blood run down into a basin."

It was that gentle hour when the soul of a city rests from the affairs of a busy day, when the rush of machinery subsides and friends sit with cooling drinks or stroll the promenades. The big market in the Place was closing, the ranks of little *camionettes* had fled off into the hills with departing country folk, the square was almost empty.

"No," I protested decisively. "It's an admirable idea, and I could do it with great relish. But I won't."

He scratched his ear vigorously, staring ahead at the river. His dark hair was of longer cut than that of most Americans, and slick enough with oil to gleam with sunset tints. For his smooth and regular features women might have called him handsome, but the soft, drooping mouth and tender chin were strangely ill matched to his cruel, hooded eyes.

Aye, but he would be master of his women, I reflected: and I wondered again at the lot of womankind. They worked hard in Martinique. They laboured in the fields bearing great swatches of cane on their heads, massive stems of bananas and baskets of mangoes, and sacks of vegetables. They toiled up from valley streams to hillside huts with cans of water balanced on their skulls. I had watched them by the yacht club unloading barges laden with sand. Barges pulled in there loaded to the limit with grey sand: men lifted boxes of it to the heads of women coolies who scurried to and fro, mute and weary and perspiring, to load the waiting trucks.

Other Negro women worked at clearing the city's clogged and noisome drains: Fort de France lies largely on flat ground and the system of waste elimination is sluggish, so that accumulations of solids block the seaward flow, causing foul morass on city roads as slime backs up and leaks from manhole covers. Teams of women raked the drains, shovelling sludge onto the streets in mounds, fly-infested and gently pulsing with great worms, and then transferred it onto trucks. They worked with the quiet courage of those who, swept on eddies close to the fringe of life, had seized with determination on the last link with survival.

"Goddammit, you don't have to marry the broad," he complained. "Just tie her hands in—"

"No. Let's forget it."

"But why not? You can sleep with her too."

"Thanks. Where's Pelée Mountain from here?"

"Her husband's a conch, he's drunk all the time."

At the edge of the river we leant on iron railings to watch two men on a landing-stage below struggling to drag a great fish from a long dugout canoe. This was the Madame River, a narrow channel skirting the city's northern edge under residential heights, a stinking artery of bubbling black dross which leads canoes in from the sea with provender for the nearby market. They had a huge marlin in the canoe, all of three hundred pounds: though how such a large fish came to be in such a slim canoe strained the imagination. The bill was solidly wedged under a seat, so they had to hack it off, but even then they could not lift it ashore without danger of the craft overturning.

"Come..."

Larry and I went down to the landing-stage and helped, holding the canoe firmly while they heaved at the fish, and in this manner it was landed safely. They thanked us, and we strolled on down the canal towards the waterfront.

"You could have my girl too," he persisted. "I'll turn her over to you. She's Puerto Rican, hot as a pickled chilli. Damn it, I've got to find someone."

Hell's fires, could he talk of nothing else? We had chanced to meet in a small café barely an hour before, and already he required me to cut up women and catch their blood in basins.

"*Fumez Bastos,*" a poster read. *Duquesne Rhum. Vins de table Cocara. "La Moucharde"* was playing at the Parnasse. This was Martinique, I should be with its people, not an argumentative American.

"It's a magnificent notion," I agreed. "It appeals to me. Nothing would give me greater pleasure than to cut her in half, and in halves again, until the pieces were small enough to stuff in sausage casings. I wouldn't even have to be paid; I'd do it for the sheer delight. But just to perform a parlour trick with mirrors, eight or nine times every afternoon and evening in front of a tentful of goggling strangers—no. Get someone who wants the job."

He sighed dispiritedly, hands deep in his pockets. He belonged to a Coney Island circus group called Pan-American Amusements, on permanent tour of the Caribbean, which had arrived in Fort de France for a three-week visit aboard a landing-barge, and had its tents planted by Boulevarde Alfassa along the seafront. Larry was chief operator in the magician's sideshow, but hoped to quit and return to the States to join a more sophisticated group. But first, according to his contract, he had to find some fool to train and take his place.

"Good money," he mourned, "All the mickey a man could want. See every city in the Caribbean. All you've got to do is learn a few easy tricks and the patter, and you knock it back. I'm crazy, I should be selling the job, not tryin' to give it away. You rich, or somethin'?"

"Rich enough, for now." Why work before the need arose?

"You make like you're a bum," he said resentfully.

"Thanks. At least I'm not a bloody Yank. Or even a Puerto Rican." Most of the circus people were Puerto Ricans, hard-driving mercenaries who competed bitterly for the best sideshow sites and quarrelled incessantly over imagined grievances. But likeable folk, withal.

"Wanna make something of it?" he growled, pausing to eye me evilly. Make something of it? Fight? Hell's devils, was I about to bleed again?

"No," I said earnestly. "I've been coming off second best a little too often, lately. I'm a bum, you're a gentleman, but let's get off the subject of women. I'll even buy you a drink, if you pretend you're not

American for a while."

He grinned as we walked on. "Good. I was getting nervous. Every time I have a fight, I get killed. I know a place in Liberty Street...."

Walking with more purpose, we turned left along the seafront while Larry described the delights of bars and honky-tonks throughout the length and breadth of Fort de France. Once or twice he paused to peer through open doorways, but continued on towards the Parc Savanne. We passed by the clutter of tents and lights and the Ferris wheel of Pan-American Amusements, already warming up for the nightly programme of events, and I pondered how it would be if I were to take the job he offered, and circuit the Caribbean as a sort of synthetic magician amusing troops of strangers. Opportunity was standing at my elbow: why did I refuse? Normally I would have accepted it, without great regard for the money involved, for any new occupation always held a strong appeal.

Did I really want to stay on Martinique?

"Tourists!" Larry muttered in disgust, moving away from a noisy bar. "Tourists and queers, funny how they always shack up at the same places. But, brother, you've got to meet a queen bee down at the Europe Café, black as a fiddler's bitch and twice as fast. And Felix, every time he opens his wallet someone else's money falls inside, but you can't help liking him. And there's Jac the Junkie, and Pappi...."

The setting sun fired the swollen undersides of swollen purple storm-clouds, and eddies of cool air sucked at the dust of the Boulevarde. Out in the bay *Renegade* was cruising in to anchorage, a red yacht I recognized from the Virgin Islands; gusts of wind whipped leaves from the headland of Fort St Louis, and scattered them about the broad Savanne. The city converges on this park from two sides, hemming it to the sea; the cafés of Avenue Duparquet and the hotel-restaurants of Rue de la Liberté line adjacent sides, and citizens on promenade wander abroad on the grassy field or sit by the emperor palms.

Café de l'Europe was a bright modern *estaminet* glittering with nickel-plate and mirrors, busily engaged with its evening clientele. Most of them were *békés*, white folk of local birth, and some Negroes; the radio was pouring forth a popular island ballad.

When you arrive in Martinique...
You arrive at your mother's home....

Two barmen were at work devising the needs of clients, cups of
fragrant coffee were whisked from some recess by two lively waitresses,
Mutzig Pils and *bière d'Alsace* stood on several tables, while others
savoured strong aperitifs, or even sweet island rum. *Jus d'ananas, goyave,
cythère, corossol*—surely this café would have its finger on the pulse of
Fort de France. I glanced around in delighted approval, and Larry
grasped my arm.

"Look!"

He indicated a Negro girl standing by a table on the far side of the
room: and at once it was evident that this was no ordinary wench.
She was tall, her body finely proportioned to suggest fluid grace and
supple movement, but these endowments were merely the setting for
the perfection of her face. She had the classic Ibo profile, an exquisite
balance of prominent feline tones blending with the deftly sculpted
valleys to be found in the old artifacts of eastern Nigeria; yet her back
was not too hollow, nor her bosom so swollen as to mar her elegance.
The fine straight nose, the enormous Picasso eyes, the delicately ridged
lips and smoothly flowing throat suggested throwback to some ancient
race when Arab blood first mingled with the sub-Saharan Bantus.

"Five thousand francs," Larry said in awe. "And she gets it, too." For
one brief moment I could have thrust a knife through his heart. "But
there's something about her, nothing can spoil her. Funny. Like as if she
was some thoroughbred, and no one can take it away." He gazed about
the room, then grinned and slapped my shoulder. "Come and meet
these types."

He led the way to a table occupied by two men and a girl, and they
received him gladly.

"I found this wandering round loose," he said expansively, and
introduced me. "I told him he was a bum and he wanted to kill me,
so pretend he isn't." He glanced at me mischievously. "This is Felix,
the one with the long fingers, and Pappi. Pappi's a birdwatcher, or
something." And then, as we found chairs and joined the group at
table, "I don't know who the broad is."

Felix laughed. "She's mine, circus man. Be careful under the table, or

I cut your hands off, eh?"

Larry squinted at her appraisingly. She was young and overly slim, her mouth pinched with conceit, and her manner suggesting self-approval that she would condescend to sit with common folk.

"What do you call yourself?" he inquired. She met his wolfish gaze uncertainly, then dropped her eyes and pursed her lips to a chaste and reproachful button, but was silent.

"What are you drinking?" Pappi asked.

"*Cap Corsé*," I said, inspecting a row of bottles by the bar.

"Ricard," said Larry. And turning anew to the girl, "Open your mouth and wobble your tongue as you breathe out, and see if you can talk."

Her eyes widened with hostility and she glanced at Felix for support, but he shrugged.

"She paints," he said. "She's an undiscovered genius. You can't expect her to talk to circus riff-raff." And addressing me, "You're not taking over his act, are you?"

"No. I just want to—"

The girl interrupted with a squeal of protest, flinching away from Larry.

"Keep your hands to yourself, you pig-thing! Felix, he touched me!"

"She's untouchable," Felix soberly intoned. He winked covertly at Larry, and turned to ask me a familiar litany of questions- where from, why, where to, how I liked Martinique. The lbo girl came across the room to visit us, but, although she embraced us all with her gracious smile, her tenderest expression was for the gentle Pappi. He had risen as she came and kissed her hand, and I wondered if perhaps they had been lovers. Her voice was a rush of honeyed whisper, her nearness brought a subtle jasmine fragrance, her nails were artfully manicured, her skin fine and pure and her kinky hair coiffured in cunning rolls. She stayed but a moment, and then went away.

"You realize what that woman is?" the white girl whispered fiercely to Felix.

"Of course. She's—"

"And yet you receive her at our table? While I am here? Do you realize how you insult me? She's a...a...."

147

"She's talented and charming and generous," Larry interrupted smoothly. "Are you talented and charming and generous, my sweet?"

"Oh!" she cried indignantly, and added with withering scorn, "And a black woman! Felix, I am very disappointed."

Pappi ordered drinks. "I missed out on my chance to go to your country," he said to Larry. "They want two things I can't produce. They want a police clearance to say I'm not a criminal, and proof that the university here will sponsor me, approve of my going."

Turning to me, he explained, "You see I am a botanist. I was hoping to attend a course in America, at the Mississippi Institute of Technology. All about stimulated mutations of tuber roots; they're doing wonderful things over there." He was a small man of perhaps forty-five, with a wide, bronzed face creased by the passage of many smiles; his eyes were grey and friendly under beetling brows. "Our university here is very academic. The Americans are so practical; they take wild leaps into fantastic new experiments. Such a wonderful course it would be."

"And you are prevented from going because you can't—"

"Why do they want a police clearance?" Felix interrupted. "*Paperasses*, red tape!"

"I don't know. Perhaps they fear I might steal the college cutlery. The clearance I got from the *Gendarmerie* mentions I was once in prison. And, of course, the university doesn't want me to go; they'll take no responsibility. So!"

But even as men invent barriers to deny their fellows liberty, so are means devised to circumvent these barriers. There were ways, sometimes, to dodge around documentary troubles.

"The police clearance," I inquired, "is it made out on a printed form? Are the remarks about prison typed, or written in ink?"

Felix flashed me a quick glance of appraisal, and Pappi frowned in thoughtful surprise.

"Well, written in ink. Yes, on the regular form."

"On white paper?"

"Yes."

"Then bleach out the remarks, and put in those which should be there. Just leave the signature."

"Bleach them out?" He stared at me with a faraway look in his eyes. "Bleach them out how?"

"With any bleaching agent. Ordinary washing bleach, or strong peroxide. Use a fine brush, a little at a time. If the ink is new, only a few days old, you can bleach it out in a few minutes. Then carefully wash the bleach away with applications of water, not enough to crinkle the paper, and when it's perfectly dry write 'No Record' on it, or something like that. No one will ever know the difference."

Gradually a great smile possessed his face. He chuckled, and Larry and Felix grinned.

"It will work?"

"It will work. Unless they used black marking-ink, and that leaves a yellow stain."

The drinks arrived, and Pappi paid. But the girl sat stiffly in her chair, outraged.

"I've never heard anything so dishonest in my life," she said tartly.

I sipped my drink and studied her a moment, failing to discover any reason why a man should like her.

"A woman's opinion in such matters," I said carefully, "as in most other matters, is completely without significance."

She gave another little gasp, and Larry laughed delightedly. Felix's face was expressionless.

"Oh!" she cried, rising. "It's…it's….Oh!"

Turning quickly, she marched off, collided heavily with a waitress who tossed a malediction in her face, and hurried from the café.

"Bitch," said Felix, smiling. He raised his glass. "To peace."

"Yes," said Pappi anxiously, "but what about the letter I must have from the university?"

Well, I reflected, here I am in the company of men. I could understand men, and they would soon be my friends; already I had a drink in my hand, and a chance to help one solve a little problem.

"That's the easy part," I said smiling.

"You can forge, then? You can forge a letter?"

"Not exactly. And you can do it yourself, quite easily, and the result will be perfect. You don't need any special skill. First, you have to get some kind of letter from the university, with the proper signature at the bottom. Can you do that? The letterhead at the top of the page, and the signature at the bottom? It doesn't matter what text is in between."

"Yes. I already have that, a letter of refusal from them."

"Good. Now type out the text you would like to appear on that page, saying that the university gladly approves of you taking a course in America, or something. Type it on heavy bond, or cartridge paper. Cut it to fit, and gum it over the original text of the university letter you have. Proper letterhead at the top, genuine signature at the bottom, and the text you want in between."

"Yes," he protested, "but—"

"Wait. Then all you have to do is have a photostat made. Photostats are accepted as valid copies of important documents. You send the photostat to the institute in America. Get the idea?"

He gaped for a moment, then threw back his head and burst forth in peals of rich laughter.

"*Mon Dieu*, but it is enormous!" he cried. "But it is magnificent, so easy. Hey, why can't it work? Why did no one think of that?" He reached out and shook my hand, while Felix grinned and Larry shook with laughter, but then a wariness subdued him.

"But you think no one would find out?"

"Why should they? But be careful. When you make the photostat, you must powder the places where the paper joins, so that no shadow appears. Ordinary talc will do. How can anyone find out? It is not a forgery, it is a photograph of a perfect original."

He wagged his head merrily.

"But...but you can produce any form of document you want, like that. Any form of testimonial, anything at all."

"The photo-copy, yes. But when you have to send a document by mail, the photostat looks even more important. Professionally important. It's the accepted practice. No one likes sending an original document through the mails."

"You think it will work? Eh, Felix, you think it will work?"

Felix raised his glass. "Success to Pappi," he said. "And to all criminals."

We drank. But scarcely had conversation resumed more normal channels, concerning the Ibo profile and the recent invasion of girls from Guadeloupe, than discourse was interrupted by the arrival of an elegant male escorting two young ladies. As he led them to our table, he glanced about the room with a lofty unconcern for lesser folk; tall and slim, haughtily correct in tropical suit and tie, he moved with the nonchalant grace of an aristocrat abroad in baronial grounds among the peasants.

"Felix, *mon vieux*," he murmured. "Pappi. Permit me the pleasure...."

There followed the scraping of chairs and the pronouncing of courtesies as introductions were offered, and soon we were all seated with another round of drinks ordered, it would seem, by myself.

"Larry's from the American circus," Felix explained. "A magic man. He plucks flowers from pretty girls, don't you, Larry?"

"And *billets doux* from their purses, no doubt," the newcomer remarked with barely concealed disdain. His face was gaunt, his complexion an olive shade, he was roughly my own age: something vaguely familiar was there which stirred my memory. His name, Sainte-Claude, meant nothing. Had I not met him somewhere, years ago?

"But how enchanting," cried Anne, the smaller girl. "Oh, I must watch. Can you—"

"I must confess," Sainte-Claude interrupted loudly, "I have never met a circus clown before. Felix, my dear, that's my foot you're playing with, not Yselle's. She's not available, you know; she comes from a very good family. Tell me, are you still living with that emaciated creature who paints?"

Felix grinned wryly. "I doubt it. I'll find out in an hour or two."

"Claude," said Anne with an engaging smile, "take me to the circus tonight?"

"I am not interested in circuses, my pet. I meet sufficient clowns in the course of an ordinary day. Waitress!" He caught the attention of a passing waitress and indicated his glass of beer. "Take away this vile concoction, it's quite flat, and bring me a Pernod."

He had ordered beer for the two girls, but did not offer to replace their drinks as well. Who was he? His manner, his face—there was something familiar there. Where had I met him before? What had we done? Resentment seemed to be allied with some old memory of

this posturing mountebank. Yselle was eyeing him thoughtfully as she
toyed with her glass of beer. She was not so petite nor pretty as Anne,
but the scholarly cast of her features, pale skin artfully framed by
luxurious blue-black hair, suggested an inquiring mind too quick to be
deceived for long by a *poseur* like Sainte-Claude. Our glances locked
for a moment, but neither she nor I yielded any form of recognition;
and Claude seemed possessively inclined towards each girl in turn, as if
confident of himself and yet suspicious of other men.

The Pernod came and conversation wandered through the city
on small domestic errands, discussion of theatre and personalities
and Liberal Government. Once, when Claude's attention was turned
elsewhere, Yselle deftly switched her beer for his Pernod, but be seemed
too involved in creating an impression to remark upon the change.

In one of the other French colonies, perhaps; or even in France
itself. Marseilles, Paris? That mannerism of stroking his chin with the
top knuckle of his forefinger, and blending unction to his arrogance.
Something unholy....

Ah, there it was! Unholiness! The picture of him came to me, the
Claude I had known years before. What had he called himself? Jack?
Jacques? In France, Lourdes, in the spring of 1954, so many years
ago. Neither of us had money, and for a week we had worked for food
and lodging at the hospital of Notre Dame des Douleurs, tending the
paralytics in the St Camille ward. Two meals a day and a place to sleep,
no money: and we were glad enough of the chance. Even seasonal
workers had come there to gain blessings, from Belgium and Holland
and Italy, even England and Denmark, and during that week we had
cared for the bedridden among nine hundred suffering Irish pilgrims,
wheeling them down to the grotto and the baths.

"Lourdes," I said abruptly. "We met at Lourdes."

"What?" He was startled, and immediately on guard.

"We were looking after those Irish pilgrims. I was wearing a beard.
Remember?"

"Oh?" His manner was uncertain as he searched my face. "Lourdes?
You were the Australian?"

"Aye."

He had stolen my watch, and a thin little dagger with a blade of

Damascus steel. He knew I had nothing and yet contrived to steal from me, from a comrade who for seven days had worked and eaten with him. If there is any city in the world which has an atmosphere of brotherhood it is Lourdes. Apart from the unhallowed huckstering of religious manufactures—trinkets, scapulas, statuettes, bottled water, barrowloads of nonsense—there was an atmosphere at once warm and welcoming, friendly and spiritual, something of the essence of Christianity. To steal in Lourdes was tantamount to spitting on an altar.

"You remember wheeling the cripples down to the grotto?"

He was unhappy, restive under the interested gaze of the others.

"But how wonderful," Anne exclaimed. "You helped the sick, Claude? I didn't think—"

"Well," he said with returning confidence, "one must do these things at times. I'm not entirely without feeling for less fortunate people, you know. Oh yes, we used to wheel patients down to the grotto twice a day, with processions of priests and nuns and daughters of the Virgin, singing *O Salutaris Hostia* with churchbells pealing, and a bishop under a scarlet canopy carrying the blessed sacrament. Quite colourful, really. And the master of ceremonies leading the parade, with a Napoleonic hat and a huge silver mitre." He stroked his chin. "Naturally, we accepted no money for what we did."

"Oh, but what fun!" Anne cried, gazing eagerly up at him.

Aye, what fun. The wheelchairs, the stretchers, the grave medics: the drawn faces, the dead eyes, the horrible eruptions, slack drooling mouths; some with half a body, or a twisted, shapeless travesty of gnarled and knotted flesh. Faces twitching and grimacing, others shaking uncontrollably, some young and beautiful and others aged beyond the years of man. Hollow-eyed and yellow-skinned with bony, parchment faces: a pitiful column of the crippled, the mad, the diseased, a shadow of the dread apocalypse: the opening of graves.

Such fun....

After morning mass at the grotto, an indifferent crypt hung with old discoloured crutches and sticks—none of them new—the invalids were taken to the nearby baths.

"You remember Mother Vincent, and Sister Patrick?" I demanded.

"Oh yes, quite charming. Sister Patrick was a dear, an angel. Such a lovely face. And all the men wanting *pigeons* (urinals), and not daring to ask her because she was so adorable. Ah yes, most rewarding work. I think everyone should work in Lourdes for a week or so."

There were two baths, one for the walking and one for the bedridden. From Ireland itself these men had come hoping to be cured. The cripples were undressed as quickly as possible, thrust naked on a web mat and hurriedly immersed in freezing water in a stone bath, while prayers were gabbled by bored attendants. The special prayer was inscribed in five languages on tablets in the wall. Each victim in the bath successively, blue with chill, was rapped on the mouth with a nine-inch silver image of the Virgin, then snatched out of the water to make room for the next. The pilgrims looked dazed, shocked, disappointed, but yet retained a sense of awe.

"And we were both broke," I said unkindly. "Remember? Neither of us had a sou. But somehow you managed to go out and get drunk, and spilled that old man out of his wheelchair and broke his thigh. Remember?"

I eyed him savagely, and he flushed.

"But you're lying!" he hissed.

"He was paralysed, he couldn't even talk, so you got away with it. And then next day you stole my watch. Remember that too?"

His olive complexion had paled with passion, his eyes were dark with hate. Felix and the two girls stared at him, Yselle in horror and little Anne in a confusion of despair and unbelief. Pappi's tormented gaze shuttled between Claude's face and mine like a newly trapped mink. Claude's thin lips grew white with fury.

"You faeces of a diseased swine!" He gritted.

"You were seen, Jack. Or Claude, or whatever you call yourself now. Mother Vincent and Sister Patrick saw you. They were watching out, because money was missing from some of the patients' clothing. They saw you take my watch, when I was showering. Remember? You said it was yours. Then you disappeared. No one knew—"

Half a glass of beer splashed in my face, and the tumbler bounced off my head to crash somewhere behind. Chairs scraped, angry voices were raised in curses and shrill protest. I rose to my feet and stood there, trembling.

"Knock 'im, Aussie!" Larry cried. "Flatten the sonuvabitch!"

"*Meutre* of a dog!" Claude shouted. "*Salaud!*"

Yselle shrank from him in loathing as he gained his feet babbling obscenities. People at nearby tables, splashed with beer, had risen to shout protests; Pappi was rooted to his chair in shock, and Felix stared wildly at the growing disorder. God's peace, I could kill him, but where would violence end?

"Go," I said shakily. "Go now, get out if you love yourself!"

His mouth twitched with emotion, his face was a malignant mask.

"Come!" he said to Yselle, and shook Anne's shoulder roughly. "Come on, let's leave. He's mad. Mad!"

They refused to go, for he was in such a state as any woman might well fear.

"I forbid it!" he cried. "I forbid you to stay! I—"

Two men seized him, one by the ear and the other by the coat, and amid a hubbub of shouts and imprecations he was hustled across the room and hurled into the street. Heavy rain was falling.

Disorder began to quieten, men and women resumed their seats eyeing us resentfully. I sat down wearily to stare at my glass and wait for normalcy to rein my nerves. Aye, he had deserved it: but why must it happen at all? I sat with friends to drink, and brought humiliation on their heads. It was I who should have left: I had deliberately set out to provoke him, poured dishonour on him. Anne was quietly sobbing, Yselle distraught. If I sat in a church, I felt, some demon would pop out from behind a pillar.

"True?" asked Felix.

"Should have flattened the bastard, Aussie!"

"*Poseur*. I never liked that strutting peacock," Pappi said.

"I'd like to see him live this down. Everyone'll know by morning."

"But Mother in Heaven," Yselle burst out, "he tipped a cripple from his chair? You saw him?"

"Not deliberately, I think. He was drunk. But as a thief he was deliberate enough. Damn, I'm sorry. Believe me, I didn't want to—"

"Sorry?" she echoed. "Name of a sacred flea, don't be a fool! Don't you see what's happened? He's been stripped, he's been exposed." She shuddered. "Anne, stop being a little idiot. If you don't stop crying,

I'll—"

"I'm not crying," Anne protested, dabbing at her eyes with a tissue. "I'm just thinking he wanted to marry me, he said he would marry me if…if…."

"He says that to every new girl he meets. Be happy you found out what he really is." We locked glances again, Yselle and I, but this time there was a softness in her expression, and the gay sharing of a brisk encounter. "Holy Mother," she said, "one never knows what will happen next. You've done a good thing, you know that? Oh, but the news will be all round town by morning. And you didn't hit him, I'm grateful for that. I know you wanted to. I think I know why you didn't, and I feel…I feel proud."

To the devil with the woman, she knew nothing. Anne grew calm, Pappi ordered another round of drinks, even Larry relaxed and laughed again, and Anne permitted him to stroke her hair.

"Life's just one big circus," he declared, "with guys like Claude taking the high tumbles. But you should've busted him. Where you staying in this town, anyway?"

"Small hotel, in Rue Bouillé."

"But no!" Felix demurred. "I've plenty of room. I've a whole heap of rooms above a *quincaillerie* (hardware shop). And Pappi lives next door. Why don't we all go there now? And you get your bags and come and stay?"

The girls could not come, they had to go home, and Larry soon had to appear for the magic show.

"Then tomorrow?" he insisted. "Let's see, we need two more girls. All right, Saturday tomorrow, we can all meet here at three o'clock and go to my place. We'll have a party, to celebrate the routing of Sainte-Claude. Agreed?"

It was agreed. There would be a party at his place on the morrow. The hour was growing late and the girls now had to leave; Anne allowed Larry to kiss her cheek, Yselle pressed my hand and shafted back a significant smile as she walked away.

During the night there had been disturbances in the corridor outside my room, shoutings and scufflings and someone thrown down the stairs. Once a girl had opened my door to ask, to the sounds of muffled giggling behind her, if I would prefer a massage or a pink mango, and the bed in the next room had creaked in continual complaint. An uneasy night. Should I go and stay with Felix? There was to be a party this afternoon and evening in the privacy of his several rooms, with at least four men and a girl for every man. It might be amusing to treat some simpering female as if she was a wooden post—but Yselle would be there, bright eyes smiling secretly from under long, dark lashes.

But many things might happen before evening. Faring abroad on the avenue, I remarked with approval how men sat to breakfast at small tables on the sidewalk: Negroes, *békés*, a few foreigners, lounging at ease and discussing small affairs. I would find a café to my liking and sit at peace among them, and order some…but what were they eating, these people? They had no food before them, nothing at all. Each table had a bottle of rum; they were drinking white rum for breakfast! How could de Gaulle control overseas possessions where men drank rum for breakfast?

In a pleasing café I ordered coffee and croissants, traditional French salute to each new day.

"Coffee?" madame inquired. "Croissants?" It was as if she had never heard of them. She seemed dismayed, and went off wringing her hands and murmuring as if I might be mad. I heard her lighting a paraffin stove. What, breakfast time already, and the stove not yet lit? Café time, and here is a café which has no café ready? But worse to come. Madame sent two small girls out into the street on errands: one in this direction to purchase coffee, the other in that direction to buy a few centilitres of milk. What had I done? Simply asked for coffee, as one well might in a coffee-house, and thrown the place into confusion.

And when the girls returned, running and wide-eyed, one had to be sent out again to borrow a cup and saucer. Finally madame brought me coffee.

"Croissants?"

"No croissants, monsieur. There is only bread."

"Ah. Bread will be excellent, thanks."

Near by a man was mixing bitter absinth with powerful local rum. It was a Parisian who once declared that wine on its proper occasion lends emphasis to one's personality: but what of a personality, I pondered, which habitually challenges each new day with a flourish of rum and absinth?

From one corner of the Savanne a headland of immense black rock thrusts strongly south into the sea. The cliffs are surmounted by the walls and battlements of a formidable old fortress, fabled Fort St Louis. Beyond a thicket of trees and tucked away behind a corner, I found a gloomy entrance in the stonework. A notice stated, "Entry fifty francs."

One shilling. But what was there inside?

"What is this place?" I asked an elderly gentleman near by, and he smiled kindly.

"But it is the museum, it is a place of great history. There you will find the history of La Martinique."

Two rough mulatto scoundrels passed us bearing a basket of raw meat between them, offal and bones which gave forth a sour smell and dripped darkly on the gravel.

"There are some animals too," he explained. "But they are not of great interest. The museum is unique, and well worth fifty francs."

I thanked him and followed the two men through the arched stone entrance. In a tall and cavernous antechamber there was a ticket-seller's booth, but no one yet in attendance, so I turned and made my way up the shallow stone stairs of a gently sloping tunnel. This would be the entrance to the fortress works above, a narrow, winding tunnel contrived for easy defence. In alcoves and small chambers were history's souvenirs, paintings of old ships, and instruments of torture, early and excellent lithographs—mementoes of the eighteenth century.

An iron-barred gate led to a sunlit eminence above, and here, at peace from prodding crowds and washed by the sea breeze, were the animals and birds and reptiles of Martinique's two-year-old zoo. One could look down on the city rooves, and shipping in the harbour; over there beyond the Savanne was Café de l'Europe.

There were cages holding birds and I paused by one; inside was a diver, black and white, but a sorry specimen. His plumage was in disarray, one eye was sightless, and the rough concrete had worn his webbed feet away to stumps, so that he only moved when aroused, and

Beach scene, Martinique

River scene, Martinique

Section of the zoo, Fort de France

Trade winds

immediately sat down. Poor diver then: instead of the wide ocean, he had only a quarter inch of slime in a shallow trough, but at least he had protection from his natural enemies.

Next door was a malfini, a goshawk, sleeping in the sun. I had swum in the sea below the Fort, and the sun was warm on my back. But did the goshawk have no water? His dish was dry. Well, they would give him water during the morning rounds.

There was an egret. One leg appeared to be broken, and its frail body was racked with recurring spasms. It tottered back and forth on one leg, thrusting at shadows with its beak, attacking unseen enemies: if ever a bird was mad, it was mad. Could isolation from its kind affect a creature thus? Could birds be afflicted with neuroses such as plagued us humans?

Two deer were in a small, fenced enclosure, dainty creatures which nuzzled among the straw and ate the fragrant mauve blossoms which fell from a cedar-tree above. There were two manicou, or possums, in a cage and both were sick, but one of them lay in its dry water trough in deathly lassitude, heedless of drying scraps of meat near by. It was almost hairless, and a great ulcer at its brow prevented it from closing its right eye. I found the half of a banana and tossed it near the creature's head. Perhaps a minute passed. Then in horrible, slow pantomine it tried to rise, moving its hideous, hairless head to and fro, blindly bumped the banana several times with its nose, and as slowly opened its mouth and commenced to weakly mumble the food. It experienced much difficulty in pulping and swallowing even a peeled portion of a ripe banana; its entire machinery had slowed, run down, until scarcely a spark of life remained.

A shiver of revulsion trickled down my spine and I moved on to the next cage, and the next. What kind of place was this? The baboon had only his urine to drink, the wildcat next door had nothing at all, their cages were foul with the stench of accumulated dung, and their fur matted with the squashed faeces on which they walked and lay. Did no one clean these cages? Was water never provided, did they merely live on rain? Something was terribly wrong. Grimly I stalked here and there to confirm my worst suspicions. This zoo was nothing more nor less than a concentration camp of hapless creatures, enduring varying degrees of hunger, thirst, sickness, filth, and misery.

Birds of diverse nature were caged together, so confined that the weaker could not escape the strong; a constant social torture reduced the weaker to shivering, jerking neurotics. Pecking, feather-pulling, blinding one another: birds could be quite human, I discovered. For hours on end one seabird offered a single straw to his crazed mate. The hope, the pathetic dead hope! Always the slime to drink, or nothing. Some monkeys were crammed in tiny, stinking cages with nothing to eat or drink; they mewed piteously as I passed, and thrust out tiny, clutching hands.

Saurians and reptiles existed in a form of catatonic suspension: the birds and animals were the ones to suffer. Until, like humans, suffering became unendurable, and they went out of their minds. Many animals had no water, a few carnivores had nothing but rotting, unwanted bread or bananas to eat. Apparently the attendants feared many of the beasts, and those cages were never cleaned; the inmates lived in an evil-smelling swamp of their own filth, often with nothing to eat but rotting garbage, and their only drink was slime befouled with urine.

How could they have survived for two long years in these conditions? How many had died? How many were dying now?

The white rats, the pacas, and those monkeys in larger cages seemed well fed, special pets perhaps, with plenty of stale bread and water too. But the two racoons: two hapless sentries endlessly pacing opposite ends of their cage ankle-deep in filth: their water trough held nothing but a dried dark-green scum....Shall one have pity for a jackal? The ceaseless hunt up and down, three paces one way and three paces back from dawn to dusk; he drank when it happened to rain. Some bird of exotic plumage was so weak, it fell with its head twisted underneath its body, quivering.

I approached one of the attendants, stretched out asleep on a bench; the basket of offal was gathering flies in the sun. I nudged him roughly, and he sat up.

"When do you feed them?" I demanded.

"Uh?" He looked around sleepily, and stared at me. "You done buy ticket?"

"I'll buy one. When do you feed the animals?"

"Soon, maybe. When people come. Saturday, maybe visitors come, then I give food. You want buy soft drink? Ice-cream? I got for sale."

So the week-ends, when the visitors came, were the big days for the zoo's unfortunates. They were fed then.

"When do you give them water?"

"Uh?" He squinted at me malevolently. "Who you? What you asking for? Why you want know when I give water?"

"I want to know. You'd better tell me."

Sweet blue eyes, must there be another fight?

"Rain every day," he said in disinterest, and lay back again on the bench. "What I care for damn' animals? If you no want to buy something, I got no interest for talk."

A squall of temper sizzled through me. No care for animals? Why, this piece of idle filth was only concerned with selling refreshments to visitors: he had no concern for suffering creatures. They could slowly die of thirst and misery and disease, and he would pay no heed. Deliberately I put my hands in my pockets and kept them there.

Turning on my heel, I walked away, down the stone tunnel and out of the Fort. In a nearby market I purchased a sackful of fruit, returned, apportioned it among the herbivores, and commenced filling the drinking troughs with a hose which I discovered by a tap. The churl came and tried to snatch the hose from my hand.

"*Meutre alors!*" he cried angrily. "I don't need no help. What you think you doing, you own this place? Hey?"

He wrenched at the hose, and I resisted, so then he went to turn off the tap. I watched him quietly as the hose fell slack, the flow of water ceased. He stood waiting to see what I would do.

The familiar repetition of a pattern: the strength of my own convictions hurled bodily against those of another man. What form of selfish conceit possessed me, that I sought to take the affairs of the zoo in my own hands? For two whole years it had survived without me: why must my arrival precipitate a crisis?

Setting down the hose, I walked towards him, and he darted glances about as if seeking for a weapon. Drawing close to him, I halted, took my wallet forth, and offered him a note for one hundred francs.

"If you would be so good," I asked politely, "as to permit my little madness, and accept this small gift for the loan of the hose, I would be grateful."

He eyed me warily, gingerly reached for the note and his dark face creased with an engaging smile.

"But of course, monsieur," he said with satisfaction, pocketing the bill. "Any time, monsieur, any time."

When the water troughs were full and the cages hosed to a cleaner state, I went away. It was not, after all, my affair. What possible concern could an Australian have with a zoo on Martinique? Here I was a guest in this pleasant city, already I had grossly humiliated one man, and had been tempted to damage another. What disease did I carry? Was it something in my blood? What possible excuse could I have for interfering in the affairs of others? The zoo was the private affair of the people who lived on this island: I was an intruder, it had nothing to do with me.

Every day a locust-swarm of little buses descends on Fort de France, caroming through the streets to market-places, there to shuffle and fidget restlessly and jostle and change places, until suddenly they erupt in a jarring crisis of klaxons and crashing gears and frantically race away again, dispersing along the coast and among the hills. In early afternoon I escaped with one of them, a small bus called a *bompe*—barely leapt aboard as it pulled out—and let the sweetness of the countryside flow through the darkness of my mind. I had not bothered to ask where it was going, all destinations were equally desirable, behind me the zoo was abandoned; and Felix and Larry and Pappi, and Yselle, were left to their own devices.

Diamant was twenty-five miles to the south, on the southern coast. Hills and gullies rich with sugar-cane and fruits gave way to windswept hills of scrub, and the bompe went no farther than Diamant. As well, perhaps, for my strained back had suffered the pains of hell in that galloping, hardsprung hearse.

The village was spread along a sudden glittering sweep of beach washed by moderate surf, striped with the trunks of leaning coconuts and green-feathered with their plumes. Huts and bungalows lay astride a single sandy lane, housing a couple of hundred souls who advertised their trade in the nets that hung to dry, and the curiously shaped dugout canoes which were drawn up high on the beach. I swam in the sea, and a laughing shoal of suntanned youngsters came to join me; occasionally folk peered out anxiously from the shelter of their huts.

A gomier came in from the sea, a fishing canoe powered by an outboard and artfully manoeuvred through the surf by its single occupant, a bronzed and dark-haired *béké*. Since I was near, I held the craft steady while he left it, and helped him drag it up beyond the tide-line.

"Ho, and thank you," he cried, laughing, and shook my hand. "Ya-ya, but there's wind out there by the Big Rock. Maurice, my name is, Augustin Maurice. Hey?" He looked at me inquiringly. "You are from Fort de France? On visit?"

As he unfastened the motor and hefted it to his shoulder, I introduced myself; children clustered around giggling among themselves, until Maurice boxed one softly on the ear with fierce pretence, and ordered two young lads and a girl to gather up the fish. The name of the gomier was *Si Dieu Veut* (If God Wills).

"Drink?" he asked me, nodding towards the village. "Come, let's have some juice. A man gets dry out there. *Meutre*, but it's hot. The sea is better, every time. Are you a seaman?"

I was already putting my jeans on over my wet trunks.

"Yes." Why not?

"Good, good. I've been all over in the merchant marine, but I still like Diamant."

The two lads had each taken up dorados which were almost as large as themselves, the girl had a string of mackerel and schnapper, and I grasped a three-foot shark. We trudged through the sand to the central lane and he led the way to a restaurant, so newly built that it had as yet no name.

"My place," he said gaily. "Good, no? Pretty?" It was of hideous raw concrete, uncertainly daubed with whitewash and a sickly measle-pink. "But my wife's place really, not mine. She and the kids, they're boss here." He soundly bussed an attractive mulatto lady, who came to meet him.

"Guests!" he cried, setting down the motor. "Food, my pretty sweetheart, but first a thing to drink. Hey—" turning to me—"you drink Martinique rum?"

"The best in the world." I smiled, infected by his bubbling lust for life.

"Ho, I think so too. Makes strong men stronger, and weak men die."

And indeed it was excellent rum. He was a gay and well-muscled *bon vivant*, beloved of the children and the master of his life—even, superficially, the master of his wife, who tended all his needs with gentle humour. For a time we drank while he discussed seaports he had known, and the curious fore and aft fins which gave local dugout canoes the means to counter drift, when sails were used. After dining we drank again in the company of friends; and finally the inevitable gendarme came.

He was slight and stooped, with a tendency to suck at and puff his waxen cheeks, and worried his sad moustache with slender fingers. He asked me who I was, and said I would have to go with him, "To be examined."

Maurice regarded me inquiringly.

"You must have done something," he suggested with rising interest. "What did you do?"

"Nothing."

He peered at me suspiciously.

"Some crime in Fort de France? Drunk? Fighting? You jumped ship, maybe?"

"But nothing at all," I insisted. Almost something, perhaps. "Or if I did, I must congratulate myself on having committed a crime with such discretion that I myself do not know what it was."

"So!" He turned on the gendarme. "What do you want with him, Antoine? Hey? That fat imbecile of a wife sent you here to make trouble, yes?"

The gendarme shrugged unhappily.

"*Alors*, she said, here is a stranger, I should go and—"

"Tchah, the fat porpoise!" And addressing me, "He has an ambitious wife. You know how it is, when a woman holds the whip? She turns a man into a fool."

Aye, I had some knowledge of women who turned men into fools.

"Sit down," I said to Antoine. "Have a drink, it's on the house, and forget her for a while."

He hesitated, glancing at the door as if she might be lurking there.

"Come, come!" Maurice pulled a chair towards him, and I poured him a glass of rum. Then suddenly I paused, staring blankly into space, the bottle still poised. Hell's angels, but my brain must be diseased! Here was I offering free liquor to policemen! What was happening? Never in my life had I....

But the others were staring at me curiously. I set the bottle down, raised my glass, and we drank. Some time during the evening she appeared at the door like an avenging bison, shrilling and shaking her wattles, but a dozen of us pushed her from the room and trundled her into the night. For a time she stood at a distance bellowing, but her policeman was happily asleep, and there was shouting and ribald laughter, and we sang.

"*Un coin de mon île...vive le bonheur, vive Sainte Luce, vive Sainte Anne, vive la plage....*"

Vive la plage, indeed!

Late on Sunday morning I awoke on the bar-room floor, and it was something akin to regaining consciousness in Fort Young at Roseau. My back was brittle as a straw, my head a steaming cauldron. But various children brought me coffee and rum, with biscuits freshly baked; others helped me shave with a borrowed razor; there seemed to be no toilet, and they followed me out into the street and along the beach, inquiring among themselves as to where I might be going, until perforce I was obliged to piddle with nine of them on hand.

Vive la plage! I would have swum in the sea to clear my throbbing head, but discovered that the village had flung a formidable accumulation of Saturday manure into the sea, and the sea had understandably flung it right back on the beach.

Breakfast consisted of soft, dark sausage made from the hot blood of slaughtered beasts, mixed with spices and crumbled bread and stuffed inside the purged intestines of a pig. But there was also rum, and anything can be eaten along with a glass of Martinique rum.

Folk passed on their way to church as we sat in the bar.

"Tomorrow," Maurice said, "we go fishing."

"Tomorrow?"

"Today is the Lord's day, no fishing today."

"But I was thinking of leaving today, and—"

"Tomorrow," he repeated with some firmness, "we go fishing. You and I." He glanced at me severely. "I don't often meet a seaman from big ships, like I used to sail on. Tomorrow we go fishing, and if you try to run out, I'll put Antoine's wife onto you. Eh?"

"But of course," I said quickly. "Tomorrow we go fishing. You and I."

No one in his right mind would wish to be assailed by that mountainous virago. Earlier in the morning she had invaded the bar, snatched Antoine from the floor without a word, and borne him off across her shoulder to devour in privacy.

Old men with nothing but the tattered remnants of the peasant uniform- loose white shirt—coat and cotton trousers, wide straw hat and sandals—would slip into the bar like anxious ghosts, apologies and courtesies exuding from their attitude, with quiet conviction drink a tot of rum-and-absinth, not bother to linger for syrup or sugared water to erase the bitterness, and slip outside again *en route* to church smiling slyly to themselves.

"Tomorrow," Maurice said, already drowsy. "Fishing."

"Quite still, quite still," he admonished me. The gomier creamed in on a breaker amid a flurry of bursting spray. The day had passed, we had our fish, but the wind had risen and the return to shore was treacherous. Apart from the danger of the slender craft broaching and rolling in the surf, there was some risk of a following sea swamping the motor.

"Quite still."

I sat rigid as a rock in the bottom of the craft, hunched low, pretending I was ballast; there was nothing that I could do, which Maurice could not do much better. The canoe sagged back behind a passing wave, and he gunned the motor again to challenge the authority of another breaker which had burst in thunder close astern. The gomier writhed and twisted in a rush of hissing foam, borne fast towards the beach…and we were safe. Leaping from the craft, we held it against the backwash, motor idle, and handled her up the beach on the following surge.

"Ya-ya!" he cried triumphantly. "How you like it, hey?"

"I'm not a brave man," I shouted above the rush of the wind and the sea. "Only porpoises and *békés* would lead a life like this!"

He laughed delightedly. "Not always so bad. My heart jump sometimes too."

As we dragged the gomier up on the beach, there was someone standing there, a young European woman with freckled, sunburnt face, white ointment on her nose, and ginger hair. She wore black slacks and a dark-blue blouse, and now she was squinting through the eyepiece of a camera. Some sort of tourist, come to watch the natives; and I grinned as I bent to gather fish. In a moment she approached us.

"*Pardonnez moi, s'il vous plait,*" she began formally, "do you permit me to take a picture, closely?"

There was a heavy accent there, but my knowledge was not advanced enough to place it. Maurice exchanged a glance with me, and raised an inquiring brow.

"*Ecossaise?*" he muttered.

"*Sais pas.*" I winked, and we stood there as she took her photo.

Maurice bowed, and with chivalry declared, "An honour, ma'm'selle. From what country do you come?"

"Kashmir, monsieur." A Kashmiri, with frizzled ginger hair and freckles? But she continued with textbook precision, "I am born in Hong Kong, but my father and my mother now live in Kashmir."

She smiled at him gladly. He was a handsome rogue, with an engaging manner designed to disturb the hearts of lonely girls.

"Ah. Breeteesh," he said, pronouncing the English word with satisfaction.

"Er, *Anglaise, oui*. I am making auto-stop around your lovely island."

A hitch-hiker, then, cutting loose from the normal routes.

"So. You like La Martinique?" With our burdens we began walking towards the village.

"Yes, monsieur. It is a very beautiful island. The people are very agreeable. I am very content to be here."

Maurice questioned me with a glance, but I shook my head.

Presently she thanked us, and turned away along the street.

"You don't want her?" he asked, puzzled.

"Want her? White ointment on her nose, and that terrible ginger hair?" I shuddered. Blue eyes, a large pleasant mouth, but a boldness in her face suggesting an aggressive independence. "No, I travel alone. I am finding my own company on the road difficult enough without ginger-haired females."

Later we discovered that Antoine, the gendarme, had found occasion to address her. Her name was Gwen.

"I don't understand it," he confessed. "Her father is a professor in India, but she was born in China and has a British passport. It says she is a student, but she is twenty-eight years old. A student, and so old? And wandering about alone, on two feet…very strange. She came from Trinidad. I asked her what she studied there, and she said she had studied Trinidad. I asked her what she was studying here, and she said she was studying Martinique. Eh?"

He scratched at his drooping moustache, and I suppressed a grin.

"I asked her if she had money, and she said, yes, and that she had underpants as well, and called me an inquisitive imbecile!"

I laughed aloud, and wished she had not gone. Maurice grinned.

"She is a woman, Antoine," he said. "And you, surely, should know what women are!"

For a week I wandered wherever the road might go, pausing here to swim and there to gather fruit. Once I slept beneath an upturned boat on a storm-swept beach, and woke half buried in fine sand. Another time I sheltered in a great barn full of hens. Pandemonium broke loose within the barn, when an early housewife attacked me just on dawn with the rough end of a broom, stabbing and beating at my head; for, as I scrambled up and fled, a cloud of pullets hurled themselves in the air in a vast cackling and squawking and flourishing of wings and stirred feathers, until at last I found a window, forced it open, and galloped out of sight across a field.

In a small village I had purchased a string bag to carry rum and food; my cushion cover and its meagre contents had been left in Fort de France, and indeed it mattered little if everything was stolen; perhaps someone would care for them in case I should return. I wandered freely, sometimes eating mangoes which had fallen by the road, occasionally invited into homes, meeting folk in fields and taverns: the world was contained in Martinique, my heart was in a pot on Pelée Mountain. Tall, rich mountains, gentle people, magnificent coasts of shining sand: there was solitude and peace, hours of silence listening to a silver hillside stream or watching liquid moonlight gild the restless sea. There was the sudden violence of evening storms, the rumbling industry of sugar-mills, the undemanding companionship of folk at rest from their labours in the fields.

There was a sweetness in this fragrant countryside, a quietness of life, a harmony of people with roots deep in a rich and generous land.

Where the cane of the lowlands fell away and forestry began, there were also the cottages of those who tended cane, humble one- and two-roomed shacks of wood and thatch or corrugated iron almost lost amid the foliage. For about them, on the heights and in ravines, pressed enormous mango- and breadfruit-trees ready to plop their fruit on the ground if you threw a stick; thickets of bananas hemmed them in, oranges, guavas, hibiscus and frangipani, taros and pineapples; and always, if one troubled to glance below, a princely panorama of ocean and valley and indented coast.

The creole patois spoken in the hills of Martinique is difficult for the stranger to comprehend; grammatical rules are thrown out, words are strung together as a stripped, utilitarian form of basic communication. Little room is given to rhetoric or the finer phrase; meaning is driven home with a pointed hammer, and one man's method of stringing words (tense, gender, sequence) may differ from his neighbour's. People I met were kind enough to accept my poor French as some new form of patois, or an obscure provincial dialect from metropolitan France. They would listen with a mildly fascinated air, analysing clumsy phrases and doubtless shuffling words to a more familiar pattern, stripping away unnecessary padding. But, if they were so good as to mistake me for a Frenchman, it could be understood how a foreigner came to do the same.

It happened on the east coast, close to Trinité. In a stonemason's house I had eaten a meal of blaf, a local dish of boiled and spiced fish, together with a pathetic little lobster which had fouled itself and not been cleaned: and now I rode a country bompe towards the coast. But there was only the driver and his girl besides myself, and a dozen times the driver nearly killed us. The girl insisted on flirting, transparently determined to arouse him, rolling her eyes and giggling and delighting in his discomfort. He was an angry young man, part European, with a thin, hungry face and little black tufts of curly hair on his chin. In one rear-vision mirror he observed his fickle sweetheart with increasing rage, and by squirming to one side he used a second mirror to stab at me with dark, envenomed glances.

We hurtled down through Trinité on the coast and out onto an isthmus ten miles long. He scowled and muttered, she primped and fluttered her eyes, I sat despairing in my seat hoping we would live. The bompe began careering drunkenly around tight corners with two wheels on the edge of outer space, and on three occasions held collision course with other vehicles while the driver shuttled frantically from one mirror to the next.

Then we passed the girl with the ginger hair, far out on the isthmus, and this was excuse enough to quit the bompe. I had paid to travel farther, but alighted with relief; the bompe roared off, and I sat down by the road. The girl with the hair—Gwen, as I recalled—was half a mile behind, but walking strongly. I could find out who and what she was, and then leave her: there could be no harm in that? Surely it would be safer than riding to destruction on the bompe?

She strode at ease along the road, black trousers and dark-blue shirt, carrying a satchel on her back. A modest sort of haversack, not more than half the size of a case of Scotch. One of the gifts the traveller has is to assume a different guise as he sees fit, and now I decided to be a *béké* and plague her with the questions so many folk asked me. And if she recognized me, having seen me on the beach, so much the better. I would be a fisherman.

She saw me sitting there, but held her course to pass close by, when she might have edged away.

"*Bonjour,*" she said, pausing.

"*Bonsoir,*" I agreed, rising. "But you are walking?"

She tossed me a quizzical glance. "*Mais non,* monsieur, I am standing on my head. How many kilometres are there to Tartané?"

Well, her lance was quick. And I had no idea how far this Tartané might be.

"It is a matter of opinion," I hedged. "But you will walk there? On both feet?"

She stifled a smile. "Both feet, yes. It is my custom."

"Ah. Permit me to go with you. We will find out how many kilometres there are. I was going to Trinité, but no matter. You are English, of course."

"Why?"

"Who else but an Englishwoman would walk about with white paint on her nose? How old are you?"

"I refuse to say."

"By your teeth, I should say about twenty-eight. I had a horse who lived till he was twenty-eight; his teeth were just like yours. Do you like Martinique?"

We were walking on together, at a somewhat more leisurely pace than hers had been.

"Oh yes, monsieur. It is a very beautiful island. The people are—"

"Yes, yes, I know, the people are very agreeable, I am very content to be here. And gendarmes are inquisitive imbeciles, no? Quite right." I pretended to study her face. "You were not born in England."

"No, I was—"

"The East has left its mark upon your face."

"Pardon?" She blinked in surprise.

"You were born in the East. Permit me to see the palm of your left hand."

"What? Why?"

"Because I am a teller of fortunes, ma'm'selle. Your hand, if you please." She held out her left hand. "I am a reader of the Book of Life, I interpret symbols which other people cannot understand. Ah, see, you were born on an island. The sign of the island is jade. But the land you now call home is a land of snow-capped mountains, and its sign is turquoise. Am I correct?"

She was fascinated. "But yes, I was born on Hong Kong, that's the jade part. And I live in Kashmir now, that's the turquoise part. *Bon*

173

Dieu, how do you…how do you know?"

"There is more, much more."

"Oh, please tell me."

"My fee is very large, would you pay?"

"Pay what?"

"One hundred francs."

"Phoof, that's not two shillings." She found a hundred francs in her pocket and passed it to me. A tingle of pleasure stole through me. Why, the return flow had already started, now women were presenting me with gifts!

"You are aggressive and independent. See how strong this line is. You have determination, but you have no tact. You are a woman of decision, but once you make up your mind you plunge straight towards your goal, and if anyone gets in the way you walk right over the top of him. You are scornful towards men. Men are toys to you. When they cease to amuse you, you throw them aside."

"Oh!"

"Yes, see the strong mound of Venus: you control your men. You don't mind sticking hatpins into men. Your father—see here- your father is a great scholar, but you are too dogmatic, your thinking is selfish. You don't even care much what people think about you, you just go ahead. And—"

"That's very true. Very true."

"And you have the gipsy sign."

"The gipsy sign?"

"The little cross there, but a diagonal cross. It means crossroads, restlessness, the urge to be a gipsy. You were probably of a gipsy clan in some former life, and it's still strong in you. And you will have…eleven children."

"Good grief!"

"And then marry."

She laughed. "Oh you…you're absurd!"

"Your husband will look like a goat. Big yellow eyes and small white beard. A vegetarian."

She laughed delightedly. "Oh, you're crazy. Besides I already have thirteen children. What do you do for a living?"

"I tell fortunes."

"Pish. You will make no money, telling things like that to women.

"Talk English. I can understand a little."

"Oh?"

"Yes. You are not afraid, travelling alone?"

"I'll try English, then. Afraid? Of men, you mean?" switching to her own tongue. "No. I have long nails and sharp teeth and a tongue like the edge of a razor, if need be. And anyway men like me, in spite of what my hand reads. I can sense that even you like me; and I like men, as a rule. They're feeble, but they're friendly, they don't make trouble for me."

"You must be rich?"

"No, I work. I work here and there, save my money, and use it to travel on somewhere else. And then, when I'm broke again, I find another job."

"What kind of jobs?"

"Oh, as a waitress, governess, English tutor, maid. I made hats in Rio and artificial flowers in Lima. I had a job as a masseuse in Panama, until I found the place was a sort of high-class girlie-house. In Trinidad I dressed up as a boy and tried to get a job at Government House, but somehow they got wind of it."

"And how long," I pronounced the familiar question, "do you propose to continue in this fashion?"

"How long? Well, when do you stop doing a thing you like? When you find something better, I suppose."

"When you marry?"

"I suppose so. But what do you really do?"

"I'm a thief, if you insist."

"It wouldn't surprise me one bit. You French are gifted in strange ways; and you look as if you might be almost anything."

Satan's eyes, did a shadow walk behind me?

"When will I marry?" She tendered her hand anew, and I examined it.

"At six o'clock in the evening. It doesn't say what day."

"You're impossible," she smiled, withdrawing it again.

"Not at all, it would make me sad if I knew."

"Sad?"

"For the man. He would find you a difficult woman to control."

"So? "

"And what is the kind of man you want?"

She sighed, and eased a shoulder-strap. There were signs of life ahead, huts and tents and groups of people, some sort of holiday crowd.

"Well, the man I will marry must be strong; he must be stronger than me. I don't care much what he looks like, but he must have a strong mind, strong character. A man of decision and good judgement. A good man. Not a social bootlick; he must be a man with the strength to act as he believes is right, regardless of consequences. A real man, not just someone in an expensive suit with a cigar and and an expense account, pretending. I want a man who stands out among men, and there aren't many of them. I haven't met one in a long time now."

"You wouldn't want to be more equal than him? Dominate him?"

"Dear God, if he's the kind of man I want, I wouldn't be able to. I wouldn't want him to be my slave, I'd just want his company and love. Compulsion in anything is undesirable; the human nature backs off in suspicion, when it's threatened with any new limitation of its freedom. If you introduce a sense of compulsion into marriage, you sabotage the entire relationship. You can't compel anyone to love you; all the king's horses can't do that. You can only encourage your man, try to deserve his love, make yourself worthy of his desire. Am I talking too fast?"

"Oh no, no."

"And you?" she asked. "I suppose you want the perfect woman?"

I laughed shortly. "You mean she exists?"

"Only as a vision. I once knew a man who had loved all kinds of women, hundreds. He found a little perfection in each one. Finally, he only wanted the single woman who had all these perfections, and of course he would never find her. He was terribly unhappy. He could only love a vision, and the vision refused to love him in return, because he, himself, had only a small fragment of perfection."

I glanced at her with mounting interest. An uncommon girl, I reflected. She talked on, enlarging on her theme of the lover's need to avoid compulsion, discussing the moral right of the individual to selectively resist social pressures and the freedom of the thinking man to lead the sacred cows by the nose. Bones of a spotted mule, I was thinking, is this a woman speaking? How did these intelligent words find their way to a woman's tongue? What a singular species she must be. Aye, but too long had I lived close to American women: like the wounded hyena which devoured its dragging entrails, so American women sucked at their hearts with anxious despair in search of the strength to dominate their men…then fed on the hearts of their prey.

Angular, freckled, frizzy-haired: why, this woman at my side might make some manly Titan a most worthy mate. I had met her on a lonely road to secretly laugh at her: and now her wisdom mocked me for…a weak degenerate?

"I like your words," I said at length. "It's a long time since I met a woman with these beliefs."

If there was a town called Tartané, we never managed to find it: we found instead a great concourse of folk abandoned to high pleasure. They must have come in the morning and early afternoon in cars and bompes and *camionettes* from the farthest reaches of the island—St Pierre, Lamentin, Fort de France, from coastal towns and mountain villages. They swarmed along the gentle beach, picnicked under trees, caroused in groups and gathered in packs to gamble, and wandered off in couples to make love.

"It's like an Italian election," she said. "Half the island must be here. What's happening?"

We inquired of a man who passed, and he drew himself up in surprise.

"But you make a joke?" he asked aggrievedly, staring at us each in turn. "It is Pentecost, the holiday of Pentecost."

Gwen laughed as we walked on. "A religious holiday. Well, to look at it you'd certainly never suspect."

Swimming, eating, drinking, dancing, gambling and singing and fighting: it was an area devoted for this day entirely to lusts and pleasures, and one expected at any moment to glimpse the sign of the cloven hoof. There were sheds, which passed for dance-halls, so densely packed that the very walls gave the illusion of bulging, and jogging Negroes threatened to spill out through the doors: one could not see inside, for there was nothing but a solid thickness of humanity throbbing to the rhythm of bumpy music coming from somewhere within the gloomed interior. Black faces glistened damply, male and female bodies jammed together belly to belly and flank to flank, perspiring hugely, and even holding their arms in the air to gain a little room.

Smaller shacks posed as restaurants and bars. They had tables and chairs outside under trees, where beer and rum were served; and men had gathered in crowds to joust and gamble. Gwen glanced around until she caught the smile of a Negro lady serving beer, then slipped the haversack from her shoulders and gave it to the lady for safe keeping.

"Bad enough having ginger hair," she said to me, "without looking like a refugee from a North Pole expedition. My, what fun they're having! Come on!"

She took my arm, and we buried ourselves in a throng of spectators grouped around a small arena of beaten earth. A single drummer sat to one side beating a fast tattoo with the fingertips and heels of his hands, and to the duel-toned rhythm men were dancing strange mimes. Local and visiting men and youths in various stages of drink performed for their fellows, provoking gales of laughter. Two lads might strut and posture like hostile fighting cocks, with fluffing feathers and darting heads, then in stiff and stylized fashion test their strength on one another, flat feet shuffling in the dust to the rhythm of the drum. Or two old dogs in wine might stage a comedy of errors, clowning with outrageous improvisation, never still; the first might bite the second on the buttock, the second might seize his partner's hat and hurl it on the ground and repeatedly bound in the air on top of it. The first would leap on his back and tumble him in the dust, then both would whoop around the circle in a stiff-legged dance. At intervals some spectator might be seized by the leg and dragged, staggering wildly amid huge laughter, right across the ring. Other clowns would take their turn to whirl and twirl, shuffling and jogging, staggering in drink, shouting bawdy jests and challenges and tumbling other revellers in the dust.

But always with good humour, a wonderful sense of looseness and release.

The English girl was enthralled, even when some young blade raised gusts of merry laughter by pretending to couple with his partner, and then make water on his head.

"We've forgotten how to do this," she said, eyes shining with excitement. "We've forgotten how to relax, we've become too conscious of dignity. Look at them! Completely absorbed in the moment, nothing else exists. And you know, this is the kind of place where the folk-dance is born. Crude, rough, mixed with dirt…and every now and then, quite unexpectedly, a polished gem of a dance suddenly appears."

A toothless old scoundrel was at her side slyly patting the coins in her trouser pocket, winking and smiling, asking if madame would gamble with him. In front of a large cantina were some thirty diminutive tables set under trees, where men could play at craps, cards, dominoes, red-and-black and over-and-under, and they were attended by an argumentative bedlam of shouting and scuffling, click of dominoes and rattle of dice, hoarse cries and drunken laughter.

"We play, we play," he insisted, and patted her pocket again. She laughed happily.

"Those wicked eyes," she murmured to me. "Isn't he sweet?"

Rough and grizzled, stooped with years, his face scarred and eroded by the passage of tears and sweat and laughter, abrasive with bleached stubble like a field of harvested wheat: aye, if she meant he was an earthy rascal loved by God and the Devil alike, probably she was right.

She put her arm around him and gave him a little hug.

"Come," she said. "We play."

She backed the red, he gambled on the black: and when he began to cheat, she cheated too. He scratched his head inquiringly when he found himself outplayed, and glanced at her with growing admiration. Her hands were even quicker than his, and once when he spoke to a passer-by she stole a ten-franc piece. He had lost twenty francs, almost sixpence, when he finally gave up.

"I cheated," she said with an impish grin. He shrugged.

"Of course, and so did I. It is the custom."

"But I cheated better."

"And so you won, it must be so."

"Then will you let me give you back the twenty?"

His eyes twinkled. "But no. If I could steal them back, and another twenty too, that would be all right."

"Then come and have a drink," I suggested, and at once he stood up straighter.

"Of course, of course."

We sat in the crowded cantina to drink *punch blanc*, white rum, as one does at evening on Martinique. For the sum of a single shilling we received five things: a bottle of rum, on trust, and a bottle of cold water; a bowl of cracked ice, slivers of lime, a jar of cane syrup and, of course, a glass. A dash of syrup was poured in the glass, then rum and ice and some drops of lime, and there was water if one desired it for a chaser. It was easy to sneak a second or even third drink of rum free of charge, or even fill one's glass up to the brim, but I never saw anyone do this and nobody bothered to check. The *rhum vieux* was better, a mellow and malty rum with authority disguised by exquisite flavour: but this was half the price again, and rarely used.

While Gwen questioned the old man on his seventy years in the hills of Martinique, I pondered how we might spend the approaching night. The afternoon was growing late, already folk were speeding home in bompes and *camionettes*. We could sleep on the beach, perhaps, the sky was clear. This girl possessed a gift, and I would have it: her intellect was keen, her judgement balanced, she had a reassuring quality which fed some obscure hunger in my heart. We could lie on the beach tonight, if she would, and talk; and very early in the morning, before she was awake, I would go.

The breeze and the smouldering fire kept mosquitoes away, and only the whisper of little waves and the clicking of feeding crabs broke the silence. Some time, later on, the moon would rise. We had eaten in the cantina with the old man, and when he went away we bought a bottle of wine and found a cosy hollow on the beach to spend the night. She had come without the slightest hesitation.

"Besides," she was saying, as she stared into the fire, "travelling just for the sake of travel is largely a waste of time. If you're running away from something, dodging responsibilities or just satisfying curiosity, you're only the victim of your own weakness. It's got to be much more than a seeking of sensation, or an emotional adventure. The world's a textbook, an encyclopaedia crammed with knowledge and instruction, not just a sexy novel or a bunch of pretty postcards."

Firelight lacquered her face and arms with luminous glints, and touched her hair with a soft, metallic sheen.

"Tourists waste their time, you think?"

"You can't pile people into groups and call them by a single name, and judge them thus," she said impatiently. "Take a thousand tourists, and you have a thousand different minds. It's what happens inside their minds, not their cameras, which is important. But if you keep on travelling for years with an inquiring mind, exposed to the whole world, if you have the enthusiasm to make it a way of life, well, you come to recognize the value it can give. You learn three important fundamental things. You learn how to survive, how to recognize and improve on your own limitations, and what magnificent creatures the world's humans really are. Nationality, colour, or creeds don't seem at all important, when you've eaten bread and salt with all of them."

I passed her the bottle and she drank, wiping her mouth on the back of her hand.

"Maybe faith moves mountains, but it's enthusiasm that moves people."

There was a sincerity in her mood, a lack of affectation in her voice, which invited one to believe in what she said.

"But what of security?" I asked. "If you don't have a regular income, where's your security?"

She glanced at me with something approaching pity in her eyes.

"Look," she began, "I was in Greece a while back. Someone told me a story. Before the world war you paid one drachma to ride on a tram in Athens. Life was normal, people toiled and saved money for security in old age. Then the Germans came. Suddenly a tram ride cost five hundred thousand drachmae, and people carried worthless money in flour-sacks. Two thousand sterling pounds to ride on a tram. Security? What would happen tomorrow if Russia minted gold roubles? She has the gold now, she could do it. What would happen to the dollar and the pound? Security doesn't live in bank vaults. Money isn't the currency of happiness."

"I see," I said, smiling. "Then what is security?"

She pursed her lips and considered the question. "Oh, perhaps it could be described as…as the ability to survive successfully under any given conditions. Successful survival, based on ability and adaptability. Resulting in freedom from fear. And God knows, shoestring travel teaches one an awful lot about survival."

Aye, she was right. One learnt to find food, somehow; to find shelter, somewhere; one sifted fragments of wisdom from discussions with total strangers. It helped if you could learn to pick a lock, start a car without a key, tickle a slot-machine with a magnet or use educated dice, or cross a river in a borrowed skiff without oars; but the greatest gift of all was freely given in discussion with wise men.

"You're learning all the time," she went on. "You're continually exposed to new cultures, new ideas and philosophies, new attitudes to life. Education in the purest and best sense. There's a creeping paralysis of academic education trying to standardize everyone in the world, but you can learn to challenge it. We gain our learning out of books, but later begin to fear books because there are too many of them, and we give our lives in the hands of specialists. But, good heavens, if travel teaches you nothing else, it teaches you to think for yourself, to formulate your own opinions, and be self-reliant."

"And to act accordingly? Even if your act be antisocial? Or even lawless?"

She hesitated. "Not so much antisocial as aware of the imperfections of opportune social law. There are times when profound personal convictions of right oblige one to be selectively lawless, against man-made law. Only a coward will compromise what he thinks is right. I nearly provoked a riot in a Danish restaurant where they were bringing live lobsters to a slow boil. I nearly turned the place upside-down, and everyone hated me; they thought I was completely out of my mind. But they finally agreed to boil the water first, for the next batch, and drop the poor wretches in to a quick death. I'm not particularly proud of putting on such an act, but I'd have despised myself for ever if I hadn't."

I felt a fine companionship for her; this, surely, was a woman to my taste. There was spark and spirit there, and crystal-pure conviction in the individual's moral right to seize a burning brand and fire the rotten haystacks of social perfidy.

"One of the things I try to do," she said, "is to be the observer, not the observed. With this mad ginger hair it's difficult, but I try to hide in the crowd, to observe others and yet remain unnoticed. But that isn't enough either, merely being an observer. You have to enter into their lives as well, live in their houses and work beside them, share their sorrows and laughter, and be one of them. You learn quite a lot about people, doing that."

"But you don't find yourself limited, being a girl? I mean, sleeping on the beach with me, for instance: you don't care what people think?"

"Oh, fiddlesticks to people! I love 'em, but I'm damned if I'll narrow my conduct down to fit in with narrow minds. If you believe in yourself, and that what you wish to do is right, then for heaven's sake do it and to the devil with what other people think. Don't hurt yourself morally, and certainly don't hurt anyone else; but if you haven't got the courage to stand up in front of a crowd and be counted, you're a lost cause. Or do you think society is some form of golden calf? Lord, I kick social pressures in the teeth every day. I'm 'peculiar', because I put starch on my hair to stop myself from looking like a golliwog. White folk think I'm a strumpet, because I sleep in black folk's houses. Black people laugh, because I wash my face in the village frogpond. What of it? Should I keep dirt on my face merely to deny them the pleasure of laughing? I laugh too, we all laugh together. If I can leave a trickle of laughter behind me, and a friend or two as well, I've done a darn' sight better than any baby-kissing electioneer."

This woman dispensed joy. What rich delight it was to meet a fellow traveller who confirmed one's most precious beliefs!

"But when you come across a serious problem which stinks like a hatful of dead worms, but which everyone else accepts as a matter of course, do you do something about it? Or do you walk around it like all the rest?"

"Like the lobsters, you mean? Look, it's no use deceiving yourself by shuffling your principles to fit the situation. That's like rubbing the palm of your hand with alum, and then having your fortune read. Situations vary, but principles don't. You can kill the nerve of an eyetooth from the constant shock of biting through cotton thread- and you can numb your conscience too if you keep on snipping principles to more comforting shapes. You have to confront a problem boldly and examine it, like an ulcer: if you hide it under a sock, it'll only fester. If you push it to the edge of your mind, that's where it'll feed. You have to sterilize it with applied principle, and cure it with the proper solution. You can't walk away from a pain, it travels with you."

True, how very true! She talked on gladly, as might one who discourses on a favourite theme, and I listened. She talked of the freedoms which were morally desirable within the framework of institutional law, pointing out that even a traveller was not free until he ceased to cast back glances towards his native land, and discovered that he could successfully survive in the most remote and unlikely corners of the world. She spoke of democracy's tendency to numb its sense of failure with the soporific of applied socialism, and the tendency of men, shrinking from the fire of world-wide hate which fed on mankind's moral failures, to yield their heritage as humans into the fearsome stewardship of military fools.

We finished off the bottle and threw it in the sea; the breeze was falling off and soon the moon would rise.

"There's thousands and tens of thousands just like me," she said in a low, earnest voice. "Young people, mostly, 'seagulls', travelling on a shoestring wherever they can go. Eager to learn, anxious to make friends, weaving a web of human understanding across the nations of the world. Young folk from every country in the world are on the move, almost as if they realized their elders had failed, and that now it was up to them. Internationalists, slowly wearing holes in closed frontiers, little termites eating away at nationalistic cults, each one carries with him the reflection of his country, plus a little understanding, plus a little hope, and takes it to new friends in foreign lands. It's not organized it's not any kind of brotherhood, it's just a quiet and obscure social movement which seems to have grown and spread during the blackest and most terrifying years the world has ever known."

We sat in silence for a time, and I considered the beauty of her words. Strange, this game that Fortune played with men. One woman thrust a lance inside one's heart, so that confidence and the strength of cherished beliefs drained away in the sand, and the love for womankind was turned to gall. The next woman came and put a plaster on the hole, even against your will, and unwittingly supplied you with transfusions of human warmth from the abundance she held within herself. And yet again, like some work of modern art, she provided stimulus and challenge rather than mere comfort. Poor Myers, what a sorry rag she made him seem! How she would have pitied his childish postulations: I imagined her there that night, with Jacob and the girl. And then again I measured her with Tic-Tac, placing her wealth of subjective and spiritual goodness beside the exquisite corruption of sensuous, empty flesh. Aye, a thousand women, a thousand different minds....

Presently she said, "You know, you've been speaking English all evening with me, and you've quite forgotten your accent."

Devil, so I had! She unlaced her haversack, drew out a thin cotton sleeping-sack and wriggled her legs inside.

"So?" she inquired, pausing to smile at me. "What country do you come from? You're certainly not French."

I was silent, staring out to sea. "Stand up in front of a crowd and be counted....Or do you think society is some form of golden calf?" Courage she had returned to me, and the strength to be ashamed.

"Are you a seagull too?" she asked, bedding down in the sand; but I was reflecting on the things which she had said, and it was a long time before I replied.

"I don't know. A counterfeit seagull, perhaps, at best. But I'm more grateful than you'll ever realize that you think I might be one."

I was uncertain if she heard me, for already she seemed to be asleep. After a long time I also slept; but, although I woke before the sun came up, she had already gone, and there was only the hollow in the sand where she had lain. But as I stretched and yawned joy was a tide in my breast. Dawn was cool and the breeze was fresh, and I laughed exultantly: ginger hair and freckles had swept a sickly infection from my brain. I stripped and swam in the sea, then walked back along the road to cross the island to Fort de France.

God's peace upon the girl. I never saw her again.

Felix was in Le Ramier, where he normally ate lunch, and he started in surprise when he saw me.

"*Meutre!*" he cried. "But you've been gone two weeks. What happened?"

"I went away," I said laughing, and sat with him. "I met an angel."

"But we…you said you'd be there, at the party! Balls of a frog, but Yselle was almost weeping. We even went to your hotel. Where did you go? Why? What angel?"

I drank a glass of his wine, for the dust of the road was still in my mouth, and chuckled happily.

"An English angel, in heavy disguise. Frizzy ginger hair, long teeth, freckles, peeled nose."

"*Dieu!*" he exclaimed. "This is an angel?"

"We spent a night on the beach, and—"

"But her figure, yes?" His eyes gleamed, he described curves in the air with his knife. "Magnificent? Enchanting?"

"Like a diamond. All sharp angles and flat surfaces. Elbows and knees like door-knobs and feet like the flippers of an elderly seal. Ah, but she refreshed me!"

He blinked in amazement. "And you slept on the beach with this… this apparition?"

"Yes, and drank wine, and talked."

"And you made love?"

"Oh no, not that."

He stared at me bleakly for a moment, then peered down at his plate and nudged a potato with his fork, as if the answer might be hidden underneath.

"I'm afraid," he said levelly, "that I do not understand."

"Ah well, no matter. Is Larry still here?"

"No, he's gone. The circus left. But you're back, at least. Well. Yselle will want to see you."

"Devil take Yselle. I came back to commit a crime."

He dropped his knife. "Sacred name! You what? What crime? Where?"

"Secret. I'll tell you tomorrow. I have to go now and spy out the land. See you at the Europe, then? Tomorrow evening?"

He opened his mouth twice as if to say something, and then shrugged in eloquent despair. I left him sitting there staring bleakly at the empty wineglass.

As dusk drew nigh, I entered the Fort and concealed myself in a tiny room adjoining the long stone tunnel. No one had seen me, no one could know I was there; the girl who sold tickets had gone home, the two attendants were up in the zoo. The time was five minutes to seven. At seven o'clock the Fort's huge doors would be closed and locked for the night.

During the afternoon I had wandered through the zoo, to discover that conditions were possibly even worse than they were two weeks ago. The malfini was dead, the diver lay on its side with glazed eyes, two of the monkeys were close to death and surely the wretched manicou could not last the night. Few of the creatures had any water, none of the cages had been cleaned. I distributed fruit and water, paying another hundred francs, then made a careful reconnaissance which assured me the attendants slept elsewhere, and withdrew. Now I had slipped back inside the Fort intent on committing a crime.

The three-minute warning-bell rang, and half a dozen visitors shuffled down the tunnel. I crouched low behind an empty showcase, but if anyone entered the tiny room I must be seen. Minutes passed. Somewhere an iron gate clanged, and the two attendants walked briskly down the tunnel.

What excitement there would be, if they found me crouching there.

There was the click of a master switch somewhere near at hand, and all the lights were doused. They made their way down to the antechamber, footsteps echoing through the dark stone vault: the main doors slammed with a clatter, and a key rattled in the lock.

I was inside the Fort alone, and the entire night was at my disposal. I could fire this social haystack at my leisure, then doubtless devise some means of escaping over the walls.

Blood of a ghoul, but it was dark!

Night had fixed itself batlike on the Fort, and the tunnel was of unrelieved blackness. Gingerly I groped my way from the little room and moved up the steps with quickened pulse, through a cloistered series of chambers and on to the upper exit which gave onto the zoo. The ghost of a ginger-haired girl was surely not far away.

Entrance to the zoo was blocked. There was a heavy gate of stout iron bars, securely locked: I was a prisoner in the tunnel. Damn, why could I not have foreseen this? But I had all night. There must be a way: surely the end of the adventure had not come so soon? I had no sort of wire, and the lock was old and large and doubtless stiff. Could one squeeze between the iron bars? A three-legged dog had come to watch me, and for a moment I paused to coax it into friendship; then placed my back against one wall, and tried to force the bars by thrusting powerfully with my legs.

Nothing happened.

Stripping off my clothes, I attempted to force my hips and torso through. I only succeeded in scraping skin from my back, and suffering dizzy pain as I bruised my fractured ribs. Dressing again, I considered the problem anew.

Might there be a key near by?

Searching with my fingers in the darkness, I discovered only spiderwebs, picture-frames, and dust. Ah, but I was a sorry amateur: I had brought no form of light, not even matches, just walked in as I was bringing nothing that might be needed. There was no strong wire on hand, nor any form of plank or bench with which to force the bars.

Perhaps I could force a way out through the Fort's main door, secure the things I needed, and return. This might entail some risk, but better far than spending an idle night entombed within the tunnel. Stepping carefully in the blackness, I groped my way back down the tunnel. Five stone steps, across a flagstoned chamber, seventeen steps, then twenty-six more…and I found myself in the vaulted entrance chamber. Here was the little sentry-box of a ticket booth.

What?

Well now, here were two large keys!

Twenty-six steps up, then seventeen, across the cloistered chambers, and up five more. One of the keys immediately unlocked the gate. I entered the zoo enclosure, perhaps fifty yards by eighty, and went towards the cages which held birds. Most of the cage doors were held by simple latches, some swinging out on common hinges and others sliding up like traps; and now I set myself to releasing all those creatures whose conditions were the worst. But not the carnivores, or animals which might endanger children who came to play in the Savanne close by the Fort.

The seagulls first: there was symbolism there, for she had referred to youthful travellers as seagulls. They were sleepy and suspicious, and refused to leave their cages until I disturbed them with a stick. Terns and gulls and others limped and fluttered from open doors and blundered off in the night: there was the joy of a strong conviction in my heart as I watched them go. An owl was next, and he went quickly; the egret with the broken leg seemed unable to move. Many other birds I freed, but left all those which were healthier than the rest.

The deer were nervous as I moved about, and three ducks chittered softly in alarm. Beyond the deer's enclosure was a low stone parapet and a brace of ancient cannon, and from here one could look down on a sports arena where girls were playing basketball in the light of powerful arc-lamps. This way, I suspected, would provide me with escape.

Two large boa constrictors were examining their cage inch by inch, rats scampered about the grounds searching for scraps of food. I opened the door of the skunk's cage. He could not escape the zoo, but there were many places to hide, and I grinned as I envisioned the protest he might make at being captured. The foxes, no, I would leave them, they would slaughter the weaker ones. The two racoons were freed; bewildered for a minute, they finally scurried off at desperate speed. Two pacas were loosed, and hurtled around the compound with the three-legged dog lolloping uncertainly in pursuit.

Ha, there would be panic in the morning!

Steps led down to a sunken pit where carnivores and a crocodile were kept, and other beasts. The wildcat and the large baboon I did not dare release, but there were miserable monkeys dying of neglect, and these were given freedom. Some could scarcely be coaxed from their filthy dens, so weak and diseased they were, but others began to move about and consider the walls and trees. The spider monkeys I left alone, they had a large cage and seemed to be keepers' pets. The surviving possum I chased from its sty, and it furtively stole away and disappeared. Other creatures I might have chosen were secured behind stout locks, and neither of the keys I had would fit.

A certain amount of subdued excitement was growing throughout the zoo. There were rustlings in the trees and a scampering through grass, and furry bodies darted to and fro in a dither of agitation. A heinous act? I laughed delightedly and wished them well. They could thank the English girl, I was prepared to stand up and be counted.

By the time my rounds had come to an end and the keys had been replaced, the basketball game was finished and the players sat to watch an amateur baseball movie being shown on a screen in the arena. Perhaps one could leave while they were occupied? The floodlights had been doused, the wall below the parapet was dark. It led down to a ledge thick with shrubs and trees, but although refuse had been thrown down there to form a tall, soft mound of leaves and grass it was still too far to jump. I found some long rods of soft iron, twisted one around the muzzle of a cannon, and by securing a second rod to the first made myself an iron rope which led over the parapet to the ledge below.

Cautious of my weak wrist, I eased over the parapet like some mediaeval villain escaping prison walls, and carefully slid down to the ledge below. Along the ledge, through a hazard of brush: and ahead was a flight of steps leading down to Boulevarde Chevalier and the Parc Savanne beyond. It was hardly nine o'clock and the crime was well begun; the rest would have to follow in the morning. Dripping with perspiration, I sat a while to rest, and comb my hair; then chose a moment when the headlights of a car had just passed by to scale the gates at the foot of the step, drop lightly to the street and walk away in darkness.

By the gods, what a strange way to spend an evening on Martinique! I went to the hotel, where *patron* had guarded my chattels the past two weeks, and in mute alarm he watched his guest, in sweatsoaked shirt and filthy jeans, wander through the bar-room and wearily climb the stairs.

Weary, aye: but the thing was done or at least begun, as certain astonished persons would discover in the morning.

In the morning the campaign was carried into the heart of the enemy's camp. In the office of Chez Chêneaux Reynal I found some fat sow slumped at her desk, wolfing food. She slithered a bleak, suspicious glance at me, and after perhaps a minute felt obliged to demand, "Is someone attending you?"

I glanced around, wondering who else might be there, and there was no one, no one at all.

"I don't think so," I said carefully.

After another mouthful or two she rumbled, "Charles, are you attending to this customer?"

Charles dutifully appeared from behind the screen like a gaunt little bandicoot sidling across the floor of the House of Commons, and hoping not to be noticed.

"I look for a Monsieur Roget Petit-Jean," I informed him. "I understand he is President of the Historical and Geographical Society."

The society was in command of the museum and the zoo. The bandicoot twittered politely and escorted me upstairs to the Olivetti agency, and here I discovered Monsieur Petit-Jean: a bland-faced gentleman of about fifty, sufficiently polite, who listened with composure to my questions. Yes, he was the President, and the society was responsible for the zoo. Would I not sit down?

"Have you been there lately?" I inquired.

He was puzzled. "Well, no. No. I am occupied with pressing affairs, you understand."

"Then permit me to inform you that the condition of the animals there is absolutely criminal," I said severely. Aye, I would stand up and be counted. "Animals and birds there are dying of neglect. Are you aware of this?"

He was agreeably polite. "But no. You see, I have no direct—"

"And yet you are supposed to be in charge? Then permit me to inform you further. Last night I entered the zoo and released a number of birds and animals. Let them loose from their cages. You comprehend?"

He regarded me with mild astonishment. "You released them?"

"Yes. And furthermore, if conditions do not rapidly improve, I shall go there again and let the rest go, including the carnivores."

But he evidenced no spasm of excitement. He gazed at me inquiringly, as if wondering what advantage I might hope to gain by this invasion, and protested calmly:

"But…it is not my affair, monsieur. Yes, I am President, but I am not the supervisor of the zoo. I have no direct dealings with it. And I am quite sure…the supervisor is an admirable man. I am sure—"

"Who is the supervisor?"

"Père Pinchon, of the Seminary College. He is a qualified naturalist, a most admirable man."

"Then I shall go to him. And, remember, you've been given fair warning."

Outside in Rue Ernest Deproge I hailed a taxi and was carried off towards the college on heights above the city. Fair warning, indeed, I smiled to myself: who the devil was I to go around giving presidents fair warning? And he had not even thrown me down the stairs. But merely releasing a few birds and animals was not enough; taken by itself, it was only an act of mischief, which would certainly not produce lasting good. Discovery of the outrage would be muffled by the thick walls of the Fort, the crime would be buried in silence away from the gaze of men, no one would ever see it as a form of angry protest. Attention must be drawn to the zoo's miserable state, or my action would be no more than indulgence in irresponsible folly.

Alors, I would beard this Père Pinchon.

On the third floor of one wing of the college the priest was engaged in lecturing a classroom full of boys; I waited a few minutes while he finished. As I stood on the balcony, I could see him through a window, a stout young man with a fine spade beard, a rich full-throated voice and twinkling eyes, attired in khaki shirt and shorts. He seemed vigorous and intelligent and glad of his role as tutor: why then had he let the zoo become such a wretched shambles?

I greeted him as he came out from the classroom, and he beamed with instant courtesy and came to grasp my hand. The zoo? He observed me warily. Yes he agreed, he was in charge; and his smile faded, his eyes narrowed in a level, flinty stare.

"Conditions there are a disgrace to everything you stand for," I stated flatly. "It is a scene of criminal negligence. I came to ask you why."

"Why is what?" he boomed, and glared at me from head to toe. "What right do you have to make this accusation?"

"By the right of any man to protest the torture of animals. The cages are swamps of excreta, the two cretins you employ as keepers never fill the water troughs, and when they think to pass around food they don't even know which animals eat meat and which are herbivores."

"Nonsense!" he exploded. "*Mon Dieu*, but it is *formidable*. Nonsense, I say!" He gazed at me indignantly. "Who are you? What gives you the right to come here with…this.…"

"I'm no one of importance," I snapped. "Just a flea in your ear: but I'm out for blood. I'm not here to entertain you with mistruths. I've made a detailed inspection of your zoo. It's incredible! It's inexcusable! Most animals have had no water at all for two whole weeks, except rain," I pointed out, wondering if this was actually true. "They only survive, because it rains. The fox doesn't even have a water dish, and the racoons' dish is broken. What of that?"

He hesitated. Doubt appeared in his attitude.

"Well," he hedged, "sometimes there is no water. The zoo is at a height, the water mains are faulty, they are sometimes under repair."

Ah, so I had him there! I stared at him cynically until he looked away. Father Pinchon, a dominating figure to a classroom of small boys, did not care to be challenged in this fashion. Good.

"That compound is a private little hell of misery, filth, and torment. Why do you starve the animals? Why are they given no medical attention? You're a naturalist, you look fairly intelligent, why do you let them die?"

"What animals?" he demanded with renewed vigour. "Come now, be specific. What animals?"

"The malfini; it died of neglect. The diver, it died of neglect. The egret with the broken leg. A manicou that had an ulcerated eye has died. Two rhesus monkeys are almost dead. Shall I go on?"

He stared out over the balcony at boys playing in the yard below, and doubtless he wished that he was with them.

"How can we manage everything," he said finally, "on the few funds we have? I have not the time. I must teach my classes, and there is not enough money. There are many things besides the zoo. We have to struggle along with what we have, as best we can."

He was fat enough; he looked as if he struggled very well.

"Then if you can't find the time, and you can't afford a zoo," I said bitterly, "get rid of it. Give the creatures away, destroy them cleanly, anything. You have no right to take God's creatures and condemn them to slow death by starvation, thirst and disease, just because you don't have the time or the money to give them proper care. There's a quarter of a million people on this island. If each contributed five francs every year, you'd have enough to make that zoo a decent, well-run place. And if the people of Martinique aren't sufficiently interested to contribute a penny a year, they're obviously not interested in having a zoo at all."

"Oh, but they are interested. Many people visit the zoo."

"At fifty francs a visit. What happens to the money?"

He fidgeted uncomfortably. There was a long moment of silence.

"And here's something else," I said "If you don't improve conditions in your zoo, I'm going to liberate all the birds and animals. Every last one of them. You comprehend?"

At once he snapped to attention. He fixed me with a piercing gaze and jabbed his finger at my chest.

"You are the imbecile!" he cried excitedly. "Eh? You were the one? You released the animals and birds last night?"

"But, of course, who else?"

He was dumbfounded. This kind of nonsense appeared to be beyond his experience. He opened his mouth several times before he found words to put in it.

"But this is a matter for the police!" he burst forth.

"Of course."

"I will have to inform the police, you understand. I have no other recourse, I am obliged to report you."

"*D'accord*, let's both go at once to the police. You can tell them about my crime, and I'll tell them about yours."

He led the way along the balcony, but paused with a worried frown.

"It is very serious, he insisted, glancing at me strangely.

"It is," I agreed. "That is why I am here."

He went a little farther and stopped again, asking for my name.

"My name is unimportant, and so am I, and so are you. Only our crimes are important."

"But I must give your name to the police," he declared, pausing afresh at the head of a flight of steps.

"I will do that for you. And you can tell them yours."

For a moment he seemed lost in thought, frowning down at the steps, then abruptly turned and disappeared inside a room near by. I waited about a minute, then went to see what held him. He was standing unhappily by a littered desk disconsolately picking at a few papers, seeds, dead leaves.

"Come," I invited him. He shrugged impatiently and refused to look at me.

"I lack the time," he growled. Ho-ho, so I had called his bluff, and found it as empty as some of his open cages.

"So, Père Pinchon," I said derisively, relishing the moment, "it seems you never have the time for anything worth while. Or perhaps you are ashamed? You don't want to expose your shame to public view?"

He was silent, he would not come. Perhaps he was making plans against me, but deciding first to put his zoo in order. One might hope so. Yes, I felt sure he was not a bad man; weak, perhaps, or thoughtless, needing to be bearded now and then.

Laughing at his discomfort, I left the room and went away, back to the city. Pappi was home, and let me use a typewriter I found in Felix's room. I made out a press release, handed it to the editor of a bi-weekly called *l'Information*, and wondered what would happen when police and Père Pinchon read the paper in the morning.

Light rain was falling as I made my way across the Savanne towards Rue de la Liberté. A heavy evening squall had just passed by with buffeting winds and short, sharp bursts of drenching rain, so that the lights of Avenue Duparquet now gleamed merrily from wet surfaces and the park was rich with the fresh straw smells of saturated grass; heavy drops plopped from the tall emperor palms, and the smells of lavender and choked sewers mingled with the salt air of the sea. Wet grass, night air, gentle rain, and company waiting in the tavern just ahead: aye, such freedom as a man could find was a precious sweetness in the nostrils and the heart. And the animals in the hulking blackness of the Fort near by. Well, a few of them were free, and at least the others would drink tonight. If I traded their freedom for my own, at least I would know the reason for the prison walls and bars, and a few days or a week or a month would see me free again.

Music from the cafés drifted through the mist of rain, lights sparkled and winked damply, the hum of laughter and conversation sounded from l'Impératrice and the Central, and waiters were drying the seats at sidewalk tables. Ah, La Martinique! Such an island this was, with its soaring green volcanic peaks and deep secluded valleys, her forested heights and fertile slopes and champagne bays of palms and caramel sand. Zanzibar, Crete, Madeira, Ceylon: I had left my heart on none of these, on any mountain top.

And Yselle: would she be waiting? Dark eyes, pale smooth skin, luxurious black hair…how would it be with us, now that I had found myself again? There had been promise in that single backward glance she gave me: but that was only a single glance, two long weeks ago.

Crossing the street, I entered Café de l'Europe and immediately found Pappi and Yselle.

"Hola!" Pappi cried in greeting, and rose to shake my hand. "We've been waiting, Felix told us. He'll be here soon. What have you been up to, hey?"

Yselle, with her smooth, bare shoulders pale above a strapless sheath of plain black nylon which revealed the becoming firmness of her bosom, glanced at me incuriously and let her glance slide away to fix on some distant point with studied boredom. So? My fond smile of welcome became a waxen grimace. Why, I was nothing to her, of course: but what had I done to merit her insolence? With a sense of loss and disappointment I sat down by Pappi.

"What have you been doing?" he asked. "Felix said you were going to commit a robbery or something. Yes? Did you do it? You weren't caught?"

Was she angry that I had ignored my invitation to the party? Again her glance drifted across my face and rested elsewhere, as if she had not noticed I was there. Why, her attitude was one of unconcealed contempt. What had I done now?

"Yselle?"

She permitted herself to study me briefly, pouting her full red lips with an expression of disdain. There was some form of problem here, it seemed: and a problem must be confronted, preferably at once. When in doubt, attack.

Pappi said, "Felix told us that you'd come back to—"

I silenced him gently with upraised hand.

"Alsace beer, Pappi. Yselle?" But she did not appear to be listening. "Yselle, your mother owes me an apology. I shall demand it from her."

"My mother what?" Her eyes sparked with subdued hostility. "You've never met my mother, I don't know what you're talking about."

"Then permit me to explain. In Guadeloupe I was the victim of a beautiful, exciting, seductive woman, who savaged my heart like a wildcat. I ran away. When I arrived at Martinique the first woman I met was you: beautiful, exciting, seductive. Another wildcat, I thought, so I ran away again. But during these past two weeks I realized my mistake, so I came back."

She took a Bastos from a packet and, as I lit it for her, I noticed her hands were trembling faintly. Why, why? For a moment she regarded me with frowning interest, then shrugged and looked away.

"It's a matter of no importance to me, whether you come back or not. Why should it be? And why does my mother owe you an apology?"

"She doesn't, I just threw that in to make you listen. You seemed to like me when we first met. Something has happened since to make you change your mind, and even despise me. What is it?"

One might as well have attacked a wall of stone with a wooden rapier.

"Is it because Felix said I'd returned to do something unlawful?"

"I said before, it is not a matter of importance to me what you do."

Pappi and I exchanged helpless glances, and gratefully I accepted a glass of beer from the waitress. Ah well, not every problem was a bag of wind to be pricked with a pin; some were ravelled knots, which only time and care could straighten out.

"But what unlawful thing?" Pappi asked impatiently. "Have you done it or not, hey? Ho yes, and that photostat, I had it made. Not so easy, it had to be done after working hours, but it came out perfectly. I sent it off, now all I have to—"

"Felix!" I murmured a quick apology to Pappi. Felix had arrived in company with a stout little woman some years older than himself, and brought her to our table.

"Elène," he announced grandly, "meet my disreputable friends. Except of course Yselle," bowing slightly. "She is the only one of them with a reputation. You know Pappi of course, and this one is Australian. He's come to Martinique to rob the rich, and buy us all Pernod."

So I ordered two Pernods in the current round, and wondered where Felix might have found Elène. She was a round and hairy little person with coarse dark curls, bushy brows which almost met, a fine dark moustache, and bristling black tufts sprouting from two moles on her chin. But despite the slight hook of her nose, keen black eyes and a general swarthiness to rounded cheeks and chin, she yet contrived to appear of gentle personality with quick appreciation of almost any form of humour.

Felix touched his glass to hers, and she dimpled happily.

"To love," she said, and we drank.

"She's fisheries research," Felix explained. "Comes from Point-à-Pitre. Pappi found her and gave her to me."

Presumably his thin artistic girlfriend had abandoned him.

"You know Point-à-Pitre?" Elène asked me.

"A little. A graveyard full of wildcats. I avoid graveyards and I'm cagy about wildcats." And since she seemed startled, I added gallantly, "Though your presence there would lend the place considerable attraction. Tell me, you are from fisheries research and Pappi is a naturalist. Has either of you been to the zoo in Fort St Louis?"

"No," said Elène.

"Yes," said Pappi, inspecting me with interest. "Why?"

"Yselle? Felix?"

Yselle had been there once. "I was sick all the rest of the afternoon," she admitted, "from the smell. I never realized animals could stink so much. And the rotten meat...." She shuddered.

"Pappi?"

"I was there a couple of times."

"What do you think of the place?"

"Think?"

"Do you feel it's clean enough? That the beasts are well cared for?"

He shrugged, obviously marvelling that such questions should be asked.

"It is a zoo. If you keep wild animals, you must put them in cages, no?"

"And feed them, and water them, and keep the cages clean. Right?"

He shifted uneasily. "Yes, yes, but it is only a small place, there is nothing important there. No elephants, no lions or big animals."

Disappointment enfolded me like damp sacking. Here was Pappi, a naturalist, a good man and familiar with the zoo, and yet reluctant to recognize the degradation existing there. Then how could one expect ordinary folk to be critical of the zoo's authorities? To Yselle the zoo meant smells to be avoided; to Pappi it meant a vague embarrassment.

"To hell with the zoo," said Felix. He touched his glass to Elène's and grinned. "To crime!"

We drank to crime.

"Yesterday you said you were going to—"

"I've been asking him for five minutes," said Pappi, glad enough to change the subject. "He won't say what he's done. All he does is make eyes at Yselle."

"She hates me. I've been trying to find out why."

Elène asked, "Did you really do something wicked? Or can't you tell us?"

I glanced around at them. Elène was observing me as if prepared to laugh at some happy indiscretion. Felix was poised to absorb some new sensation. Pappi looked suspicious, and Yselle was toying with her glass as she frowned intently across the room at nothing in particular.

"I went into the zoo last night," I said, "and let a lot of animals and birds out of their cages."

Elène gave a shrill squeal of delight and clapped her hand to her mouth, gazing wide-eyed at me, but otherwise there was a moment of utter silence. They all stared, unbelieving. Certainly they did not approve, they gave no sign of any understanding. What had I done? Their eyes condemned me for a madman. How many were there who would understand?

"Let them go? Animals and birds?" Pappi breathed. "You...you?"

Yselle was gazing at me as if I had suddenly turned into a trotting spoonbill. Then Felix began laughing, leaning back in his chair with his hands limp by his sides, gales of laughter which seemed to fill the room, and Elène likewise gave way to convulsions of hilarity. Quite unable to speak Felix raised one hand to point at me, and as if the effort were too great let it fall again. Elène's bosom heaved with peals of delighted mirth, quaking jellylike from her shoulders to her hips.

"Ho-ho," Felix cried at length. "Ho-ho-ho, he let…he let…*meutre alors*, he came all the way from Australia to…ha-ha! Oh name of a sacred dog! Oh, great Gaul, but that's…*c'est formidable!*" He wiped his eyes with the back of one hand and shook helplessly.

"But, but, but," stammered Pappi, groping for words, "why? what… what for? It's an…they'll get you. By all that's holy, if they find out! Hey?"

Yselle had her head bowed, quaking and biting hard on her bottom lip. Elène was smothering spasms of happy giggles with both her hands, and every time she peered at me a fresh wave of giggling began. So, here was social comment on my act: laughter. Amazement. One man's protest against the suffering of animals was condemned outright as magnificent, laughable folly.

"How many?" cried Pappi. "How did you get in? How many did you let go? But why, why?"

Well, then, I was on trial by my peers. Briefly, brutally, I described the appalling conditions I had found in the zoo; how I had entered, what I had done.

"Birds," I said tersely. "Lots of birds, the ones that were suffering most. Monkeys, racoons, pacas. Possums, squirrels. A skunk, two—"

"Skunk!" howled Felix. "Oh, sweet wine of life, but I wish I'd—"

"But how did you get out?" asked Pappi.

"Over the wall."

"Did they see you, anyone?"

"No one."

"But if they find out, hey?"

"They've already found out."

"Hey? What?" He glanced nervously at the door.

"Found out?" echoed Felix. "Who found out?"

"The zoo authorities."

"But how? How?"

I permitted myself a weary grin, remembering Père Pinchon's incredulous dismay.

"I told them."

Felix stared, closed his eyes and shook his head, and stared again. "Mad," he whispered. Pappi was slack-jawed, Yselle gazed with brittle fascination. Damn them all, I had no respect left for their tender feelings.

"I told Petit-Jean, the President; and said why I'd done it, and that if conditions didn't improve quickly I'd let the rest go, even the dangerous ones. I told the same thing to Père Pinchon, the naturalist who's in charge of—"

"Père Pinchon?" Pappi whinnied, distraught. "I know him. You told *him*? But he eats fire, that one! Holy angels, but if you made him angry…oh!"

"I made him angry, yes. And then I typed out a press release and gave it to *l'Information* for good measure, to make sure the whole thing couldn't be hushed up."

"Mad!" said Felix with happy conviction. "It is a man who is mad, absolutely! What in the devil can you gain?"

"Better conditions for the animals. Shut up, Elène, you sound like something from outer space."

"And you gave the whole story to *l'Information*?" he persisted, vigorously scratching his head with both hands.

"It'll be printed tomorrow. Thanks for the loan of the typewriter. I used yours."

"Eh? Oh, that's Claude's. We haven't seen him for two weeks. *Meutre*, but releasing animals in the middle of the night, and escaping, and then reporting it yourself…but it is fantastic. And you told them your name?"

"No. Only my nationality."

"But of course they will find out, you will be arrested."

"Perhaps. But they can't arrest the ginger-haired angel I told you about, and she's half to blame."

"The one you slept with, on the beach?"

"She slept in her sleeping-sack; she wasn't interested in me. But I was still suffering from wildcats at the time, and she brought things back into perspective."

"Animals, angels, breaking into forts. It's too much. Waitress? Five Pernods. But double!"

"Sleeping-sack?" said Yselle inquiringly. "This…this creature Felix spoke about…."

"Yes. She gave me nothing, except a few things I had lost. She looked like a straw broom with wooden arms and legs, but she gave me back the convictions I had lost."

"Oh," she murmured, and smiled diffidently. "I thought…oh."

So, the knot was beginning to unravel.

"I would defy anyone to make love to a broom," I declared. "Her quality was of the intellect, rather than elsewhere. Felix, you said that was Claude's typewriter?"

"Yes, it's his."

"I find that interesting."

"Why?"

"He once stole my watch, I feel inclined to return the compliment. I think I could be persuaded to steal his typewriter."

He shrugged. "As you wish. But when he asks, I shall have to tell him. You won't mind?"

"On the contrary, I wish you to. In fact you might just tell him I've borrowed it. Permanently. You may also tell him, if you see him, that I have every intention of borrowing Yselle." I met her steady gaze, and for a long moment our minds were locked in a secret embrace which everyone could see. Aye, she must earlier have thought me a piece of driftwood to lie on the beach with such company as offered; and now we were each the closer for having shared the raw distress of lonely disappointment.

"And listen, mad Australian," Felix added, "you can spend the night at my place. In fact you may spend all your nights at my place, and your days as well. But, if you walk around in Fort de France with the gendarmes looking for you, no one will be able to protect you. And they'll be looking for you. There can't be too many idiot vagabonds around here wearing jeans and a crazy shirt."

"They'll be looking," Pappi chimed in, worried. "That Père Pinchon—"

"All right, then I'll sleep at your place. It is a spare room?"

"Everything you need, for as long as you want. Even a typewriter. But no animals, please."

The others began discussing Father Pinchon and his formidable reputation. Catching Yselle's glance, I offered her the matchbox sign: for a moment she was puzzled by the quaint device, but then a faint flush touched her cheeks with colour and she lowered her eyes. After a time she slowly pushed her glass to the centre of the table; I pushed mine forward until they touched, and we raised them in silent toast.

South America seemed very far away.

The denouement of the affair came rapidly enough.

Early the following morning I went down into the street, and made my way through the city towards the hotel. I would claim my sack of goods, pay the rent, change into my other shirt and disappear from the sight of gendarmes and zoo authorities. Ah, but it was wonderful to fall in love again: every hour was rich and full, the minutes were intensified, the very seconds marked the vibrant pulse of joy. No purpose could be accomplished by throwing myself at the law, nothing could be gained by being captured.

En route to the hotel I purchased a copy of *l'Information*, and there in the centre of the front page was the story: *Au Zoo du Fort St Louis.* UN HOMME OUVRE DES CAGES ET LAISSE S'ENFUIR DES ANIMAUX.

Well, perhaps it would do some good, one could only hope so. In a few days or a week the police would forget the matter in the face of more pressing affairs, and then the pleasure of the city would be mine once more; in the meantime Yselle would spend her free time with me, so that I would merely be confined to paradise in the apartment above the *quincaillerie*.

Who could have known that a wildcat could have such tender claws? What man would not be snared by such enchantment as she had?

Prison would be folly now, and separation vile; for a chosen time I would live with caution, eschewing public life for private ecstasy…and every day, as she had promised, she would come. This last journey, then: later on today, perhaps tomorrow, police search their records and discover a single Australian lived at a certain small hotel.

The hotel itself was hard by the Quartier Bouillé, a high-walled compound tenanted by the military and police, but the hour was still early and none were in the street near at hand. In fifteen minutes' time they could come and search in vain. *Patron* was sweeping the bar-room as I entered, and started in alarm when he saw me. He paused to pass one hand across his glabrous dome, his Adam's apple joggling up and down, and consternation bulged his eyes like those of a trodden toad.

"Monsieur," he pleaded. "Monsieur."

Two figures arose from chairs near by. Ten thousand demons—the police! So early? They waited already? Sudden beads of sweat pricked my scalp, a clamour for quick flight or violent action roused my blood. Could I turn and run? But they were too close! Gods, who would have thought....

"Monsieur," said one curtly, "your papers, please."

Papers? So it had begun, it always began thus. But my passport was back in the apartment.

"Uh, I don't have them with me." I hedged. "May I be of service to you in any way?"

Dung of a whistling bee, it might be days before I saw her again. Perhaps I could get bail?

"You are Australian, yes?" the officer queried. His *confrère* had moved to prevent me from darting through the door. Well, it had happened, Pinchon had reported me and they had probably waited all night. I was caught.

"Yes, I am."

Patron continued to goggle. What use was there in concealing facts? I could not regret what I had done, but was merely reluctant to be parted, even briefly, from Yselle. Lies would not only be futile, but would cast an odour of shame on a worthy act.

"And will you inform us of your activities during the night before last?"

Why not? They would find out.

"I was busy with affairs in the zoo," I stated.

The officer blinked his surprise, and exchanged a significant glance with his companion.

"You opened the cages? You are the man who let the animals free?"

"But of course, monsieur. Who else?"

Such naïve candour disturbed the logical trend of his inquisition, and for a moment be seemed uncertain what to say. Obviously there was no point in seizing and handcuffing this fool. He was offering no resistance.

"You are aware, of course, that this is forbidden?"

"Forbidden, monsieur?" I feigned surprise. "But forbidden by whom?"

"By law. By the police."

"Liberating suffering animals is certainly not forbidden by *le bon Dieu*, monsieur. And I believe His authority is still in advance of yours. The torture of animals is surely wrong; how then can the release of tortured animals be equally wrong?"

He studied me carefully for a moment, possibly wondering if I was some obscure form of evangelist come to deliver the animal kingdom from the thrall of mankind. Then he indicated the door.

"You will come with us. I must advise you not to offer any resistance."

They took me to the *gendarmerie* hard by the prison in Rue Amiral de Gueydon, and a morning of intermittent interrogation commenced. The usual questions were asked and repeated in various guises designed to trick the truth from the mouths of liars, and at one point I was escorted to Felix's apartment to retrieve my passport. There was no one there. Yselle had not yet arrived, and I was not permitted to leave any form of note. On a thought I took Claude's typewriter too, not knowing how many days I might be obliged to spend in jail; the police already had my cushion cover, with its few remaining contents, in their custody.

The morning was confined within a small, bare whitewashed room with nothing but several chairs and a single desk. Two officers took turns at the questioning, and then I was left alone without lunch; there had been no breakfast either. I was briefly interrogated by a stout middle-aged major, who appeared vaguely amused to be in the presence of such a quaintly afflicted foreigner; but tempers grew short as the hours grew long. To the most frequent query, "Why did you free the animals?" I would finally only reply "Because there was no one else to do it", and this seemed to confuse them. But confusion exploded about us in shouts and excited abuse when, having laboriously typed out a

205

twisted confession for me to sign, they handed it to me and I tore it up without bothering to read it.

A conference was held beyond my hearing. Yselle would be wondering what had happened; by now she would have arrived at the apartment. She would find me absent, my passport and the typewriter missing. But what would she think? That again I had run away? That I had wandered off into the hills, casually forsaking her? But, no, it would be impossible for her to consider such a thing: she was intelligent, and surely she would realize something had happened to me, that I would return as quickly as I could.

Ah, Yselle, but brief separation would only bring us closer.

"Monsieur!"

An officer came to the door and observed me coldly.

"It has been decided that your presence is not required on Martinique. You will, therefore, be deported."

Deported? The word burst through my brain like a pistol-shot. Deported to where? But away from Yselle? No, impossible!

"But look," I protested, "it's only a—"

"We have been in contact with your consul. You have a certain amount of money, which will be used for your transportation. There is a ship in two days' time. You will remain in custody until that time."

A ship to where? Dominica? Barbados? One of the British islands? I would slip away from the ship before it sailed. I would come back, somehow. On a native sloop, I'd pay them to land me secretly.

"Where to?" I asked angrily.

"As far as possible, towards Australia. To the Pacific at least, away from the Caribbean. It has been agreed that you may find your peculiar talents of more service to you in your native Oceania."

7

TAHITI

The Lotus is Bruised

SEVERAL years had passed since police in eastern Canada arrested a South African gemmologist, and charged her with illegally entering the country by means of an altered passport. She refused to reveal the artist's identity and was remanded for deportation.

The investigation was switched towards the man who had accompanied her from Europe: and since nothing could be done, and the cause was already lost, I abandoned her and fled. Besides, I had emigrated as a carpenter, and officials had recently been threatening to find me a job as such. Thousands of miles west I found a twelve-foot canoe, purchased a light rifle and supplies, and set off down the Peace, Slave, and Mackenzie rivers north to the Arctic Sea. The journey took three months and more than two thousand miles, until at last I reached the sea and paddled into a haven holding a seasonal Eskimo camp.

Here there was peace for a while. There was the stillness of the summer *tundra*, hammocked mosses starred with clustered button flowers, endless days when the sun would never set; sometimes the thrill of the chase as we pursued white whales in asthmatic ancient luggers, and the smell of the driftwood fires as women rendered blubber. The law had been left far behind, and the nearest white woman was five hundred miles away.

And now, as the ship from Martinique approached Tahiti, I thought I could feel this peculiar peace steal over me again. In the distance Tahiti resembled Martinique, although smaller and more compact, a scarab of green and purple mountains ringed with reefs and creaming surf, companioned by Moorea with a splendid sense of world's-end isolation. Once more the pressure of police had forced me to leave my woman behind, this time to quit the Caribbean and journey over water for a month to mid Pacific. I had no woman now and wanted none. Yselle had been too close, as the South African had been, but the weeks of clean salt air had rinsed bitterness away, leaving only the luxuries of memories and regrets. And this time I had altered my own passport, carefully and vindictively bleaching out remarks the Martinique gendarmes had written there.

Travellers arriving at Tahiti were required to have some form of onward ticket, and I had none. In order to gain a permit to land and stay a while, one had to produce a non-refundable ticket guaranteeing transport to some other destination, in case one embarrassed the Government by running short of funds. If I could produce no ticket, I would not be permitted to stay. And yet again, as I had no onward ticket and lacked the funds to purchase one, who would agree to carry me on to somewhere else?

But there was bound to be some chance, as four hundred passengers jostled their way ashore. Certainly something would happen, even if I had to lower myself over the side at night. I would stay here on Tahiti, to the devil with gendarmes. All was behind, the past was a fragrant vision hidden behind a wall thousands of miles away. All was ahead, the future was waiting ahead there on Tahiti's lovely shores, a tranquil tropical haven as serenely beautiful as the Arctic's *tundra* coast. Aye, Tahiti was endeared to the traveller's heart, one of the distant places like Samarkand, and Mandalay, and Timbuktu. Already I had learnt that Tahiti had no zoo; she was a woman, but she slept, and a man might sleep in peace with her even as she slept.

"Looks deserted," said Cliff. He glanced inquiringly at Denny and Hal, who had pulled up beside us on the second motor-bike. "Whaddya reckon, fellers?"

"Could be," Denny surmised cautiously.

"What if it is?" asked Hal with customary petulance. Hal seemed to droop through life burdened by the notion that laughter was a form of adolescent weakness and approval of anything a sin: he was American, soft and emasculate, and younger than either of the Canadians or myself.

"Then we take the joint over," Cliff announced. "Or you wanna go climbing through windows again, and get chucked out in the street?"

We were five miles out on the road south from Papeete, riding double on two powerful 650 BSAs, which Cliff and Denny were using on a tour around the world. Accommodation in Papeete had proved both scarce and expensive because of the coming festival: on our first night ashore three of us had climbed through a hotel window to share a single room hired by the fourth, but on the second night we were discovered, and ejected in the wee hours of the morning.

Now we were on reconnaissance, determined to discover some friendlier and less expensive refuge, where we might stay for a month or more without pawning our arms and legs. And here, in this old estate beside the road, with ranks of coconut palms parading off into the hills, was a grand, old wooden mansion with turrets and cornices, columns and architraves, with an old wrought-iron hitching-post beside a broad flight of steps, and a scattering of statues in the grounds. But the place seemed untended and untenanted; cows were grazing freely, windows were broken and doors askew, scabrous old paint was flaking from the walls and the roof was stained with rust. No sign of any human could be seen.

"House of Frankenstein," Cliff murmured, frowning. "Spooks, cobwebs, buggers howling in the night. Come on."

We left the motor-bikes by the road and squeezed by the sagging main gate. The place held an air of complete abandonment and the only signs of life were the grazing cows, chirruping birds in the shrubbery, and the breeze which stirred the sun-drenched palms to pattern the grass with moving shadow-stars.

The veranda was bare, the planks loose and rotten underfoot. The original house had been rectangular, but three curious hexagonal rooms had been added later on, and joined to the main building by covered wooden walkways. One might have been a bandstand, another the kitchen; what the third could have been we never did decide.

"Hey, beds!" Denny had found a room with the frames of three old beds. Broken crockery and glass were scattered on the floor. "We got it made, we can start a colony here. Dames, dames and more dames, bring 'em all out here."

"Good trick. Charge 'em a dollar a time," suggested Cliff. "Gee, a regular vag's hotel."

He was the only man I ever knew who could effectively combine a ferocious scowl with a happy elfin grin, a combination which had an electric effect on susceptible women. Overly tall, with strong bones sparsely fleshed, the scowl was constant reminder of the temper which lurked an inch behind his sudden smile. His eyes were intense, deep-set, and shadowed by beetling brows, and the backswept crop of coarse dark hair strangely supplemented the sallow, angular face. He came from Vancouver, in Canada, where he built and raced small cars, but his trade was panel-beating.

Hal glanced disconsolately at the dust on the sprung floors, the cobwebs festooning dim corners, the termite tracks on the riddled walls, the creeping vines invading the veranda.

"Goddam shambles," he lamented. "You guys going to live here?"

No one bothered to answer him. Two years in the United States peacetime army had apparently not succeeded in prying his fingers loose from the sacrosanct apronstrings of pragmatic Americana. Recently discharged, he was drifting now without apparent purpose or direction, continually dismayed to find himself in the rough and profane company of aliens and foreigners.

"Sh-h-h!"

Denny had paused on the rear veranda, grimacing drolly and stabbing his finger at some target beyond our sight.

"A dame!" he whispered hoarsely. "A female woman!"

Quickly we moved to cluster by him. Just beyond the veranda a young Tahitian lass, long blue-black hair and nut-brown skin, was hanging freshly laundered clothes on a line. Near by was a set of washtubs holding yet more clothes.

"Hell," Cliff breathed, "we got us a housemaid too."

Her bosom was only restrained by a narrow strip of cloth, her pareo had slipped so low on her hips that modesty had rushed away to hide. Well now: did she live here? Was she a fringe benefit, along with the three old beds? Warily we stalked her, padding along the veranda and through the back door, and the three of us approached her in a group with Hal loitering vaguely in the rear. Her back was to us. We stood behind her, a yard away, and Cliff loudly coughed.

"Ooh!"

She jumped several inches in surprise and swung to face us, grasping wildly at the pareo as it slithered towards her knees. But here was no nervous nidget, for as soon as she saw us, and briefly scanned our faces, she broke forth in delighted peals of laughter.

"Ooh, mama, you scare me into a tree!" she cried in French. "Sacred name, oh!" She stooped to retrieve some laundered garment she had dropped on the grass, and giggled happily. "Yes? Who you are?"

"Friends," I said. "Come to visit you." Cliff and Denny had little French, so I introduced them.

"Ah good, and I call myself Nita," she declared. "And you are making visit?"

"What the hell's she saying?" Cliff demanded. "Damn, I wish I'd studied."

"She says her name's Nita and wants to know if we're making a visit."

He scowled at her with a predatory smile. "Well, tell her I think she's a good-looking babe and she's hired. And for crys-sake ask her to cover up those boobs before my eyes drop out. And tell her we live here, as from now, and see if she throws a mickey."

"Ooh!" she cried, giggling again, and adjusted the strip of coloured cloth across her chest. "You see, I spik Eenglish, a leetle."

He clasped one hand to his eyes in mock dismay, and Denny and I burst out laughing.

"Ooh my," she said to the pair of us in husky confidence, "I like heem!" She eyed him admiringly from head to toe. "He is so beeg, an' he look nice, no?"

Cliff took his hand away and blinked at her like a wounded owl. Two days and nights in Papeete had not been enough to condition us to the frank and unsubtle approach of the *vahinés* to sex.

"An' you say you will leeve here?"

"Who owns the place?" Denny asked.

"Who owns?" She shrugged and glanced about the grounds, as if the owner might be peering from a bush. "Somebody, I theenk. I don' know. You like stay here?"

"Yes, we like."

"For sleep?"

"For sleep, wash, eat, and...everything."

"Everything?" She gurgled delightedly. "Ooh my! O.K., you can stay. I am happy if you stay, my house is not far." She glanced at Denny appraisingly. "Nice. You pretty, also. I 'ave one sister. You like?"

Denny squinted down at his feet and shuffled them once or twice, and scratched his nose, shaking with suppressed mirth.

"Er, well, maybe." He caught Cliff's eye and suddenly they both burst out laughing.

"Oh, my smothered uncle," said Denny presently, "I love this damn' island. I'm never going to leave the place. Gee, what a bunch of hairy-minded dames." And turning to Nita, "O.K., bring on your sister, let's have a look at her. So it's O.K. if we all live here, eh? The four of us?"

"Four?"

He indicated Hal, sitting behind us on the steps of the veranda, and she observed him carefully.

"I don't see heem before. He mahoo, that one?"

"Mahoo? What's that?"

"You don' know what is mahoo?" She stared at Hal again, and then shrugged. "If he not mahoo, he can stay. O.K., tomorrow I bring some eggs and my sister, Vickie, yes?"

Thus it was that we settled down to live in the House of Tamaraa. Cliff and Denny, who had ridden their motor-bikes overland from Canada to Panama and then shipped out for Tahiti, had fitted their machines with brackets on either side to hold stout wooden boxes; in these they stored the necessities for life on the open road. Hal had an enormous United States Army pack, almost as large as the kitbag he had been obliged to leave in town, crammed with sufficient surplus of clothes and gadgets to furnish a thieves' bazaar. I had a portable typewriter, blanket, shorts and shirt, and a large sheet I had smuggled off the ship. Cliff and Denny and I claimed beds and permitted Hal to sleep on the floor; as a mattress I used bags stuffed with grass, and they had their sleeping-sacks.

Later on we learnt that the House of Tamaraa was the oldest of all the buildings on Tahiti, built by a Monsieur Goupil in 1873, and the estate was second only to Atimaono in size, with fifteen thousand coconut palms and a hundred and twenty cattle. And somehow it seemed fitting that this long-abandoned mansion should, in extreme old age, be blessed with the daily gratitude of strangers who had chosen her in preference to all the fine and pompous hotels on the island.

"O.K.," cried Denny later, "so let's hit the big smoke, boys! Five o'clock and we gotta find chow, and there's all those dames there waiting in Papeete." He sat on the edge of his bed combing his hair, and the light of impending conquest gleamed in his calm grey eyes.

"What dames?" Hal asked petulantly, lying on the floor, and we stared at him amazed.

"Only about ten thousand of 'em," said Cliff, frowning darkly. "All passionate and panting."

"Glance at 'em sideways, and they fall into bed."

Hal was good-looking in a lustreless and listless fashion. He walked with caution on the edge of life, wary of perils and skeptical of joy; his body was soft with tender curves as if from lack use, his cheeks were round and girlish and with his dark abundance of artfully waved hair lent him the suggestion of a youthfully effete gigolo. He was suspicious of women, yet attracted them with ease.

"Probably all jacked up," he said glumly. "And, anyway, the tourists and M.G.M. have sucked up most of the talent. What would girls want with bums like us?"

Cliff glowered, his eyes hard and shiny as black agate.

"You make my heart bleed, Hal. So you want to stay here, maybe? And read up your jungle warfare book?"

"Ah, well, there's nothing to eat here. I guess I might as well go."

The thunder of the BSAs burst upon the peace like cannon-fire: never had such powerful motor-bikes been seen in the Society Islands. Black and silver, heavy and aggressive, their machine-gun detonations racked the gentle silence of Punaavia and the clustered huts of Faaa. The coast was rich with the abundance of palms and groves of mangoes, thickets of bananas swarmed with flowering vines, palm-thatch huts were sweetly set amid flourishing coppices of frangipani and hibiscus and vanilla. The evening air was cool and spiced with the fragrance of flowers and woodsmoke, and folk who heard us coming ran from their huts, or paused on the road to wave their greetings and laugh in delighted alarm.

The motor-bikes went slower, and slower. Neither Cliff nor Denny could maintain speed and fully savour the smiles of the many pretty girls without running off the road into a tree. Tawny-skinned, with long black hair and the gentle regular features and leisurely grace of Polynesia, their laughter came as easily as the taunting flick of a hip, and every smile implied an invitation.

"Crys-sakes," Cliff shouted over his shoulder, "a man'll never get back to Canada! Oh-la-la, look at them two…and that one!" The machine veered as he passed a girl who smiled at him from under thick, dark lashes. "Oh, mother, save me!"

"Crazy dames!" Denny yelled, coming up beside us. Hal rode behind him like an expressionless blancmange. "What a crazy, goddam island. Enough to drive a man to drink."

"Don't worry, we're drivin'. Hinano, here we come!"

In certain respects the town of Papeete is an obvious intruder, a conglomerate of alien commerce and control never fully accepted in the Tahitian way of life. It holds the seat of Government—but the Government is French, and Tahitians like to pretend that the French are merely visitors in transit. Too courteous and apathetic to openly protest at French control, they gravely consider the pompous pronouncements of imported codes and precepts, and then carry on exactly as if nothing had been said. The town also holds the seat of commerce, but the commerce is largely Chinese, and since the islanders love life too well to spend it counting silver, or cutting cloth, or cleaning out cafés, they permit the orientals to fulfil these boring roles. But Papeete remains a stranger with one foot on the land and the other on the decks of passing ships.

Rambling wooden structures with red or rusty rooves lend Papeete the aspect of a sprawling shanty town, untidily sliced by narrow streets and wedded to the sea, yet seasoned with the dignities so dear to Europeans and salted with smart and modern shops.

The intrusion of iron and asphalt is rapidly stemmed at the edge of town by the luxuriance of native palms and flowers crowding about villas and small huts: the waterfront faces a broad lagoon screened by distant reefs.

Preparations were afoot for Bastille Week celebrations, streets and public buildings were hung with flags and bunting, and trim white yachts from overseas were moored by the esplanade. The lowering sun was firing the sea and the sky with shafts of copper-crimson incandescence when we arrived at the waterfront. The motor-bikes were parked, and for a little time we lingered to gaze on the beauty of the sunset lagoon, and let our glances rove along the festive avenue of Bir-Hackeim. Folk were taking their evening pleasure along the esplanade and sitting at cafe tables, which overflowed the sidewalks to the street.

"Hot baby," Denny sighed. "I wouldn't be dead if it killed me. Man, just look at that!"

Three Chinese-Tahitian girls drifted by quietly talking, with piled blue-black hair and creamy skins. Their delicate features were touched with a subtle hint of Polynesia, their slim figures were sheathed in fine brocade. He studied the roll of their hips with a practised eye.

"You can see the Tahitian in 'em. They'd get pinched if they walked down Robson Street like that."

Denny, like Cliff, came from Vancouver where he was an elevator technician by trade. He was a man of reflective silences, but easily roused to the drama or delight of any opportune occasion; sensitive and pensive, he was the observer who quietly waited with a fine sense of timing to fling himself in the midst of the local scene. This relish of opportunity provoked his present eager state, rather than mere lust for taking women. Women tended to trust him for his frank and pleasant face, and level gaze; and, since he was a worthy man, their trust was not misplaced. As a rule.

"Fan-bloody-tastic!" murmured Cliff, gazing hungrily at a pair of venturesome vahinés. And dragging his eyes away he added, "Let's see if we can find a place at Vaima's."

Hal was combing his wind-ruffled hair as he inspected the row of yachts, but followed us over to Vaima's Restaurant. All the tables were taken, but we found four chairs inside and strangers on the sidewalk made room for us to sit. Tables, girls, and conversation were freely exchanged among the Vaima's international clientele. A Tahitian waitress in the inevitable pareo brought four large bottles of cold Hinano beer, playfully ruffled Hal's hair and quizzed Cliff with a raised brow before she went away. Hal combed his hair again, and stared back at the yachts. They bore the flags of New Zealand, Australia, Britain, and the United States.

"Think I'll go and make some inquiries tomorrow," he commented, "among those yachts."

"Sure. Buy one for me too," said Cliff. Hal permitted himself a vague smile.

"No, but I was thinking I might be able to get a job on one. Go somewhere. There's American yachts there."

We stared at him, incredulous. None of us really liked him, yet there was a compelling fascination about his unlikely approach to life.

"Go somewhere?"

"Holy crud," Cliff cried in pain, "you want to leave? You only just got here, and you want to leave? Goddam, Hal, you get some original ideas."

"And all these dames." Denny sighed happily. "If I had a thousand million dollars, I still couldn't think of any place I'd rather be. And Hinano beer."

Hal shrugged sheepishly, and I wondered what it was that could bring him peace and joy. He had certainly not enjoyed the voyage from Panama. The ship we had all arrived on was still in port, tied up at the Commerce Quay a few hundred yards along the waterfront. Her name was *Caledonien*, some seventeen thousand tons, one of three vessels that made the Marseilles-Sydney run for Messageries Maritimes. We had travelled fourth class on wire bunks in the forward hold, and certainly Cliff and Denny and I had seen enough of ships for a time. The matter of coming ashore had been easy, after all: an acquaintance had passed through immigration on board, showing his onward ticket to Australia, then slipped it back to me and I had used it too. Engrossed as they were in passport data, they had merely glanced at the ticket's destination and failed to notice that someone else's name was written there.

"Dig the bad, bold mutineers," Denny remarked, indicating four long-haired men seated at a nearby table. The shining wealth of their uncut hair hung down to touch their shoulders, and one of them had tied his long, unruly curls with thin black ribbon. They were Americans, *Bounty* men, part of the cast being used by M.G.M in the filming of *Mutiny on the Bounty*. Bronzed and youthful, they were churlish with awareness of the critical appraisal of tourists.

"M.G.M., go home," Cliff said dryly. "They've been here nine months now, and they reckon the price of everything has doubled since they came." The price of a large bottle of beer had risen to as much as fifty francs, almost five shillings. "And that new jet-strip: the Yanks are going to bugger this place, like they bugger everything else. They say the—Hey, who the hell are you, honey?"

I had watched the Tahitian girl wander over to us from another table, leaving two men there staring after her, and now she blithely sat down on Cliff's lap to grin mischievously and fondly stroke his neck.

"'Andsome baby," she said blandly, and finished his glass of beer as he fixed her with a threatening black scowl. "You like pussy?"

Denny choked in his beer and froth sputtered from his glass, and Hal surveyed the girl in open dismay. Cliff's mouth twitched into a broad, villainous grin, and suddenly the girl squealed and slapped a trespassing hand.

"Hey, what you t'ink?" she cried in distress, and as suddenly kissed his nose. "You like pussy-pussy, eh?" she murmured huskily.

"Some cat," said Denny.

Cliff untwined her arm from his neck and pushed her to her feet.

"Bugger off, sweetheart. You're interfering with my beer. No pussy-pussy now."

She gazed at him pouting, and smoothed her pareo.

"Mahoo," she said accusingly. "You bloody mahoo." She returned to the two men she had left.

"What's this mahoo business?" Cliff inquired; and I turned to an American woman who sat beside me, a visitor who by her conversation appeared to have been on the island several weeks.

"Pardon, could you tell me what mahoo means?"

But she was shocked. She recoiled a little, questing the expression on my face.

"Br-rother! That's the strangest pass I've ever had."

Her husband, a plump little man with crafty eyes and olive jowls, leant forward to speak across her.

"Means a fruit," he said in a confidential rasp. "A fairy, see? A queer. For the love of Mike don't ever let 'em think you're mahoo, or they'll give you a real hard time. Tahitian men are undersexed and the women are oversexed, and they want slap-and-tickle all the time, see?"

"Really, Martin! I don't think—"

"Pussy-cats," he said, ignoring her, "the lot of 'em. If you don't shack up with one of 'em inside your first week here, they all reckon you're definitely mahoo. They pass the word around, see? Carry a cucumber in your pocket, and they'll buy you drinks for ever."

"Indeed."

"Martin! Really, you're disgusting."

The sun had set and coloured lights were shining in the branches of trees above our heads; groups of yachtsmen were entertaining friends aboard their vessels, and the esplanade was populous with strollers. How like an American to impute the easy friendship of vahinés to an urgency arising from their loins. Any person must be judged, if at all, within the social context of his own environment; and the standards of the United States, contrived with brittle artifice to measure the neuroses of sophisticated cynics, were shivered into splinters by the Polynesians' natural and candid way of life. It was incomprehensible that a woman might give herself to men, and yet remain unspoilt and innocent. It was unthinkable that brown-skinned islanders who gave their lives to pleasure with no great care for work, and who regarded the act of love as part of the natural pattern of affection, could be anything but immoral profligates.

Long of hair, proud-breasted, softly feminine and usually barefoot, they walked with a fluid, leisurely grace which mocked the stiff-legged strut of Europeans. Some had flowers in their hair, most of them were clad in gay pareos which barely sat their hips; their squat and handsome faces contrasted with the doll-like delicacy of the pale Chinese.

In the pleasure of companionship and idle conversation we finished our beer, and Hal said "I'm going to eat. You guys coming, or what?"

"Sock-suckin' mahoo," Cliff muttered, still smouldering at the insult. "I just might give her a big surprise, if only she had a little finesse. Yeah, let's go eat."

Later, when we had dined in a modest Chinese café frequented by country folk and shunned by tourists, we fared abroad in search of the night's affairs. The previous evening we had spent in Quinn's, but until the *Caledonien* sailed the place would be infested by a throng of determined tourists. Afflicted ourselves with the snobbery of those who travel on the edge of vagrancy, we preferred to assume that tourists were the Others.

For a time we drifted from bar to bar and finally came to rest in a populous dance-tavern largely given over to Tahitians. The tables were of worn, scrubbed boards, the room was a cavernous shed hung with faded streamers, the orchestra was a gramophone and two men with wooden drums; but the happy babble of islanders softened the scratchy music, and beer was only two and six a bottle. We shared a table with two Tahitian men and their girls.

"'Allo," said a fat little waitress, nudging Denny with her hip. "*Américain?*"

"Canadian, honey."

"Ah, *Canadien? Canadien* O.K., *Américain* no O.K. You beer?"

She brought us beer, and having joined the four Tahitians in a toast to mutual health, and another to Hitiaa from whence they came, and a third to Canada which they imagined as some European princedom, we settled down to watch the crowded scene. The lights were dim, the air already fogged with smoke, and a quarter of the room was given over to the throbbing rendition of the island's uninhibited form of dance. Basically the dance consisted of the male holding his arms aloft and rapidly flapping his knees as he crouched: and the girl, quite stationary upwards from the waist, was violently in motion downstairs with hips frenetically twitching to the tempo of fast rhythm, weaving and thrusting and shaking with such broad suggestion that sometimes a girl would leave the floor half-way through, shyly covering her face with her hands.

Cliff groaned aloud as if in pain, and wriggled in his chair. The Tahitians nudged each other and grinned, slyly observing him.

"Fan-bloody-tastic!" he exclaimed. "Monkey's nuts, they're damn' nearly...they're almost...."

"Look, look!" cried Denny urgently. The pareo was slipping from the hips of one young girl, gradually working loose and sliding down the flare of her pulsing thighs. Completely absorbed in the dance, hypnotized for the moment by the compelling drums, she made no move to adjust it and we watched, fascinated, as it inched down her throbbing buttocks and dropped about her ankles on the floor. Her partner laughed delightedly as she danced on with pagan abandon, thrusting her hips towards him even as he thrust his, then shaking them like castinets at incredible half-beat speed. Men and girls who watched her smiled approval. She was only attired in black lace briefs the size of a handkerchief.

Even Hal's brow gleamed with beads of perspiration as he watched, slack-mouthed and pale, and Denny's grey eyes were fired with imagination. Abruptly the dance finished, and girls went back to their tables either excited and laughing or with downcast eyes and flushed cheeks, hiding secret smiles. The girl who had lost her pareo stood there for a moment drooping with fatigue and anti-climax—and then, as if suddenly aware of her condition, squealed in dismay and snatched up her garment amid a chorus of compliments and laughter.

"Sufferin' cods," murmured Denny, "now I've seen everything. Now I can go home. But I'll never go home, I'll stay on this crazy island for ever."

"You like?" asked the Tahitian lad seated next to Cliff.

"Like?" he echoed trenchantly. "Oh-h, brother! Hey, you understand English, eh?"

"Yes, I unnerstan'. My name Manutahi. You want dance with my girl? She want dance with you."

"Huh? Aw, buddy, you keep her. I'll find a babe in a minute."

Manutahi spoke to his girl, who pouted and buried her nose in a glass of beer.

"Canadian man can dance with my girl," he said. "But not American."

Hal bridled instantly. "Why?"

He shrugged. "We say, American go home."

"Yes, but why?"

"Tahiti too small, too much American come. M.G.M. come, pay too much for beer, too much for taxi, too much for all things; now everybody else must pay too much. Now tourist come, aeroplane come every day from America, more money and more money, and soon everybody else must pay too much, too much."

"They spend their dollars here," Hal argued. "That must help Tahiti's economy."

"Help economy? I am not economy. Tahitian people not economy. Chinese, French, maybe. Big hotels, restaurants, banks, that is economy: is not Tahitian people. But de Gaulle—you know de Gaulle, Big Nose?—he say France give no more money to Tahiti. He say Tahiti must support her own self. Must pay price for French gendarmes, price for French officials, price for French Government. What to do? We got some vanilla, we got some coconut, we got some pearlshell. Not enough. So the French he say we must having tourists for bring dollars. We say them, no, we don' want tourists, we ask protection from too many tourists. French say, no. Build new hotels, big airstrip, all things. Now everybody got too many tourists, but only French and Chinese got dollars. Where is economy for poor foolish Tahitian?"

"Work, then," said Hal. "Produce stuff to sell for dollars."

"Work?" Manutahi received the suggestion as a novel approach to the problem, and twiddled his glass as he considered the idea. "Some work, yes, that might be good."

"I mean work every day. Hard work. Real work, to compete with the French and Chinese."

Manutahi viewed him as if he might be mad. "Every day? Every day hard work? But—" he spread his hands helplessly, appealing to all of us—"for what use is it to live, only to work? Horse work, donkey work, French work, Chinese work: you see them happy? Tahitian like to sing and dance and make love. We don't got too much time for work hard."

Ah, blessed people, I reflected. I had been looking for them for years. "We don't got too much time for work hard." Aye, what a wealth of wisdom lay behind those words. The island was rich with natural fruits, even fence-posts sprouted branches, what need was there to work? Only the slavish addicts of manufactured goods would feel obliged to work more than an hour or two each day on such an island.

Bastille Week celebrations, which by custom set Papeete in uproar for a fortnight, provide the Society Islands with by far the grandest festival of the entire year. For months ahead of time costumes are prepared, drums are manufactured, men and girls practise songs and dancing with inter-village rivalries exciting feverish delight as the month of July approaches. Trading schooners bring folk in from distant coral atolls and obscure little islands rarely visited by whites; they come too from Morrea and Borabora, Raiatea, and even from faraway Rarotonga.

And now tourists came in steamers, and on jets from Honolulu and Los Angeles; a few hardy souls came under sail from thousands of miles away.

Strangers doubled up in hotel rooms and dossed in the corridors of boarding-houses. Polynesians overflowed from schools and recreation halls to sleep in parks, along the beaches, in the streets, or occupied floor-space in the homes of city friends.

From every corner of the town came the high tom-tom varibeat of songsters tapping rhythms on hollow wooden drums; gusts of laughter poured from open windows and dancing teams announced themselves by singing ancient songs and happily cavorting through the streets. No one but the French could wait for the Fourteenth of July: days before, though no one could say exactly when, hilarious excitement assumed such high proportions that the festival had obviously begun.

Quai de l'Uranie and tributary streets became a scene of carnival, lined on either side with stalls and tents and galleries and thronged with merrymakers attired in festive wear. The bars in the town closed down, and reopened here in great marquees, where men and girls raised merry hell from dusk to dawn, and dawn to dusk again. Barbecues kept going all night long.

During the day we would explore this lovely island, exploring far up broken roads into ravines with pools where women sometimes swam, or flirting bravely with vahinés in distant villages, or lying on black beaches tormented by devilishly sinful bikinis. French and Chinese caste girls, exquisitely proportioned, pretty and petite and with flawless tawny skin, frequented one particular beach to sun themselves and swim: and the two Canadians would sigh, and softly moan, and beat their fists on the sand in sheer frustration. Instead of their pretence of wearing a piece of ribbon across their chests, these girls so wondrously endowed might just as well have used a pair of band-aids; and the provocative silken g-string five inches below their navel was no wider than a packet of cigarettes at any point.

"I can't look," Cliff would mourn as half a dozen girls near by lay in abandoned postures. "Don't let me look! Aw, hell!" And he would bury his head in his arms for at least a minute. On one day Denny would fall helplessly in love with the dainty half-Chinese, who contrived to appear serenly unaware of his ardent gaze; next day he would lose his heart to the French-Tahitian girls, who giggled vivaciously when we were near, but ignored us just the same.

"How do those things stay up?" he would groan. "Look, they're not even tied above the swell of the hip. They glued on, or something?"

"Grafted, man. Must be grafted on."

"Must be they haven't discovered gravity out here yet. Hey, Pete, for crys-sakes make French with these two little sweethearts. I can't stand it! Get 'em talking. Or cover 'em with a blanket, do something."

But no matter how we tried, with gallantry or finesse, our attempts ended in stark failure. They became a challenge, an obsession, the subject of ecstatic dreams at night; but whether they were professional virgins, or inviolate connoisseurs of diamond rings, or already happy in the service of M.G.M., we never had the chance to discover.

Finally the strain proved too much, and we just had to keep away from that beach.

It was not until the Governor had formally opened the festival that I met little Pauline from Papénoo.

A grand ball presaged the Fourteenth of July, and folk-dances were held every afternoon and evening during the following week. A large expanse of lawn near Government House had been fenced off, and tiers of wooden benches set inside to form a square; spectators paid two hundred francs to watch successive teams of island dancers. With others of our kind we found some empty oil drums, stole some lengths of timber and a number of fencing planks, and contrived a series of perches on which we could stand and view the dancing free of charge: later we discovered we could crawl in under the benches and watch from the very edge of the arena.

To repetitious drum rhythms beaten out in the high tonk-tonk of hollowed hardwood logs, teams of fifty or more dancers, either men or women, stamped and twirled through stylized routines which only suffered, perhaps, from their unerring perfection of soldierly precision. But behind us that first night was a scene which we found ever more absorbing. The girls from Papénoo were there, slipping their flax dancing-skirts up under their pareos, then shucking off, and stripping off their tops to don brassières of woven flax embroidered with cowrie shells. The skirts were of silky flax dyed gold, as were the tops; they were barely held on the lowest curve of the hips by an artfully woven belt studded with woven flowers of a deeper gold, and swept down to the ankles with a subtle life designed to lend accent to the slightest shimmy of the hips…and the girls were constantly hitching their skirts as low as they possibly could, rather than pulling them up. Around their heads they wore a band which matched their belts, and each had a whisk of the finest flax to be held in the hand as they danced.

We easily found excuses to approach the girls and greet them, and bubbling sallies of dialect were bandied to and fro as they darted smiling glances or shyly turned away. There was one who was far too young, the baby of the group, a pretty little creature with a mischievous, pixie smile; and when I conveyed my admiration with the droll regard of a hungry man who sees an apple pie, she hid her face in her hands and fled, and joined her friends in peals of merry laughter.

Denny and Cliff were involved in close engagement with two girls, and Hal was standing sadly at a distance, so soon enough I returned to watch the dance, the war dance of Haapiti. But a moment later the little girl was less than a pace behind me, straining on tiptoe for a glimpse: and she permitted me to take her hand, and draw her up beside me on the plank.

"Where do you people come from?" I inquired.

"Papénoo."

Ah yes, the beautiful river ten miles east, cascading down a ravine and shimmering over pebbles through a coastal shelf of palms and flowering trees.

"I shall watch you dance. But you must promise me one thing."

"Promise?" She glanced up inquiringly.

"You must promise not to let me fall in love with you."

She was standing close beside me, and I felt her shake with laughter.

"Why?" she asked ingenuously. "I am not so pretty?"

"Yes, you are so pretty. But also you are so young."

She flashed me a puzzled glance, and shrugged.

"Maybe." She was silent for a while, watching the men dancing; then suddenly she was gone, running to join the Papénoo group, which was gathering near the gates for the next event.

Cliff and Denny returned to stand beside me; the Haapiti men left the square and were replaced by the Papénoo girls. She was in the

Festival spirit—the author and Pauline of Papénoo

Tahitian women dancing

M.G.M's version of H.M.S. Bounty, Papeete

second line, a quiver and ripple of brown and gold, swift and graceful as a slightly pixilated woodland nymph interpreting the frantic pipes of Pan. As I watched her, there was a peace and quiet joy in my heart and yet a sadness too, for she was too young for me to risk her close acquaintance.

"They dance once more tonight," said Denny smugly, "and then I've got a date. You find a dame?"

"No." The dance was over, the girls were leaving the square to enthusiastic accolades of clapping.

"Tough cheese," said Cliff. "Where's Hal?"

"Who cares."

Another troupe took to the square, and these were the men of Papara, also in flaxen skirts, stamping out a military ritual. But as I watched I was obliged to repeatedly slap at an ant which climbed my leg, and finally glanced down to find my Papénoo girl was there tickling me with a blade of grass and almost stifling with laughter. She held out her hand, and I pulled her up beside me.

"I should paddle your *derrière*," I said severely. She tried to smother her laughter in her hands, as if suddenly grown shy of her own boldness. "But you're even too young for that."

Again she glanced up at me curiously.

"Your dance was perfection, but it made me sad and I'm not going to watch you again. Will you be coming every night?"

"Three nights, only. How am I too young?"

I was silent.

"The men in my village do not think I am too young. And I have one husband."

One husband? Well, that was a start, at least. I studied her upturned face: she might be seventeen, I supposed, at the most. Here in these islands girls matured at an early age.

"Friend-husband," she added. "Not married."

"How long have you had him?"

"Oh, one year."

I scratched my ear reflectively and turned to watch the dancing, but all I could see was a child involved in an adult love affair.

"He my second husband," she added. "Not too young, you see."

Slaughter me gently, I decided, let's go no farther back.

"How old are you?" I asked.

"Sixteen. An' I call myself Pauline."

Pauline from Papénoo. Twice wedded to "friend-husbands" since the age of fourteen years. Aye, but she was a product of a natural way of life, not yet infected with the contagions of the West's synthetic shame. Too young, indeed. Too young for what? We stood close together, crowded on the plank by the others, and I put my arm about her waist. When I cuddled her she looked up at my face, and smiled, and cuddled me.

"Huh!" said Denny, peering at us with a waggish grin. "No dame, eh? Hot baby!"

We watched the dancing for some time, and when her troupe had performed again I escorted her back to her billets at the Kuomintong school. Once, when I questioned her concerning the intricate design of her flaxen brassières, she casually took them off and handed them to me, so that I was at a loss as to how to avoid becoming cross-eyed. And then, on a thought, I evinced keen interest in the texture of her skirt, but she merely scooped some tresses up to let me feel their silky touch.

At the gate of the school I halted. "Will you come tomorrow, night?"

"No. Next night, also afternoon."

"I'll see you then."

"Yes. Next time, I dance for you."

From the House of Tamaraa a path led down through groves of palms to the edge of a quiet lagoon, sheltered from the sea by coral reefs, and here and there small thatched huts hid shyly amid thickets of hibiscus and vanilla, screened by ferns and palms; the deep peace of sun-pierced glades tinkled with the laughter of small children. We slept in the house, but came each day to town, involved in easy friendship with Americans and Britons, New Zealanders, Australians and Tahitians, and Polynesians from outlying islands. The French we preferred to avoid, and they considered us intruders; the Chinese kept largely to themselves. During the day there were javelin contests, ranks of athletic young men shafting clouds of long, thin lances at a coconut set high on a bamboo pole; canoes and sailing catamarans raced in Motu Iti lagoon, off the waterfront of Papeete. Islanders lent us catamarans to roam the coral gardens and the reefs, and sometimes we watched the *Bounty* put to sea with personnel from M.G.M., spreading her sails as she passed beyond the break in the thundering reefs.

Bounty had been built in Nova Scotia from the same plans originally used in construction of Bligh's vessel, and a brave sight indeed she made coming in at evening, etched in detailed silhouette against the sunset sky. It was said she had cost four hundred thousand pounds; fitted with twin diesels she had motored and sailed via the Atlantic and the Panama Canal to Tahiti, and many of her crew were featuring in the film now being made.

Sometimes little Pauline was my companion, uninhibited and gay, absurdly happy to wander the fair in her costume of golden flax and tugging my hand to join with others in dancing through the streets. Her friends would smuggle her out of the Chinese school at night, tittering and giggling with shy conspiracy; and later on I would push her back through a window with sweet things for her friends.

Cliff and Denny were each involved with rendezvous of their own, and when I returned to the house alone I would cough, and whistle, and scrape my feet, wondering who might be in my bed, and if breakfast could feed us all.

"There must be a gimmick somewhere," Cliff declared with a thoughtful scowl. "They must have something painted on their feet."

The night was intensely black beyond the small arena, and evergreens around us were flushed with light from the blazing mound of fire. This was an ancient site reserved for traditional ritual, and three large stone idols solemnly faced the crackling pyre; several hundred spectators watched from tiers of benches.

"Maybe they go into a trance," suggested Rause, but the others were skeptical.

"They reckon if you wash your feet in urine every day," said Denny, "they go hard as a bullock's hide after a while."

"Asbestos paint," said Mike. "Or some kind of drug."

Rause was a gentle intravert repeatedly embarrassed by the realities of life, generous to a fault and ardently preoccupied with the welfare of those near him. Mike was a dark and intense young man of predatory cast, to whom the world was a casino peopled by the successful and the suckers. Both of them were Americans. Rause was a teacher *en route* to a position in a Tasmanian school; he was something of a recluse and seemed to live on canned sardines. Mike was too canny to advertise his talents, and appeared to live largely on his wits.

The fire occupied a space about forty feet by twenty, with great logs and stumps piled ten feet high and popping with sharp reports which tossed streams of sparks in the air. We watched as a mechanical hoist backed up; grapnels were tossed among the fire, and amid hissing flames and showers of sparks logs and stumps were dragged away from the arena.

Ten Tahitian drummers appeared and took their stand beside the three stone idols. Forty young stalwarts and their aged chief assembled to watch operations, brown skins varnished by the firelight, clad in loincloths and grinning self-consciously as people stared and murmured. These were the firewalkers. Those men selected from among them would walk barefoot across the pit of red-hot stones, which lay beneath the inferno of blazing timber. We had watched the routine carefully, Cliff and Denny and I; had seen the rectangular pit being dug two feet deep, saw the large, smooth river-bed stones and boulders dumped into it to form a fairly level bed, and stacked with brushwood. The brushwood had been lit at 4 a.m. the previous day, and we had several visits to check the progress being made. Logs were piled on top of the brushwood by the hoist, several tons of huge boulders were laid on top again, and these were covered by even more logs and stumps. The result had been a massive conflagration which gradually subsided to steady furnace heat, with an occasional boulder exploding in a hail of fragmented stone and red-hot embers.

There was, we had assured ourselves, no question about the bed of stones being intensely hot.

And now we watched again as the remaining logs were dragged away, still burning, the boulders were pried off with heavy poles and removed, and the basic bed of stones raked clear of the pile of incandescent ashes.

"Doesn't look that hot," Hal complained. Only a central patch about five feet by five was actually glowing red and white; but even towards the edges the stones were smoking with an impression of great heat.

"Try it, Hal," said Denny with careful restraint.

"Thousand dollars," Mike added. "Give you odds. A thousand bucks to one salted peanut."

Hal was silent.

"Go on," said Cliff, nudging him. "The man's offering you a thousand bucks. We'll chip in and lend you a salted peanut if you lose."

"Cold feet," said Denny, and we laughed.

The chief, loosely described by the French announcer as a sorcerer, caused the forty young men to form in line, then walk and trot about the fire to the resonance of the drums, while the announcer proclaimed the religious nature of the firewalking rite, and exhorted spectators to conduct themselves as they might in their own churches. Any form of outcry or disturbance was expressly forbidden, as such might lead to tragic consequences for those who walked the fire. The chief himself gave an oration in which he invoked the fire god.

"…who is made of the sun's fire and the heat of flames, of white and black earth, of salt and of sweetness…."

The chief himself prepared to walk the fire with twelve braves selected from the forty. They carried wands of palm in their right hands and wore garlands of palm-leaves around their heads: the old man stood at the edge of the pit and gently tapped the stones with his wand, asking the fire god to see the clean hearts of these twelve good men and to cause the heat to subside beneath their feet as they walked across.

It was impossible to know if any discreet chemical had been applied to the soles of their feet. There was no evidence of any state of trance: on the contrary, several of the men were shyly laughing, so that one or two people near us murmured in shocked tones.

As the leader stepped forward onto the stones, there was a silence of hushed and intense expectancy, broken only by the soft throbbing of the drums. Gripping their wands, the thirteen men filed across the pit, even through the glowing heart, gingerly stepping at a brisk but steady pace, and emerged unscathed on the other side.

A vast sigh of relief arose from the audience, and a restive ripple of murmuring and movement passed among us like a sudden breeze through trees. The six of us were incredulous, elated, and skeptical in turn.

They walked across the pit four times, and then they walked four times down its entire length, each time passing across the glowing stones in the centre. And, even as they walked, incandescent rocks beneath the top layer cracked and spat, spurting smoke and cinders here and there. Not one of the thirteen men showed any sign of discomfort, or limped, or even rubbed his feet on the cool grass.

Finally, some official fool announced, in both French and English, "The sorcerer has agreed that any spectators who wish to test the heat of the stones may do so. If anyone wishes to attempt to walk barefoot across the stones, he will be permitted to try." A derisive chuckle swept through the audience. "However, you are warned that anyone who makes this attempt will do so completely and utterly at his own risk."

"Gee, how silly can they get," said Denny mockingly.

"Man'd be mad."

"Have to have clay feet. Give it a whirl, Hal."

But then we were amazed to see a number of the spectators begin clambering down from the tiers of benches to gather by the pit, taking off their shoes.

"They're gonna try it," cried Cliff. "The dumb bastards, look at 'em, they're raving mad."

"They'll burn their feet to the ankles," Rause said anxiously. "Oh no, they shouldn't allow it."

"Of all the hell-bent exhibitionist fools," Mike muttered scathingly: and with horrified fascination we watched as these silly people began the attempt. One or two local French, a few tourists, some Tahitians. Aye, and they did cross too: they stepped quickly, lightly from stone to stone, but avoiding the red centre, and arrived on the other side almost running, but with few signs of real distress. One or two rolled on the grass rubbing their feet and cursing, but no one shrieked in agony.

Why, it was possible, then. But how? Even ordinary European folk, accustomed to wearing shoes and soft of foot, had incredibly managed to walk across that pit: and resentment washed through me, resentment that a supposedly sacred rite should be fouled with such offhand insolence, and that the drama of the occasion should be sabotaged successfully by fools.

But perhaps it was a good thing to do, training for the next life.

"So we can do it too," I said, rising. "Probably the only chance we'll ever get." But there was a chorus of protests from my friends.

"Why not? Look at them, they're getting across all right. See, there's even tourists. Come on, we can do it."

No, they would not. But, finally, two of them agreed, including Hal, and we went down to the pit. We took off our sandals, held them in our hands, and nervously began to walk across well to the side of the glowing centre. Hot, aye! One could not step for more than part of a second on any one stone. One had to rivet full attention on the task, selecting the stones ahead without a moment's hesitation, stepping briskly and with purpose: and the stones were black ovals seen against the fiery red flare of heat below them.

We crossed to the other side, soles of our feet tingling mightily, legs flushed with heat, but unhurt. Had it been perspiration on our feet which gave us momentary insulation? Some would leap the last few steps and go to ground on the grass to hiss and mutter and rub their soles. I went around to the other side and attempted a second crossing, closer to the centre this time, closer than most other folk attempted, and indeed great concentration was required to maintain a steady pace and keep from running, or gasping from the extraordinary heat.

I had almost crossed this second time when a girl close by slipped, cried out in terror, and sprawled on the smoking stones. Instantly she shrieked in pain: one foot had slipped down a red-hot crevice. The palms of her hands began to fry, as she scrabbled in agonized panic, screaming. I snatched at one arm and dragged her, someone behind her seized a leg, and we bore her away to a grassy place well clear of the pit.

"My sister!" she groaned, half conscious. Her hands and feet were already swollen with great blisters, one foot was badly burnt and gave off the odour of scorched meat. "Oh God, my sister, my sister...."

A doctor came at once and her sister rushed up whimpering with fear, so I left. An American, I reflected. A young American girl, perhaps twenty. Well, she would have a tale to carry home.

Twelve people were treated for burns and four hospitalized. The three stone idols winked and grimaced in the uncertain light.

At the end of festival we left Tahiti, Cliff and Denny and I, to see if we wanted to live on Raiatea. We were short of money, and now became beachcombers seeking some romantic island village where men would let us join their lives, and lovely girls would bring us endless pleasure. We carried little with us. Hal had been left behind, and the motor-bikes were stored with Tahitian friends.

Raiatea was eighteen hours away by island sloop, a long oval island of great beauty, the coast studded with clusters of huts connected by uncertain tracks, which often as not became lost in the sea or the hills. Within ten days we had walked right around the island: I carried my things in an onion bag, possibly becoming the first Australian to circumvent Raiatea bearing a typewriter on his head. But despite the hospitality of lads who took us fishing on the reefs, and men who would not let us pass their homes without taking food and drink, and families who insisted we must spend the night with them, we never found the village of our dreams and were not pursued by maidens, nor encouraged to pursue them.

"Must be the wrong goddam island," Denny suggested after a week. His feet were sore. We had had to walk for miles through lagoons and over a great headland before finding another beach. "All those stories a man reads, you know?"

"Sure as heck ain't here," Cliff agreed. "Maybe they've got civilized. Every damn' village has a Chinese store."

Indeed, the Chinese here were among the most hospitable of all.

"Fifty years too late. Or maybe the girls haven't come back from the fête." Denny was inspecting his tender feet. "But what about them hairy magazine stories you read, about guys getting shipwrecked or something on islands like this and practically being loved to death by dames?"

We pondered the problem with a growing sense of failure. The island was remote and charming, the people happy to receive us; but if the girls sometimes flirted and twitched their hips at us, no one really seemed to care whether or not we stayed.

"Maybe we better go back," said Cliff. "Raiatea's O.K., sure, but as I see it I wouldn't want to stay here for ever. Maybe we could get a job with a Chinese wine merchant back there, or something."

The Tahitien, seen in Papeete from the Bounty

Between scenes, showing ragged mutineers

Extras and technicians on board Bounty, preparing for the day

Men and women celebrating Bastille Week in Tahiti

"Wine-taster, that's it. Wine-taster in a Polynesian harem. That'd be the shot."

"We gotta do something."

"We could have a look at Tahaa, that's close by."

We had a look at Tahaa, and even Borabora farther on, but finally returned to Tahiti. Nowhere could we find the enchanting village, which lives in the mythology of shipwrecked mariners.

It was Mike who finally found us work; although, admittedly, none of us had tried very hard. It was difficult even to invent any form of relaxing employment, which would permit us to continue our leisurely way of life with only two or three hours of work every second day. Five of us were enjoying our evening beer in front of Vaima's, Denny and Cliff, Hal and Rause and I; funds were low indeed, we were almost *pousse cassé* (broke), and we had all chipped in to buy a single bottle with five glasses. Hal must have had more cash than he cared to admit, for we knew he was secretly considering taking passage to the Cook Islands on a Rhodesian yacht called *Si Ye Pambili*; and passage with her, even working, was quoted at thirty pounds.

Mike came along with a broad smile on his face, and made his triumphant announcement.

"You're all employed," he declared. "The lot of you. You start work in the morning."

"Doing what?" we choroused.

"You register tonight at eight o'clock, in their office on the third floor of the Grand. Start at seven in the morning."

"Who for? Where? Whatta we gotta do? Speak, you dumb, bloody Yank!"

"You're all movie stars. You work for M.G.M. They want extras." He chuckled richly at the expressions on our faces, and beckoned to a waitress.

"Crys-sakes!" Cliff shouted. "you mean it?"

"Marvellous." Rause laughed. "How'd you fix it?"

"Just lucky. Happens they need a lot of guys to reshoot a few scenes, on board *Bounty*."

"How much do we get?" Hal asked.

"Five hundred Pacific francs a day. Five and a half bucks. And lunch."

Denny was enthralled. "On *Bounty*? And we start work in the morning? Hey, the big deal, boys: we're in the movies!" He found the waitress quizzically eyeing our single bottle and five glasses, and assumed the grand manner of the rich. "Avast there, Mister Christian, you luscious doll, bring six big cold bottles of Hinano. The six best bottles in the house."

Each morning for the following ten days the four of us rode in early to Papeete, and joined two dozen of our fellows; some had travelled with us on the *Caledonien*, most of the others we knew from tavern revels. Within an hour the ship would power across the lagoon and put to sea, and we extras would don the colourful vestments affected by eighteenth-century sailors and marines. Piles of garments were brought on deck and dispensed by a small, slim and surprisingly efficient Tahitian girl called Teena; make-up men were on hand for certain of the officers who were required to wear wigs.

Sailors wore white bell-bottom trousers and black shoes with silver buckles, cotton sweaters banded white and blue, black silk neckerchiefs and broadbrimmed hats stiff with tar and varnish. Those of us masquerading as marines had beetle-tailed coats of collision red heavy with braid across the chest, gay epaulets and collars of blue and gold, and bayonets and ammunition pouches hanging from crossed straps. Breeches were tight and white with black gaiters, hats resembled stiff and shiny toppers with a curious white pompom to one side.

The ship rode well, deep-chested and heavy, her great masts and billowing sails easing her motion to a slow and graceful rhythm: and as we lounged around the deck admiring the view and waiting for something to happen, the general effect was that of a shipful of indolent Portuguese lion-tamers hopefully wondering what kind of a lunch there would be.

The camera, which with accessories was valued at more than a hundred thousand pounds, was carried astern on the motor vessel *Orohena*; it was mounted in a cage of gimballed scaffolding, which also seated the cameraman. At intervals during the day we would all be called upon to assume action stations, certain sails would be raised or taken in, and as the *Orohena* approached with camera at the ready such confusion would ensue on board *Bounty* as reminded one of preparations, in the army, for ceremonial march-past. Everyone was kept in suspenseful ignorance of impending events until the very last moment when various directors, each pulling rank and pretending to greater knowledge than the rest, would rush around in ever decreasing circles shouting contradictory orders until, spinning gently to a halt and wiping flecks of spittle from their mouths, they would find the situation under fair control despite their despairing and excitable instructions. The *Orohena* would cruise by anything from a hundred yards to a mile away as we performed small functions on deck, or pretended to peer ahead at land; either Moorea or certain sections of Tahiti would appear in the background, and for two of these days the vessel was disguised with panels and false housing as a fictitious craft called *Britannia*. Then we were supposed to be seen approaching the mutineers' settlement on Pitcairn Island, which was actually a cluster of huts on top of cliffs near Point Venus.

"These bloody Yanks," said an Australian called Lance one day. "You know, they're going to foul up this picture. One of the best-known sea-stories in the world, and they're putting in things that never happened."

He had come direct from Victoria on holiday, and had been to stud with half the available girls in Papeete. Copper-blonde, with gleaming matted hair on his chest and the face and build of a handsome athlete, he was playing poker with half a dozen of us as *Bounty* cruised back to port under power. Another day was over, we would collect another five hundred francs tonight.

"So who cares?" said a Californian called Ferdy. "You got shares in M.G.M.?"

"Kind of stupid, bloody remark a man'd expect from a Yank," said Lance. "This mug that plays Adams—supposed in history to be the only surviving mutineer on Pitcairn—he gets drunk, they sack him, they can't scrap all the film he's appeared in, so they put another mutineer called Brown in his place."

"Hell, so who cares?"

"And the American ship that finds Adams: for some stupid reason they make it a British ship, the *Britannia. Bounty, Britannia* and *Pandora*, all of 'em the same ship with a bit of camouflage. You reckon people won't know that? Bloody cheap skates."

"Cheap skates?" Ferdy cried in pain. "Cost 'em twenny million bucks so far, thirty-eight thousand bucks a day on Tahiti alone for nine months, and you call 'em cheap skates? How in Sam Hill're they cheap?"

"Good chow, anyway," Denny commented. Lunch had consisted of generous servings of roast pork with mashed potatoes and peas and salad, and cauliflower and apple sauce, with rainbow ice-cream and fresh milk for dessert. All of it, except the potato, had been flown from the United States.

"And during the mutiny," Lance persevered, "every schoolboy knows Christian never hurt Bligh. Nah, but that ain't good enough for the bloody Yanks. They got to have Christian skewer him in the leg and the arm with his sword, with plenty of blood around, Tchah! Hey, Teena, you little bitch!"

He swivelled and grabbed at Teena's leg, but she darted away. Lance dropped his cards and raced off in pursuit.

"Garddam Arzie," Ferdy complained. "Look a gift-hoss in the mouth, pull its teeth out too. Be a swell damn' film when it's through."

"Almost through now," said Cliff. "Group One's all gone back, with Brando and Howard and them. Only a few more days for us, I bet."

"They reckon the limeys're coming out to make a picture. Hey, you see that plug-ugly James Mason drinking at Vaima's last night? But what a little guy, eh?"

"Who'd want to work for the limeys?" Ferdy asked. "Probably charge admission to let you work, feed a man on breadfruit, and salt horse."

There were sounds of excitement farther along the deck, and suddenly Lance bounded over our heads in a prodigious leap and started scrambling up the cable ladder leading to the mainsail cross-trees. Teena was in hot pursuit squealing maledictions, and gained the foot of the ladder close on his heels. Clad as she was in tight black shirt and even tighter shorts, she made a fine and lusty figure as she climbed above the deck, and we paused in our play to watch.

She caught hold of his trousers just as he reached the main-course lookout, and held on like a terrier. He had to use both hands in his struggle to squeeze through an opening onto the lookout platform. Pulling and tugging at his trousers, one foot tucked around a ladder rung for balance, she scolded him with a litany of biting epithets, while the men on deck shouted encouragement and Lance roared in protest.

"Pull 'em off, Teena! You got 'im, undo the belt!"

She could not reach the belt, but finally something gave and the trousers slid down Lance's kicking legs, while he howled in baffled despair. But still not satisfied, and hugging her moment of triumph, she flung his trousers to the deck and now attacked his underpants, stripped them off and tossed them to the winds, while an uproar of laughter rose from all the men below, and then climbed down gleeful with rejoicing.

Lance, the vaunted woman-hound, had been assaulted by a slip of a girl in the most public possible view and suffered humiliating defeat. He took off his shirt and used it as a loincloth.

"Bloody little pussy-cat!" he cried unhappily, standing on the platform. "You stupid no-good vahiné, go home!"

"Vahiné go home?" she shrilled. "Oh!"

She rapidly shinned up the ladder again, pursued by shouts of encouragement and gusts of excited laughter. Lance began scrambling up the next ladder towards the distant topsail trees, shirt flapping loose in the breeze and presenting such a ludicrous sight that his progress was marked by howls and bellows of hilarious delight from the assembled men on deck. Teena gained on him hand over fist, passed the first lookout and sped on without pausing. Before he realized it, she was directly below him; and as he manoeuvred onto the topsail trees she grabbed wildly at his shirt.

Her aim was faulty, and Lance gave a wild howl of discomfited surprise.

Flushed with embarrassment, she began climbing down, heedless now of the derisive insults he hurled down on her bead. Then, still with his shirt wrapped around his loins, he came down on deck threatening obvious and immediate forms of manly violence to her with such torrid conviction that, terrified now of public shame, she in turn sought refuge in the rigging.

She stayed there for two hours, nervously refusing to come down until *Bounty* had docked and she had watched Lance walk off, outrageously mocking her, with the other extras.

Since returning from Raiatea we four had abandoned the House of Tamaraa to live in Tahitian quarters on a hillside just above Nita's house. There was a tiny thatched hut partitioned into two diminutive rooms with beds; a similar hut with a table and chairs, where we ate and where I camped; and a small thatched shelter just outside where we cooked on an open fire. Nita and Vickie provided us with eggs and fruit, and taught us something of the Tahitian's domestic way of life; they added laughter to our lives, and magnificently flirted with each of us in turn. Neighbouring folk would bring us gifts of plantains, or mangoes, or bananas, and in return we were sometimes able to render them small favours.

Flowers and palms and fruit-trees grew in riot about our huts, half garden and half jungle, and sometimes until late at night the clink of glasses and gusts of conversation were framed within the merriment of visiting vahinés.

Festival was over, Papeete no longer held such fascination as before, and adventures in our huts were apt to be as charmingly exciting as any to be found among the town. An evening in Papeete would begin with Chinese food for three shillings in a certain restaurant, where oriental girls would shyly sit with us and talk; from there we would go to Quinn's, or the Bar Lea or Col Bleu, to dance there until those places closed; then, with those who still survived the revels, we would continue to a coastal dance-tavern some miles out of town, called Lafayette.

We had been working for a week with M.G.M. when suddenly we realized that our attitudes to island life had undergone a distinct, if gradual, change. A number of us had gathered in Quinn's, a spacious waterfront dance-hall with a well-appointed bar set as an oval island near the entrance, cubicles with tables lining opposite walls and an orchestra to the rear. A tropical atmosphere was laboriously contrived with an abundance of bamboo, and chairs and tables crowded against the dance-floor; the men's *pissoir* was a concrete wall beyond a screen of beads, and often enough one was pushed against the wall by mischievous vahinés as they passed on their way to the women's toilets just beyond.

"Just a goddam cathouse," Mike cynically observed to the company at large. He scanned the cosmopolitan rabble; two hundred or more vahinés were at tables or the bar, consuming all the beer that foreigners would buy them. "Papeete's had it, you know? Hit fair in the fanny by the jet age."

"Pity," Denny agreed reflectively. "Nice people."

"Seems like the States picks on one place after another, builds it into a resort, saturates it with dollars, then leaves it behind in a flat spin. They reckon Hilton's gonna build a big hotel." A plump vahiné, dazed with beer, paused by his chair and he slipped his hand up under her pareo. "Hi, Lulu."

"Buy me one beer, Mike." She stood there passively as he stroked her.

"Next week."

"Huh. You damn' mahoo." She drifted off to another table.

"Joint's coming apart at the seams," said an Australasian called David. He came variously from Queensland and New Zealand. "You can see it, day by day. Too much easy money in these bars, too much free liquor, and no protection, from themselves or anyone else. The Yanks've caught them with their pareos down. Collision of the sophisticated society and the natural primitive, and the primitive hasn't got any protection."

"Take a lot to spoil them all, though," Cliff demurred. "The good-time girls, yeah; but not the country people."

"Time," said Mike. "Just a matter of time."

Several foreigners were attempting the local form of dance in company with vahinés, vacationing executives and business men jerking awkwardly and sometimes falling over drunkenly as their fellows shouted ribald encouragement and obscene jests. Many of those who came from Westernized societies, where public decorum was rigidly policed by unctuous exponents of the holier-than-thou, were apt to confuse freedom with gross licence in the liberal atmosphere of Papeete. Abruptly freed from surveillance by their neighbours, discarding

245

inhibitions like confetti and secretly amazed at local tolerance, they shouted forbidden four-letter words in the streets and revelled in loud and obscene conversation in the bars. They fondled naughty words as if stroking the body parts concerned, and openly practised licence and lewd gestures on befuddled vahinés who, often as not, had no idea of what they said.

But the corruption of the girls was evident.

"That time I went to Borabora," Rause reminisced with a gentle smile, "I was looking for the ideal Polynesian girl. I didn't figure I'd find her in Papeete, but I thought I might find her over there. Island of dreams, sort of thing."

We nodded, we had some idea of what he meant.

"So I checked in at a sort of hotel, and thought I'd have a beer before I went out. There was a beautiful girl there. I tell you, she was exquisite. Terrific: soft, beautiful, feminine, the ideal type. So I sat down with my beer to look at her, and she came over right away and plumped herself down in a chair opposite me, with each of her legs on an arm of the chair, and snarled, 'Hey Joe, you buy me one beer!'"

Sympathetic laughter passed among us.

"Same afternoon I was walking along the beach, feeling pretty happy in spite of that initial shock, and I found an islander lying under a tree with a jug of red wine or something, and a flower tucked behind his ear. Just like the poem, but he was by himself. I guess he was a little drunk. But I felt good, seeing him there, so I said, 'Carnival, eh?' And you know what? He got to his feet and he was going to hit me. He said, 'Cannibal, eh? Cannibal?'"

Rause waited until our mirth subsided, and then added, "That night I found two local girls ransacking my kit. Seems they're just learning to steal; they didn't even know what the word meant a year ago. I caught the next boat back to Papeete."

Aye, we agreed, the rot had set in. Nostalgia was a bar-room disease in Papeete, a raw regret for the rising costs of sinning. It was *de rigueur* for all old-timers, and for those who wished to be regarded as such, to spend several hours each day in some favourite bar or café sadly reminiscing about the good old times (pre-M.G.M.) and, by inference, condemning new arrivals as disappointed fools who had arrived a year too late. And it began to seem that we had indeed arrived too late.

"Man'd be mad to shack up with a doll from one of these places," Cliff declared.

"Claphouse," said Mike. "Every last one of 'em's clapped."

If beauty in a woman included feminine decorum, poise, and a modest ability in intellectual conversation, one would have to admit there were probably no beautiful girls in the bars of Papeete. But if beauty merely consisted of flagrant sex-appeal, attractively furnished bodies, the twitching hip and pretty face with laughing eyes, then indeed there were some and any could be had.

"Suzie!" cried Cliff. "Hey, you neglecting me?"

Suzie was a slim, young libertine of mercurial passions, just as capable of dragging a desperate stranger to the dance-floor as of tipping a glass of beer down his neck.

"Hey, *Canadien*, you pussy-pussy?"

But she ruffled his hair and sat on Denny's lap to seize his head and soundly kiss him. Denny squirmed and struggled, protesting with muffled grunts and seeking to push her away, but she held his head firmly until the chair overbalanced and crashed with both of them to the floor. She grasped him again, kissing his mouth while folk near by applauded. At length he fought free and gained his feet, wiping his mouth and staring down at her. For a moment she sat on the floor fixing him with a gaze of smouldering resentment. Then abruptly she leapt to her feet smiling, drank his glass of beer, flicked her hips at him and wandered away carolling the Quinn's anthem, "Gar-dam son of a beetch, what's a matter you?"

A passing girl tweaked Rause's ear and rubbed her thigh against him. He flinched away, mildly flushed with embarrassment.

"Mahoo," she said. Her name was Louise, and even at the early age of twenty her face was already marked with dissipation. "You lolly-lolly?" She snatched up his beer, and bore it away to sit with a group of friends and giggle at us over her shoulder. Beer-drinking in Quinn's was beset with occupational hazards.

"Sluts," Denny muttered. "Jees, what a bunch of hairy-minded dames. Imagine 'em in a beer parlour at home!"

I had talked with Lulu one day when she was sober. She had seemed to have great pity for Europeans, and I had mistaken this for a sign of intelligence. One could pour one's most precious recipes and thoughts into her head: she was a cellular morass, a consuming swamp, and they went in as if one was filling a brown jug, and later, when one peered in to see what was there and what was happening, there was nothing. Where had they gone? Only the inarticulate smiles, the revolting amity, the luscious nothingness of damp, yielding flesh, the meaningless soft glut of pity. The ideas were absorbed as by an octopus, transmuted in a braincase of unformed putty, and vomited forth as a black obscuring ink of sympathy.

"They go crazy when they come to Papeete," said Mike. "Clapped up in the first week. Guy I know reckons he's had it six times in seven months. You fellers ever seen the Penicillin Parade?"

"Ah, change the bloody subject," said Cliff, scowling.

We had seen the parade, a daily pilgrimage of diseased rakes and nervous lads filing up to the hospital, often with their girls. It was difficult to maintain sympathy with dissolute vahinés, whose English was limited to a sequence of obscenities, whose social graces were confined to erotic suggestion and stealing beer, and to whom the obvious end of social intercourse was a wriggle between sheets. But where did the blame lie? Who was there among us fit to cast the first stone? How had it been with them before the white man came with his lies and his syphilis, his dollars and his lust? Who were those sophisticates so apt in schooling others to depravity?

Once they had been gentle girls, frank and unaffected, impressionable folk as those beyond the limits of Papeete still remained. Generous, perhaps, but not licentious; delighting in the act of love, but not obscene. Laughter and the love of life is the Polynesian's birthright: and the children born of love were accepted with delight, they were never any social or economic problem, or ever born in shame; babies are always welcome on Tahiti. These good-time girls who played the game so hard according to the rules the white man brought: they were, in final analysis, soiled and misused innocents who knew little about sex beyond the obvious, and practically nothing about anything else. They ranged from twelve years of age and upwards, and were oddly lacking in finesse in their approach to prostitution, because no one had yet organized them and taught them how professional whores were supposed to act. Sometimes a girl would ask for money, but, if her man pretended he was poor, she would often enough give him half of what she carried in her purse.

The lotus was bruised, and its fragrance bitter-sweet.

Suzie had sold her house and four beef cattle to lend money to a Scandinavian seaman, whom she loved: he took the money and disappeared, and she never saw him again. An Australian had promised to marry Little Pwee, and brought her from Moorea to Papeete: but, before she bore his child, he also fled. Lulu, Jo, Marie and Three-Minute Bébé—all, for similar good reasons, were exempt from the white man's stones.

"Funny how this place hits you when you first get here," Cliff mused. "Papeete, I mean. Gay, romantic, gorgeous dolls. Sort of wears off after a time."

"Gets knocked off with a baseball bat in joints like this," said Denny dryly. Mike rose and drifted off to one of the cubicles by the wall, where two teenage vahinés were drinking lemonade and casting shy glances about the packed hall. It was probably their first time, I reflected. Cliff squinted savagely at his beer.

"Ship out, I reckon," he said. "Whaddya say, Denny?"

Denny pondered the suggestion for a moment, reluctant to leave Tahiti and yet knowing that he would not, after all, stay for ever. The gem was flawed, the golden apple had its worms.

"You want to stay?" Cliff persisted.

"No. No I guess not."

There was a sadness among us then, an invasion of obscure regrets as we looked down at the table, or at the dancers, avoiding each other's eyes. Awareness of the outside world intruded and each of us sat in loneliness to covertly consider return to reality. At that moment Denny and Cliff had already left Tahiti.

"Book on the *Tahitien*," Cliff persisted. Denny's face was sober, as he inspected his glass of beer.

"Yeah, Sydney here we come." His voice was flat with resignation. "Not much point in staying."

"Me, too," Rause said. "The *Tahitien* comes in about ten days, but you'd better book soon. Lance is going too, and a lot of the others. Work'll cut out by then. Mike's going. And Patsy and Maggie."

A hungry desolation crept through me. They would leave, all these good friends? Why, our little group of huts would then be empty: and what of life on an empty hillside without their companionship, how would it be without their grave or buoyant conversation, the delight of indiscretions shared, and the exhilarating rush of wind as we thundered forth on the motor-bikes to rendezvous with small adventures? They would go? All? "A lot of the others," Rause had said. Ah, and I could not go with them. I lacked the money for the fare, and they had arrived in possession of onward tickets. Perhaps there would be a yacht. I was competent enough to earn my passage, but most of the yachts which came for festival had already left.

"Hey, look what Santa Claus sent in." Mike had returned, bringing the two vahinés with him. "Michele and Tui. Michele's fourteen and Tui's fifteen, and they've never been here before. How's that?"

They smiled uncertainly as they sat down, faces flushed with colour which showed through the tan of their tender cheeks, and shyly whispered to each other in Tahitian.

"*Here voya oh é* (Darling, I love you)," Denny murmured confidentially to the younger. She burst into laughter and covered her face with her hands in confusion.

"*Hina ro wau apa ia oh é?*"

"Hey, chop it out Casanova," Mike protested. "They're both mine."

"*Horo mi apa, here* (Kiss me, darling)," Denny persisted, and she leant over to hide her face in Tui's lap, giggling uncontrollably. Rause had a wistful expression of deep compassion on his face, and my heart warmed to him. He knew, too. Occasionally we saw them come in, new recruits who might drift in from sheer curiosity. Before the night was out they would be helplessly drunk, half carried and half dragged off down the street like tired moths by some pot-bellied tourist, or cynically grinning adventurer.

"What's their story?" asked Cliff. There was a brittle snap of anger in his dark eyes. Neither he nor Denny had any illusions about what was in store for Michele and Tui.

"Missed their ship after festival," said Mike complacently. "Have to wait three weeks for another. Reckon I might look after 'em, sort of, until I go."

Come back in a year, and they would be the same as all the others: for, once caught up in the snare, they would stay and carry on. Well, at least Pauline had gone home to Papénoo: and I was glad she had not stayed. I had told her to go, said that I would visit her, but since then I had carefully avoided Papénoo.

And anyway, I reflected, I had left my heart on top of Pelée Mountain, safe from the claws of tigers and the hatpins of shrews. Every man, I thought, should have his Pelée Mountain, should fillet his breast and secrete his heart in a pot on a mountain top. As I had done.

Or…had I really given it to Yselle?

We worked as extras on *Bounty* for ten days. On the afternoon of the tenth day a personable M.G.M. executive called Major, who seemed to be the director of the directors, assembled thirty of us on deck and selected thirteen for special duties on the morrow. Twelve, including Cliff and Denny, would be required to play the part of ragged mutineers in scenes to be shot in three days' time. The thirteenth man would act as stand-in for Marlon Brando, who had returned to Los Angeles, and would commence work on the other side of the island next morning.

Major carefully inspected us, seeking someone whose physique resembled Brando's; some were too obviously tall, or short, or fat, and Brando was of average height and build. We had seen him on occasions in Papeete, sullen and eschewing any company but that of the most attractive women, a mortal man rather less impressive than the hero of the screen, but admirably restrained in the presence of coyly camera-clicking tourists.

"You'll do," said Major. He was pointing directly at me. "Tomorrow morning at the Grand, six o'clock."

I glanced behind me on either side.

"Yes, you," he said. "You're Brando. Location's at Taravao."

"Hey Marlon," Cliff exclaimed, "how about giving us your autograph on a cheque?" Others joined in with various jests. Cheque? But surely I was rich, they would pay me some handsome sum. Fifty dollars? A hundred perhaps? Why, I would be able to buy a ticket on the *Tahitien*, to somewhere.

I cleared my throat, and humbly asked, "Rise in salary, Major?"

"No, buddy. Five bucks fifty a day is all."

Ay-ee! Something less than Marlon's reputed five thousand dollars a day; but at least I was still employed, and more than half the others had been dropped.

Marlon Brando, indeed. How Lee's weak degenerate had come up in the world.

Early each morning for the next four days I was carried off by bus with directors and cameramen and others to a great lagoon several miles in length, and thirty miles distant on the far side of the island. Many arrived before on trucks or in private cars; Tahitian braves to don the wondrous shell-and-feather costumes of Hiti-Hiti's princes, technicians to check equipment, Director Havers and attendants, the inevitable Teena and a host of others. The harassed make-up team busied themselves adjusting bands of evergreen leaves about the warriors' heads, affixing black wigs and invisible nets to smooth down tufts of coarse, cropped hair, then turned to two of us who were to play the parts of an officer, and Brando.

Our uniforms were white ruffed shirts with tight breeches and white stockings, silver-buckled shoes, and a sword apiece which hung at the hip from a broad black leather strap across the chest and shoulder. Hair was brushed back and a fine blonde wig applied, lightly cemented to the scalp and pinned in place; powder was applied about the face on a base of ruddy grease to diminish any tendency to shine.

Ho, but this was a fancy fop, I decided as I inspected him in the mirror: my own mother would have passed me in the street. The loose shirt diminished any disparity in the build of Brando and myself, and seen behind at a little distance not even the sharpest scrutiny would discern the difference. The wig I wore was the same one he had used.

In a fine disorder of persons rushing to and fro the officer and I were hustled aboard a launch, and borne off to a distant part of the lagoon; there to wait for hours while some semblance of order overtook the various launches and canoes. That portion of the film with which we were concerned dealt largely with the occasion when, soon after Bligh's arrival at Tahiti to load breadfruit, three members of *Bounty's* crew eloped in a boat with the three Tahitian girls of their choice. Bligh called on Christian and an officer to give chase, and Hiti-Hiti obligingly lent them war canoes.

There were six war canoes all told, lashed in pairs eight feet apart with stout wooden platforms in between. The largest pair of canoes was about fifty feet long, and all were wondrously decorated with pearlshell and cowries, feathers and totems, and paddled by sturdy brown Tahitians wearing loincloths and garlands of leaves. The camera was set on an outlying reef, and scenes were taken variously of the three sets of canoes in motion one behind the other, of the officer and Christian standing on the platform in charge of a pair of canoes, and of Christian in company with the handsome and exotically attired prince, who was Hiti-Hiti's son. The canoes had been built for the occasion.

And what a grand sight it was on that wide, calm blue lagoon, with the distant smoking tumult of the reefs and the green and purple mountains, with the great canoes gliding swiftly across the water, paddles flashing and rippling brown bodies glistening with sweat. The upswept bow of each canoe was carved in the likeness of pagan gods, the tall sterns like scorpions' tails were tufted with bright feathers and glittered with mother-of-pearl; groups of arrogant bodyguards stood rigidly on the platforms gripping spears. Hiti-Hiti himself was a lordly figure in a huge feathered helmet of green and scarlet, and a sweeping cloak of green feathers. Here was a pagan scene of savage splendour, of cobalt sea and emerald coast and relentless warriors, a truly rewarding spectacle for any travelling fool!

The outboard motors between the canoes were hidden well out of sight.

A great deal of wasted time and effort was involved in shooting even the simplest scenes. Instructions had to be relayed over radios and loudspeakers in three different languages, English through French to Tahitian; and the Tahitians themselves, casual and good-natured, were indifferently puzzled by the entire affair and apt to be found asleep, or reading comics, hunting clams or nursing bottles of pop at critical moments, when everything else was in perfect preparedness for action. Occasionally we all waited for hours while squalls passed, for exactly the right lighting and perhaps a touch of breeze…and then, with every member of the company poised for action, the unpredictable would happen.

A fisherman's outboard dory might cut across the background a mile or more away. The breeze might blow a paper tissue into the middle of the scene, or a stray paper cup might be discovered floating brightly somewhere in the bay—and since we all ate lunch from paper plates, and drank innumerable cups of coffee from as many paper cups, such a thing could easily occur. And when finally the scene was shot with absolute perfection and everyone relaxed with mutual commendations of a worthy scene well played, someone would notice a warrior wearing a wristwatch. The result would be fire and brimstone via an electric megaphone from high-strung Director Havers, curses steeped in vitriol from his various acolytes, and infinitely patient grins from the unworried Tahitians. The scene would be tried again.

On the fourth day the officer and I joined the dozen others in playing the part of mutineers, clad in rags, rushing away from the camera towards a tandem pair of canoes to be paddled out towards the *Pandora*. We added so much weight to the canoes that, of course, they grounded and stuck fast, with roars of delighted laughter from the Tahitians, who would have been glad to foretell the error if anyone had bothered to consult them. This sequence was run again and again, taking two days to complete, and then our work for M.G.M. came to an end.

Once again we became ordinary people, but richer with the righteousness of having worked for at least a little while.

There was a restive sense of purpose and subdued excitement along the waterfront. The *Tahitien*, a great black and white liner *en route* from Marseilles to Sydney and sister ship of the *Caledonien*, was tied up at the Quai du Commerce and would leave at five o'clock tomorrow evening for the Hebrides, New Caledonia, and Australia. Her four hundred passengers swarmed among the restaurants, the bars, the curio shops and Chinese stores; some of them would stay until another Messageries vessel called in six weeks or two months, and their places on board would be taken by those friends and drinking partners I had known these seven weeks. All bookings had been filled, and there was now no chance of purchasing a ticket, even if the cassia blooms suddenly turned to dollars.

Denny and Cliff had packed. I had watched them neatly stowing gear in their wooden boxes, and laughed at their embarrassment when Nita and Vickie and others came with farewell gifts of coconuts and jars of octopus, garlands of flowers, and great stems of bananas: but my laughter came from a hollow vault, an echo-chamber of loneliness, for comradeship was coming to an end. Hal had disappeared; someone said he had flown to Hawaii.

This last evening as we strolled the esplanade in company with Marge and Patsy, two ebullient American girls discovering their way around the world, the problem of what decision I should make was clouded with nostalgia for other friends and comrades I had known in foreign lands. Soon, the lament was heard, there would be no more distant places, the temples were littered with candywraps, the sacred shrines of vagabonds were advertised on subway travel posters. The strongholds of seclusion were invaded by Coca Cola signs and guided tours of the tender and well-fed, who stared and clicked their Kodaks, and hurried home to show what they had seen. The most remote citadels treasured by the venturesome, only to be reached by weeks of bold journeying on foot, or by canoe, by packhorse or sheer wit, were only a few hours away by jet.

Eventually, perhaps, the diverse colours of the world would become a monochrome, standardized by the social and economic aggression of rival world powers. Mix the colours of a paintbox, the result is standard mud. Soon those ardent scatterlings who quartered the world in quest of the unknown, and themselves, might have to turn elsewhere; and who knew where else? He who for any reason becomes blasé in travel reaches a point of diminishing returns, requiring frantic endeavour for minimal reward.

But these, my friends, would travel on across the Pacific some thousands of miles to Australia. Australia, my own land- how would it be there now? There, at least, was one country in thriving civil health, where one might walk in peace without passports, or identity papers, or visas or permits or the jealousy of rival frontiers. The forests were sweet with the scent of eucalypt, the rocky coasts were girt with meadowlands and trimmed with saffron beaches bold with surf: and beyond the mountains, the prairies swept far yonder into tomorrow, and beyond.

"…the other day," Patsy was saying, "that it's just about as big as the U.S.A. Heck, I didn't know it was that big."

Her eyes were luminous with excitement, and she was already impatient to complete the three-week voyage which lay ahead.

"Dames," said Denny dreamily. "Those Aussie dames. They reckon they're all right."

Marge laughed. "That's all you men think about," she said dryly. "Hasn't Tahiti worn you out?"

"And it's pretty well civilized all around the coast," Patsy went on. "I was looking at a map; there's a whole network of roads. Gee, I bet a girl could have some fun hitching in Australia."

"But you're staying here, Pete?" Marge asked. "I think you're crazy. You're so close now."

"And they all speak English," Denny murmured.

A tingle of excitement stirred my blood. Australia, then? The great South Land, the continent down-under…mine, my own country! The years had grown many, I had gladly left her long ago: but her people were my people, her wattles were pure gold. Her rivers were brown, her hinterland vast, the whistle of the freight train was lonely in the night, her men were sunburned and her women were….

Ah yes, her women!

My pulse quickened with a surge of eager purpose. Why, I could not even be deported from Australia! That would be a new experience, indeed: even at the worst one would purchase one's indiscretions on the system of time payment. Heedless of the conversation of the others, I gazed with new interest at the ship, *Tahitien*. There she was, waiting patiently for those who wished to board her on the morrow, waiting to take them all to Vila and Noumea and Australia. And I wished to go? Purpose abruptly congealed within my breast, and I exulted with this new determination. I would go, of course, what else? The devil with tickets, I would stow away, mingle with the passengers and pretend to be one of them.

Stow away. Aye, that sounded well…but what of the Sydney police? I had some acquaintance of Sydney police; and suddenly there came the vision of their luckless prey being bundled into a black van and borne away to face a sentence of six months. Six months in Long Bay? Was that how I would return?

Noumea, then, in New Caledonia. I would leave the ship there and persuade some Australian vessel to take me on to Sydney, or Brisbane. The Solomon Islands, New Guinea, New Zealand, anywhere: but, finally, Australia. Something could be arranged. I began chuckling to myself, aware of brief scrutiny from Patsy. Ho, but this was like old times again: the challenge gladly taken up, the wits oiled and sharpened, the familiar delight of the clandestine and the zest of the fugitive. Lawless escape from paradise, needling the gendarmes who would in time discover a single name remained on their lists, and commence to search for me.

But the thing must be quietly done: Marge and Patsy must not know, for they were women and women talked. Plans could not be made; one could only use advantage as it came. Later, when we were alone, I said to Cliff and Denny, "I'm going with you. On the *Tahitien*, tomorrow."

Moments passed in silence, then a grin began to tug at the corners of Cliff's mouth. He knew I had no ticket, and that no ticket could be bought.

"Stow away, you mean?"

"Yes. As far as Noumea anyway, if I can get that far."

Denny viewed me in silence with his reflective grey eyes. Cliff grinned fiercely.

"You're gonna hide? Crys-sakes, where?" He had already been on board and reported that conditions and accommodation were almost identical with those we had experienced on *Caledonien*. "In the paint locker, or something?"

"No. Just mingle with the others and see how it goes. There'll be so many passengers joining here that no one'll realize there's one extra, for a while."

He considered the idea.

"Well, at least you know the layout. And the fellers we know would, ah, co-operate, I guess."

"H'm. But let's keep it to ourselves, for the time being. Some might gossip, or make too many wisecracks in public; and those stewards probably aren't as stupid as they look. The fewer who know, the better— at least, till we're well at sea."

Denny pensively scratched his nose and said, "Sort of hairy. What if you get caught?"

"I don't know."

"All those stewards running round checking names and destinations and tickets and health certificates...."

"And all the gendarmes here"—I laughed—"running around looking for someone who isn't here. My landing permit expired last week. They probably think I'll leave on the *Tahitien*. And they're right, but they'll never know it. I hope."

"Yeah. Well, damn' good luck anyway. Buy you a beer."

We wondered what the French would do, if they found a stowaway.

8

NEW HEBRIDES

Stowaway

COMMERCE Quay was a scene of restive pathos as a great concourse of people waited for the liner to depart. Many of them were island girls farewelling their brief lovers, to whom they had given garlands of gay flowers and coloured shells, and now as time for departure approached the passengers infesting the vessel's several decks tossed down streamers, toilet paper, *billets doux* and promises, or kissed their garlands and threw them back with unconscious irony to the ones they left behind.

Cliff and Denny were ears-deep in blooms: Nita and Vickie were gazing up from what appeared as a tossed salad of bright pareos, frothed with flowers and studded with upturned faces like brown raisins. There were tears and laughter and the listless silences of those who could find no more to say, or who were too polite to leave before the ship had sailed; the gang-plank was still down, and officials hurried to and fro on late errands.

In the third-class lounge I sat with Marge and Patsy, sharing a bottle of perfume with a vacant-eyed vahiné called Annette. Better to sit with friends, it seemed, than wander about the decks where officers and stewards were seeking those who should already be ashore.

"Heavens, I don't know how you can do it," Patsy said, and shuddered. "It tastes like…like stale embalming fluid, or something."

It was doubtful if Annette had been able to taste anything for the last hour. She had ignored the warning bell, and announcements on the broadcast system, and refused to go ashore. If any officials questioned us, I felt, their attentions would instantly centre themselves on her.

"Don't drink it all," Marge pleaded. "I thought it'd last me a year. Please?"

It was half a litre of Tiare Tahiti in an ornamental bottle, but little more than a quarter now remained. The two girls had been surprised to learn I was travelling on the *Tahitien* after all, but I explained I had taken advantage of a last-minute cancellation, and bought a ticket.

Tears began to roll down Annette's cheeks. With unsteady deliberation she lifted a garland of frangipani from her neck and placed it around Patsy's, then broke off one of the flowers and tucked it behind Marge's left ear.

"Oh, isn't she a darling?" Patsy cried, and kissed her affectionately.

"We're going to miss you, Annette. But honey, you'd better go. Or you'll end up in Australia."

"Left ear," Marge mused. "That means I haven't got a man, and I'm looking."

"And right ear means you've got a man, but you're still looking anyway," Patsy said. Passing a second flower, she added shrewdly "Maybe you'd better wear one behind each ear. That tall, good-looking steward with the bonny, dark curls is giving you the eye."

Perhaps I should leave and join the throng on deck, I reflected. It might be better to move around, rather than linger for long in one place. There were not many others in the lounge. At all events I must not be caught until well clear of port, or I might be transferred to an island vessel bound for Papeete. I had come aboard at midday, armed with a visitor's permit such as was freely given on request at the Messageries Maritimes office down near Vaima's; Cliff and Denny had brought my few belongings on board with their own, and since then I had quietly manoeuvred in such fashion as to avoid the attentions of immigration officials, ship's officers, visiting police and a host of inquisitive stewards in quest of tips.

At two o'clock the gangway was closed to any further visitors, and passengers who came aboard were obliged to show their tickets. At four o'clock all remaining visitors were urged to leave the ship, instructions to leave at once were broadcast repeatedly, the warning bell sounded and officials commenced a casual check of those who remained on board.

Annette twined both arms around my neck and damply kissed me, then buried her face at my neck and shook with gentle sobs, occasionally pausing to sniffle and wipe her nose on my shirt.

"Poor darling," said Patsy. "We'd better get her ashore, before they take the gang-plank up. You know, she told me she's a virgin? Seriously. Twenty-one years old and a virgin, imagine!"

Marge snorted skeptically.

"She won't be for long, if she goes ashore loaded to the gills with my perfume. Oh no, look who's coming!"

An American called Ralph was hurrying towards us, mildly distraught; he was a strange individual of perhaps thirty-five, tall and swarthy and loose-limbed, whose supercilious insolence estranged both men and women and whose air of disciplined dissolution suggested some sinister secret vice. Two ship's officers and a steward had entered the lounge in his wake.

"Where's Cliff and Denny?" he demanded when he saw us. "Immigration want to see them in the first-class lounge. Can't find them anywhere on the ship."

The two officers watched Annette as I disentangled myself, and issued some instruction to the steward.

"On deck," I said. It would be wise to leave the lounge at once. "I'll tell them; I know where they are."

The steward came to Annette, urging her to leave, and I rose.

"Monsieur? Your name, if you please?" One of the officers held a sheaf of lists in his hand.

My name? Quickly, what name? Well, I had known this would happen, one would have to take the chance. Moving closer to him, hoping that neither Ralph nor the girls would overhear my answer, I said, "Rause. Dan Rause. American, destination Sydney, fourth class."

He perused the fourth-class list.

"Ah yes, thank you."

He turned to Annette, who was sobbing in the arms of the patient steward, and I fled on deck to find Denny and Cliff. It evolved that small formalities were required concerning the export of their motor-bikes from the island.

Soon the gang-plank was raised, lines cast off, and amid an intense confusion of anxious farewells the *Tahitien* moved away from Commerce Quay. Papeete fell behind as we turned into the channel leading out to sea through the reefs: and the thrill of the lonely challenge coursed through my blood, feeding on the triumph of the moment. The vessel throbbed with steady power, passengers were walking the decks and gathering in saloons, or clustering at vantage points to gaze back at Papeete, and the purple mountains stroked with sunset, stoking their hearts with memories and regrets. I had wanted to stay for ever on Tahiti, and in a sense I would; I would never leave, the police would hold my name in a special "Illegally Missing" file, and wonder where I hid.

Nine days, then, to the first port of call at Vila in the New Hebrides, and another couple of days to Noumea. Among four hundred passengers I was a solitary fugitive, riding the tide of circumstance, exposed to the sensitive antennae of professionals accustomed to detecting stowaways. Aye, but I had the advantage: the advantage of being only one hidden among these hundreds, and of having good companions who would warn me of any harm, and watch my cause.

The bell for supper rang, and I took counsel with my friends.

"You going in?" Denny asked curiously.

"Yes. Best to act like everyone else. If they kept noticing me around and never saw me at meals, they'd soon figure out what was going on."

"First night. There could be some sort of check."

"Denny and I could go to the first sitting," Cliff suggested, "and see what happens."

"Good trick."

There would be three sittings in fourth class, and those who arrived in the saloon first would be the first served. Two long ranks of tables end to end ranged the centre of the hall, with ledges fixed against three walls where others ate; serving counters occupied one end and three stewards served. Cliff and Denny would attend the first sitting and report on any hazards I might face.

I occupied myself with small affairs, and after they had eaten they met me up on deck.

"Nothing," they said. "No check. Confusion all over the place, anyone sitting anywhere, and the stewards half pissed. Potage, cold cuts, and pineapple with condensed milk."

I chose a position in full view at a central table, and since no one of the fifty who sat at this sitting was aware of anything untoward, there were no whispered jests or sly smiles for the stewards to intercept.

Fourth-class passengers were distributed in perhaps a dozen cabins, each with eight bunks, and in dormitories forward in Number One hold: and, since I had not been allotted any bunk, I cast about and decided to claim one of several vacant bunks at a lower level in the hold, where ten soldiers *en route* to Noumea had established themselves. It seemed likely that inquiring stewards might not bother to come here, thinking only soldiers occupied that level: but if they did I would be trapped in a cul-de-sac, and would have to parry their questions as best I could. In order to minimize this risk, I selected two companions whom I trusted, who occupied berths of strategic value, and to them I confided my condition. One was Lance, who occupied Cabin 301 to starboard and who would be one of the first aware of any organized search or official check; the second was David, who occupied Cabin 304 in a similar position by the port corridor.

Certain signals would advise me of any form of crisis or alarm. Cliff and Denny, up above me, would provide a second line of defence against unheralded intrusion by officials.

On the first day out from Tahiti a pattern of events suggested early discovery of the vessel's uninvited guest. As I was leaving breakfast, which was more or less continuous with passengers arriving as others left the room, the portly first steward in charge of fourth-class welfare chose to address me just outside the door.

"Have you eaten well, monsieur?" he asked politely.

"Thank you, yes."

Why had he elected to accost me, in particular? Or had he addressed others in this fashion? He scrutinized my face with professional interest…or was it professional suspicion?

"Your name, monsieur?" he blandly inquired.

A little bubble of panic grew in my stomach. He knew, he knew! Why else should he be lurking there, waiting to ask my name? He had certainly not challenged either Cliff or Denny, who had eaten earlier, or they would have told me.

"Denny Clarke," I said levelly.

"Clarke," he mused. "And of what nationality?"

"Canadian."

"Then you speak some French, no?"

"No, monsieur."

"Ah. And the food, it is all right?"

Why, he was merely concerned about the food. On the *Caledonien* there had been near mutiny in fourth class when we accused the stewards, who belonged to a catering firm contracting to the shipping line, of pocketing funds which should have been used to buy fresh food at Panama. The captain had intervened, and meals improved at once.

So I shrugged and said resignedly, "It is food. I suppose it's adequate, for fourth class."

He patted my shoulder. "*D'accord*, monsieur. If I can be of any service...."

Later in the morning I was informed by a scout that everyone was being issued with certain forms to complete, landing *fiches* which demanded passport details and points of destination.

"Your *fiche*, monsieur?" demanded a steward with a thin and wolfish face. His manner was as suavely brusque as his pencil moustache.

"You've got it already," I said, preparing to move on.

"I have it?" He glanced at me skeptically. "Your name, please?" "Cliff Rich." Cliff had already handed his in. Surely this starved little mountebank would not connect faces with their names so early in the voyage?

"Ah, Rich. Yes, I have it. You are one of those with the big motor-bikes, is it not?"

"That's right." Again I moved to pass on. Damn him, I wanted no truck with stewards. They might happen to discuss me and discover I had several names.

"So powerful, eh?" he purred happily.

"Yes. Excuse me," I said, smiling agreeably, and strode off.

And yet a third time there came another steward who caught me just as I emerged on deck. The system of warning was not functioning as well as I had hoped. He carried the inevitable list in his hand.

"Have you been issued with linen, monsieur?" he asked.

"Thanks, yes." Linen had been issued the previous evening. I could hear one of the girls calling to me from the deck above.

"Pete! Oh, Pete! Here's that Stanley Gardner story."

Damn her, I could only ignore her cries.

The steward seemed doubtful. "But I don't think so, monsieur. Do I have your signature?"

"Hey, Pete, you deaf?"

"Everyone has my signature. I've done nothing but fill out papers and *fiches* ever since I came aboard."

David moved down the well-deck to intercept and hold the girl's attention. Bless David, then!

"But your name is…?"

Devil with his questions. Well, I would toss another onion in the broth.

"Lance Marsden."

"Marsden? But I don't…ah yes. Cabin 301. Very well, monsieur."

During that afternoon there was the matter of lifeboat drill. All those who had boarded at Tahiti were commanded, over the broadcast system, to don their lifebelts and assemble on the boatdeck. Should I go? Certainly I would not be missed, if I did not. Would they check off names on a list? And I had no lifebelt, I would have to find one. Aye, but perhaps it was better to be bold. A watchful steward might chance to miss me, or note that I failed to attend, and question me: and the more I was seen in public affairs, walking freely and without fear, the less likely I would be to attract suspicion. If I could last three days without being caught, I would probably be safe for as long as I chose to stay aboard.

I stole a jacket from the dormitory and followed the others to the boatdeck; persons from all classes were there. No one bothered to check any names. An officer briefly lectured us first in French and then in English, and we were dismissed. In our absence stewards had been searching out new passengers who neglected to attend the parade.

Twice during the day there were casual inspections of our quarters by officers, but each time I was warned and moved elsewhere. But at nine o'clock that night, when most of us were abed, someone rapped twice and twice again on the steel deck just above my head.

The second-phase alarm! Some form of inspection was in progress, and they were too close for me to mount two flights of stairs and escape on deck.

The soldiers near me appeared to be asleep, rocked by the easy roll of the ship and shushed by the rush of spray swishing past the hull outside from the cleaving bows. The hold was in darkness, dimly lit by lights from the upper level where Cliff and Denny were. A large tarpaulin used to cover the hatch in port was in one corner of the hold, roped in a neat roll: it was the only possible refuge which could hide me. Seizing my blanket and clothes and sandals, I darted over to the bundle and unlashed it; earlier I had assured myself that this could be easily done. A torch flashed at the head of the stairs, and the legs of two officers appeared as they began to descend.

Horns of Satan, but the warning had come late! They must have been asleep upstairs when the officers appeared, and given the signal under their very noses. Hastily I unrolled the heavy canvas, drew it back over me, and doubled up in a ball with my clothes and blanket hugged against me as the officers gained the floor of the hold. From one side I could see the light of torches flash to and fro.

"Poilus," said one. "Only soldiers."

"Have them sweep it out in the morning," said the other. "Phew, smells like a sack of oysters."

Once the beam of a torch played full on the canvas under which I lay, but the many layered fold was too stiff to suggest a body underneath and a moment later the officers went away.

For a time I lay there, in case any of the soldiers had now woken, but after twenty minutes crept back to my bunk. Thereafter I only entered the hold when the soldiers were asleep, and left before they woke in the morning, leaving nothing to suggest that anyone had been present.

"Where do you sleep?" Ralph asked on the second day. We were sitting on the forward hatch watching David and a French girl play dominoes. His tone held a note of confidential inquiry, and his beautiful, soft eyes were steadily fixed on mine. For reasons of his own he must have noted that I seemed to have no berth in any of the men's cabins or dormitories.

"On deck," I said briefly. Abroad on deck at night one stumbled over couples in odd corners, wrapped in blankets.

"Where?" he persisted. But why would he wish to know?

"What's it to you?"

He shrugged, but still regarded me with an interested yet disdainful stare.

"One of the stewards wanted to know," he said. "He was asking, earlier."

Indeed. There seemed to be more stewards than enough for the hundred and fifty fourth-class folk; and since there were less than twenty of us whose native tongue was English, we comprised a small minority which stood out from the rest. If stewards began breathing down my neck, I might have to disappear altogether, and hide myself in some crevice like a rat.

"Give him my compliments," I said irritably, "and tell him to go to hell, that I sleep on deck with a woman."

"Oh." He seemed to be disappointed. "Which one?"

Stab me softly, but he should have a list in his hand and a pencil to make notes. He would make a good steward.

"The one with the square navel. Get lost."

I rose and went amidships to the third-class quarters, and found Marge and Patsy in their cabin with an English girl. I had already noted the location of their berth as an adequate source of temporary refuge, if I found myself in flight through the ship; they would help me with no hesitation, I knew, if I revealed the need.

"Deputation," I announced. "The boys appointed me to invite you lovely people to their humble fourth-class rabbit warren. Come and sunbake on the peak."

"Who's there?" asked Marge thoughtfully.

"Oh, everyone of importance, everyone who loves you. Mike and Lance, Denny and Cliff, Rause and—"

"We'll come," Patsy announced, sparkling with a smile. "The Austrian's not there, is he?"

"No."

No one loved the Austrian. Every time he saw a man and girl strolling the deck hand in hand he would spit, or laugh maliciously, or mutter salacious comments which could barely be overheard. Women avoided him and melted away from his approach; men regarded him with uneasy distaste.

The three girls came with me to lie in the sun on blankets, on the forecastle; if I was supposed to be sleeping on deck with a woman, I decided, it would be wise to be seen in the company of women during the day. Besides, there was a pleasing irony in lying with them in the sun, engaging in mild flirtation and lazy conversation, while officers on the bridge gazed towards us with derisive envy and binoculars.

The hare was eating lettuce in the middle of the field, but the hounds were still upwind and unaware.

But when three days had passed, when the chief steward found that
all his forms and *fiches* had been filled and signed, when various
inspections had satisfied the officers that all passengers were accounted
for and no one had been found hiding in linen closets or lifeboats or
fuse lockers, this matter of being a stowaway assumed an easy and even
humdrum air of watchful boredom. We lounged at ease throughout
the days on the forecastle or forward well-deck, or played cards and
draughts and chess in the dining-hall, drinking cheap *vin rouge* in
preference to the execrable beer. Sometimes we would sit with friends
who invited us to upper-class saloons, or invade the first-class pool, or
forage through the vessel stealing fruit from better tables; occasionally I
avoided the airless hold to sleep on deck in some secluded niche.

One day, when I lay on Denny's bunk reading a borrowed novel,
I noticed the Austrian near by in company with his only friend, a
pale Swiss lad who mistook obscene manners for a worldly attitude of
savoir-faire. They were standing a few yards away, engaged in tricking
money from a puzzled, young French soldier of perhaps eighteen years.
I had met the Austrian in Papeete, lecherously admiring pornographic
pictures he had purchased, and he had spoken of the illustrated sex-
books he had bought. His brain was a breeding-ground for psychotic
purulence, and the handiwork of perverts was secreted in his luggage:
he was travelling to Sydney and planned to sell it there.

Several times I had seen him tricking the guileless with three coins,
playing a version of heads and tails which he described as crown and
boot. The game was played by three men. Each would spin a coin in the
air simultaneously, catch it, and at once slap it down on his wrist for all
to see. If three heads showed, or three tails, the coins were tossed again.
Usually the coins would fall showing two of a kind, and one odd face:
and the man with the odd coin won.

The Austrian and the Swiss cheated in such fashion that no stranger
could ever win. They "butterflied" their coins, so that they only
appeared to spin; and if the Austrian showed a head, the Swiss would
show a tail. No matter what side the third man showed his coin would
make a pair with one of the others; and the man with the odd coin, the

Austrian or the Swiss, would inevitably win.

When on promenade with the girls I had overheard the Austrian making indecent comments, but any open conflict on deck would have caused the girls embarrassment and brought undue attention to myself. Now the time seemed opportune; most folk were up on deck.

Discarding the book, I rose, and yawned, and pretended to interest in the game. They let the soldier win once, and then he began to lose again.

"What do you call it?" I inquired.

"Crown and boot," said the Austrian. He threw me a speculative glance, but seemed to decide against an invitation.

"How is it played?"

He explained the principle, and added, "You've never seen it before?"

"No." It must have been one of the commonest games in taverns throughout the world.

"Well, you like to play?"

"Oh, I don't know. I never gamble for francs, you can't buy anything with them. Besides, I'm not lucky."

"What you mean? What do you gamble for?"

"American money. Or Australian. But I'm not much of a gambler."

But the mention of dollars and pounds whetted his appetite, for francs would be useless in Australia.

"You got dollars? You want to gamble?"

"Oh, I've got dollars."

A cunning light entered his eyes, and he shrugged as if with sad reluctance.

"Well, all right, if you want." He handed me the Frenchman's coin. "But only once or twice, this isn't my lucky day. How much you want to spin for?"

I pretended to hesitate, then took money from my pocket and counted it in front of him. There were fifteen dollars I had purchased from a tourist in Papeete, the remainder was six dollars worth of francs.

"That's all I've got," I said "Twenty-one dollars' worth."

"Hey? But you want to throw for all that?" He licked his lip and gave me a strained regard.

"Might as well." I grinned. "Treble or nothing. One throw."

The Swiss fidgeted nervously, and exchanged an anxious glance with his colleague.

"All right," said the Austrian. "All right then."

I placed the money on the deck under the toe of my sandal, and each of them placed francs to the same value in front of them.

"Ready?"

We all tossed. But even as they moved to catch their coins I pushed the Swiss lad in the chest, and drove my fist against the Austrian's mouth. The Swiss stumbled against the companionway, the Austrian reeled back and fell against the framework of tiered bunks. Rapidly I scooped the three piles of currency from the floor, and stowed them in my pocket.

"Bastard!" cried the Austrian, wiping a plump hand across his mouth. "Bastard, you steal!" He scrambled to his feet, glaring wildly, and flung himself forward, head down and flailing his fists. An easy target. Again my fist crashed against his mouth, so that his head snapped back and he slowly crumpled to the floor. The Swiss lad was staring in horror, gripping the rails of the companionway and with one foot already on the lower step, as if prepared to flee; but I only glanced at him once, and then ignored him. Three male passengers near by, Frenchmen, chattered among themselves with excited inquiry.

The Austrian pushed himself to a sitting position, fumbling at his mouth with one hand.

"*Verfluchter Dreck!*" he cursed thickly. "*Hat mir die Zähne kaputt geschlagen!* Ah-h-h...."

"But...but why?" asked the young French soldier, gazing at me as if I might be mad.

"Because he cheated. And because he's no good anyway."

"Cheated?"

"Yes." I nudged the Austrian with my toe. "Isn't that so?"

But he was silent, spitting into his hand, and I nudged him in the ribs with some force.

"Tell him you cheated."

Tears were rolling down his cheeks as he glanced up, and even malice and hatred had drained from his eyes on a tide of extravagant self-pity.

"My teef!" he cried unhappily. He held out two broken teeth capped

272

with gold. "You break my teef. Why? Why? I do nothing to you."

"You called a decent girl a whore the other day, when I was walking with her. And you cheated just now. Right?"

"No, I don't. Yes, yes! All right, yes I cheat." He spat blood on the deck and stared down at it inconsolably. Would he report me to the stewards? Would there be some form of inquiry? Devil, he could do me greater harm than he knew.

"Better quit cheating," I said. "And insulting people. And don't bother making trouble. Those Sydney police are tough on characters who try and smuggle in dirty photographs and books. Understand?"

He said nothing. I nudged him again.

"You understand?"

"Yes, yes, yes, I understand. Nothing trouble."

I left him sitting there, and the Swiss lad scurried ahead as I made my way on deck. As a certain officer had remarked, there was something below that smelt like a sack of oysters.

"Strike me lucky, what a miserable-looking place!" David muttered, gazing ahead through mists of light rain. "Romance of the Pacific, look at it."

It was the afternoon of the ninth day, and we were clustered at the windows of an enclosed deck just below the bridge. Ahead of us the New Hebrides appeared as an olive smear of flat shadow dimly seen through veils of weeping mist.

"Not so bad, though," said Lance. He had called in there on his way to Tahiti. "You can get Foster's lager there, in Vila."

"Vahinés?" suggested Mike.

"Not that you'd notice. Melanesian types, I think. Frizzy, sort of Negro. But they got Foster's."

"They reckon we lie off, out in the bay," Denny said. "Mightn't be able to get ashore anyway."

"Aw, there'll be a launch or something. We'll be there all day tomorrow. We'll get ashore somehow."

"Who wants to?" David asked. "Looks like it rains for ever around here."

Personally it was a matter of small importance whether or not I could go ashore; only four persons were aware of my position, and all the others, including stewards, seemed to assume without question that I was a passenger. I watched as a seaman made his way forward on the well-deck below, clutching flags in his hand; he paused by the foremast, untied a line, and raised the French tricolour on the port flag-halyard. Crossing to the other side, he raised a British ensign on the starboard halyard.

"British?" I inquired. "What's that for?"

Lance was uncertain.

"Some kind of split-Government deal they have here, I think. French and British."

"You mean, part of the Hebrides is British territory?"

"Something like that. Trust territory or something."

This was interesting. Conceivably, then, it might be wise to land at Vila; the British were less hasty than the French, and inclined to easier tolerance of Australians. But of course, if half of the Hebrides was British, there would be Australians there; and, if Australian officials were sometimes the worst of all, there would surely be others of my nation one could easily approach. I now had thirty pounds, a goodly sum: certainly something or other could be arranged.

But someone tapped me on the shoulder, and when I saw a steward there a sudden gust of premonition fired my bowels.

"The chief. He wishes to speak with you."

Cliff and Denny studied me with brief anxiety, and turned away. Lance was suddenly stiff, pretending not to notice. But what could the chief steward want? He was standing not thirty feet away, waiting, obviously wishing to speak with me in confidence. It could be no routine matter; they employed no such finesse.

Why had I been singled out for the chief's attention? Fear enveloped me in bloodless wings, but I went to him, forcing discipline on tingling nerves.

"Yes?"

"Come, monsieur." We moved aside from a couple standing near us, and then he halted to survey me with a cynical regard.

"You are the one, eh? The Australian."

I would use David's name. If he thought I was Australian, I would be David Lawson.

"What's on your mind, chief?"

"Making trouble. You know it is forbidden?"

Many things were forbidden; such as travelling on French liners, and sleeping on French bunks, and eating French food, without paying.

"You are the one who hit the Austrian?"

Ah, so that was it.

"I hit him, yes."

"Why?"

"Because he has a serpent in his mouth."

"Fighting is strictly forbidden on board," he announced firmly.

I was silent. His statement rested well enough by itself.

"I shall have to make a report to the chief officer," he went on, and waited. Waited for what? For me to protest, or shed tears, or offer him a bribe? A pox on him, he could make his report.

"Go ahead," I said, and shrugged. I would leave the ship at the earliest possible moment. "He deserved it. I hit him twice."

He nodded with satisfaction. "And your name?"

"David Lawson."

"Lawson?" he echoed, incredulous. "You are David Lawson?" He looked at me with a strained air of disapproval. "But no, monsieur, I do not believe so." And turning to the group by the windows he cried out, "Mister Lawson!"

David turned around and left his place to come towards us. Eyes of a buttered dog, what was happening? I was caught. I had been too clever, there was no way out of this. Or could I pretend that I had lied to try and dodge his report, and give my right name as someone else?

"Monsieur," said the chief to David, "Your name is David Lawson, is it not?"

David intercepted the flicker of an eyelid.

"Er, no, chief. I'm Lance Marsden."

"Marsden? But....*Meutre!*" He was confused. As a man who doubtless prided himself on remembering names and faces, since his position would demand it daily, he suddenly found his talent ridiculed. "But I called Lawson. You answered!"

"I thought you said Marsden. You're already talking to Dave

Lawson. What's the bloody matter with you?"

"Eh? Lawson?" He fixed his eye on some distant point, twisted his mouth in a wry grimace, and gave a vast sigh. "*Eh bien*, Lawson", looking back at us.

He made a note of the name and went away shaking his head and muttering to himself. David grinned at me.

"You're on report," he said. "Or I am. Anyway David Lawson is, for flattening the Austrian."

"Proud of it. We'll play it as it goes."

I rested my hand on his shoulder, and we walked back to the others chuckling.

At dusk the vessel anchored in a cove half a mile out from the town of Vila, a small Pacific outpost steeped in early twilight and shrouded by grey clouds. Passengers were permitted ashore, and Denny and Cliff led the way amidships to the gang-plank on brief reconnaissance. There were no formalities; no papers were demanded, one merely walked down the gang-plank and boarded a waiting launch. Nor were there any formalities when we landed, and Lance led us along the wet and lugubrious waterfront to the Wailélé Hotel.

The bar was crowded, so we sat about a table on the veranda with bottles of Foster's lager: David and Lance, Denny and Cliff, Patsy and Marge, and a sad, little old-young Englishman called Guidon. Australian currency was used, but dollars were more than welcome and even Pacific francs were acceptable enough. Laughter and conversation raged for an hour or more, but I sat with an air of detachment wondering if I should stay ashore, or risk continuing on *Tahitien* to Noumea.

What part of the Hebrides was governed by the British? Did British vessels call here? What would happen if I was questioned by the chief officer? I needed some source of information, a man who had his finger on the pulse of the local scene. Thoughtfully I watched the men who came and went, those who sat with others and those who sat alone: and after some time I approached a certain man, and invited him to sit with us. We were strangers, I explained, and hoped he would honour us by settling small disputes which concerned the Hebrides.

He came from Santo in the north, and his name was Bill Giles; he was a lean and weather-tanned Australian approaching forty-five years, a laconic wit and engaging raconteur. Everyone immediately liked him for his personable manner; his conversation was direct, to the point and even bold, laced with congenial humour and the flavour of far places, yet touched with a gracious restraint for the sake of Marge and Patsy.

Later, as he came back from the restroom, I found an excuse to intercept him. If he was the man I thought he was—and I had watched him closely—he was not the type to run to the gendarmes with sly reports.

"I have a problem," I began, confronting him at a distance from our table. He considered me in watchful silence. "Point one is that someone travelled from Papeete to Vila, on the *Tahitien*, without a ticket."

He accepted this with a thoughtful nod, inspecting his fingernails.

"Point two is that this person doesn't know whether it would be best to get off here, or at Noumea."

He glanced at me swiftly. "No problem there, friend," he said gravely. "You get off here."

"Why?"

"I'll tell you why." He accepted a cigarette, and a light. "A while back I heard about two Aussies who snuk on board a French ship at Sydney—the *Caledonien*, I think—and they got caught before the ship reached Noumea. The cops grabbed 'em in Noumea, and gave them six months in the chain-gang."

"In a chain-gang? Hell's fires!"

"I'd keep the hell away from Noumea," he went on. "The French cops there are mean, and they can do what they like with you. But, now, take this place", indicating the Hebrides with a flourish of his cigarette. "It's different. It's a *condominium* for a start, under the joint rule of France and Britain. For all practical purposes this town here, Vila, is French; but, if anyone breaks the law, they can't just grab him and slap him in jail. There's a special clause that states a Spanish judge has to be present, whenever any sentence is passed on a prisoner. And no Spanish judge has been available for about ten years now. Get the picture?"

"But that's magnificent!" Nothing could happen to me; or if it did, what could it be?

A lazy grin spread across his face. "There's two arraigned murderers walking around this town quite openly. Cripes, they wouldn't worry about a stowaway. They might deport him to Sydney, but that's about all. And then it'd be up to the Sydney cops."

Ah, then there was still that.

"Better stay," he said, smiling as he squinted at me through cigarette smoke. "Want me to arrange a room for you?"

"Here, you mean?"

"I know the management. I can get it fixed without any silly questions."

"Well, yes thanks."

He arranged that I should be given a room in the annex, at moderate cost. I would stay ashore, and avoid undue attentions until the vessel sailed some time tomorrow night. All the clothes I possessed I had worn ashore, I had my passport and my razor and toothbrush; the blanket and typewriter were still aboard, but these were expendable items and a hindrance to fluid movement.

When my companions set out to return to the ship, I confided my plans to Denny and Cliff and stayed behind. Perhaps I would see them in Australia. That night I slept in the annex. Early in the morning Giles flew back to Santo, and I did not see him again.

Next day I remained a fugitive, intent on avoiding any untoward occasion which might provoke misfortune; I left the town in early morning and only returned at night, and during that night *Tahitien* sailed away. Thus, on the morning of the second day, I was the only person in town who knew who I was, or from whence I came; one could lend imagination to almost any form of story, and invent the most unlikely tales, as long as they coincided with the data in my passport: and how could anyone prove that a tale was true or false? If anyone suspected I had come aboard *Tahitien*, they had only to cable the vessel to learn that I had not. No one of that name was on their list.

Happily I rambled along the untidy waterfront with its humble native shops, its several modern stores and offices, and among attractive villas tucked away on hills behind the town. Freely I walked, unknown to any unless I chose to permit some brief acquaintance. To this person I was an artist recently returned from Santos, to the next I was a recorder of tribal ballads, to the third I was a journalist returning, after holiday, to Sydney. What did it matter? Let them gossip, if they wished, and dispute with one another: I would not be long among them, for I would go on to Noumea.

"How did you arrive?" some middle-aged hen demanded. She was like some plump, half-melted candle, with tallow arms and greasy eyes.

"There are two schools of thought," I replied. "Some think I came by *Tahitien*, others say I came by way of Santos."

"But which is right?"

"Take your choice," I offered, and she arched with indignation and went away.

A plane would leave for Noumea in two days' time, making the ninety-minute flight to Noumea, and I supposed one might need some kind of visa. But if I approached the French authorities and asked for a visa now, they would have two days to think of questions and check on my replies: better, therefore, to wait until a few hours before the plane departed. With a ticket in my hand and ready to leave at once, they might more easily be tempted to rid themselves of a fool who only promised to be a nuisance.

Towards noon on the last day I presented myself at the *gendarmerie*, explaining to the receptionist that I sought a transit visa for New Caledonia.

"If you will leave your passport," she suggested, "and call again this afternoon?"

"But the plane leaves at two o'clock. See, I have my ticket."

She consulted some inner office, and I was required to present myself to a handsome, young officer within. He accepted my passports.

"A transit visa only?" he inquired. "Transit to where?"

"Through Noumea to Australia, monsieur."

He paged briefly through the first passport, found an empty page, and stamped it with a large rubber stamp.

"Three days," he said, "in Noumea." He filled in small details with a pen.

"Thank you." Well, this was too facile: rarely had I received a visa with such expeditious ease. What an intelligent, worthy, and efficient officer, a credit to his nation: he accepted me without demur, I was once again *en règle*. But then, as he was about to hand the passports back, he looked among the pages for the entry stamp to the Hebrides. He glanced through the first book twice, frowned, flicked me an inquiring glance, and began searching through the others. Whenever he found a French entry or exit stamp, or visa, he would scan it hopefully—stamps and visas for Tunisia, Dahomey, French Morocco, the Cameroons, Algeria, French Guinea, the French Sudan, French Equatorial Africa, St Martin, and Guadeloupe and Martinique. It took some minutes.

At length he frowned thoughtfully and said, "But your entry stamp, you have none? Where did you enter the New Hebrides?"

Well, then, here it was. He would require some form of explanation, but he seemed an agreeable young blade.

"I ask your pardon, monsieur, but I don't have the faintest idea."

He leant back in his chair, rested one finger against his cheek, and regarded me with a baffled stare. He was interested rather than suspicious; obviously any *agent provocateur* would make no such admission, but would have a logical story tailored for the occasion.

"You have no idea where you entered these islands? You mean you don't remember the name of the port?"

"There was no port, monsieur. I landed on a beach."

"On a beach? What beach? Your last entry shows Tahiti. You swam here, perhaps, from Tahiti?" He was frankly astonished. One might forgive him for considering me some witless escapee from an institution.

"I was shipwrecked, more or less."

"More or less? You mean you had a yacht, a motor vessel, and you were wrecked? What was its name?"

"It was a catamaran, monsieur, a small catamaran called *Tiare Tahiti*."

"I see," he murmured vaguely, as thoughts hunted through his head like hungry rats. "A catamaran. You came from Tahiti, in a catamaran?"

"Yes."

"Alone?"

"All alone, by myself." And then added soberly, "It was a mistake."

"A mistake." He drew a hand across his mouth, smothering an urge to laugh. "You, ah, meant to go to Sydney, no doubt? But you became lost in the course of a few thousand miles by catamaran, and found yourself here instead?"

"No, no, monsieur. I mean, I'd only borrowed the boat for the day, from a friend in Papeete, but the wind was strong and blew me out to sea."

He nodded bleakly. "It blew you half-way across the Pacific Ocean to the Hebrides?"

"Yes, monsieur."

"And how long were you at sea? All night?"

I swallowed a smile. Obviously he was not one to be deceived by such nonsense. But what could he prove? Or disprove?

"Five weeks, monsieur. I was at sea five weeks."

He closed his eyes for a moment, gently massaging them with his fingertips, and then viewed me with droll mistrust.

"And, of course, you carried enough food and water for a month or two. Or perhaps you slept through the voyage? Or stopped at convenient hotels?"

"It was a hard journey, many days I don't remember at all. When it rained, I had water—" thinking of the animals in the zoo—"and I lived on fish. I had fishing equipment with me. I had gone out just beyond the reefs to fish."

It was impossible to check on such a story; and just as impossible to believe it. But how could I be punished for some indiscretion which the law could only guess at, and never hope to prove?

"But, of course," he said patiently, "you managed to bring your luggage?"

"All was left behind. The only things I have are my passport, some money, and the clothes you see me wearing."

"Oh?" He was thoughtful for a moment. "At what beach did you land?"

"Somewhere north, I think. For two days I was lost in jungle, and then I found a road. The road led here."

"H'm. It is not at all possible, of course, that you travelled illegally on the *Tahitien?*"

"Monsieur?"

He tapped his finger against his jaw, studying me with interest from under lowered brows.

"No, of course not, that would be against the law."

For some moments he was silent, gazing down in meditation at the desk. It might have been pleasant, I reflected, to take him out and have a drink, and be able to laugh together at this absurd and childish tale, but he belonged to the enemy camp, and there could be no compromise.

"I congratulate you," he said finally, "on your excellent health. It has not interfered with your imagination." He handed my passports to me. "I strongly recommend that you join the plane at two o'clock, without fail. And without luggage. *Bonjour,* Captain Bligh."

9

NEW CALEDONIA

Escape to the South Land

THE waterfronts of the world are charged with a vigorous sense of cosmopolitan collision, suggesting that those who dwell on a city's seaward fringe also live on the ravelled edges of the law: or perhaps the nightly invasion of lusty crews from foreign steamships, weaving an intricate oceanic web from port to distant port, themselves provide the illusion of social drama and burlesque.

Wandering the harbour-front with lights already twinkling in the dusk, I watched as seamen strode up from the docks to favourite taverns: Swedes and Germans, British, French, and others. Ah, but it was good to be alive: and I laughed aloud with the joy of life, flexing my muscles and stretching my arms, exulting with this freedom to be once more myself. What would happen tonight in the taverns of Noumea? I had money in my pocket, plucked from fools by the Austrian and then passed on to me, my passport gave me three whole days to find some onward transport to elsewhere; and nothing now could link me with the threat of prison, deportation, or exposure of past follies to the law.

Immigration at the airport, an hour or two before, had expressed concern that I had no onward ticket and ordered me to report to them on Monday: but Monday was far away with Sunday in between, and tonight—why, opportunity infested every tavern, anything could happen before dawn!

Australia was too close. I could look to the horizon and imagine the invitation of her smoky-blue coast. I would not stay in Noumea. Already my own country enfolded me with an unexpected fever of nostalgia, and gladly I would go to her. I must, I had to go. French New Caledonia was merely a rock in the sea to rest a passing bird. A seagull? "Weaving a web of human understanding across the nations of the world," the ginger-haired Gwen had said of seagulls, but perhaps this would hardly be my own case. Authority in any land is rigid and dogmatic, to be challenged or avoided but never understood; and perhaps, as the immigration man on St Kitts had said, I reflected no great credit on my nation. But what of the ordinary folk? Ah yes, that was a different cause. The ordinary mortals like myself I understood, and loved them well, no matter what their nation or their colour or their creed: I had lived with them and laughed with them, and even worked beside them, and, aye, most of them had loved me in return.

The evening was yet early. Turning towards the docks, I strolled down to the harbour edge and cast speculative glances at the ships. Which of them might be bound for Australian ports? That handsome Swedish freighter, perhaps: it would be good to travel again aboard a Swede. Or that small German coaster, but Germans rarely carried British crew, and anyone in the Commonwealth they classified as British, disorganized, and casual in their work. Ah, there was an Argentinian, sleek and grey, and I had never been to Argentina—but no. I had no wish to go there now. Nothing but Australia would do.

Joyful expectation raced through me. Australia—the very name was a cadence of deep music. The South Land, Terra Australis. Her name was an exclamation on the tongues of foreign folk, a word provoking quiet awe, a symbol of remote and unknown lands lying beyond the limits of the sea.

And there, why, farther along the dock was a British ship, black hull daubed with red lead and decks stained with rust, an old Liberty ship. But were there no Australian ships? And beyond the British ship, that great black liner: the *Caledonien*, perhaps, on her way back from Sydney to Marseilles? But, no, she had already returned. The *Polynésien*, then? I walked closer. Three sister ships plied the Marseilles-Sydney run. But, no, the *Polynésien* had a white stack, it was not the *Polynésien*.

But…what?

Name of a thousand murdered virgins, it was the *Tahitien*! She was still here, but, of course, this was her last French port of call before Sydney, and one of the most important.

Ho, and all my friends would be on board? Cliff and Denny and Lance and Patsy and Marge and- But I would go aboard at once! I strode towards the gangway, joyous with delighted purpose. Hey, but this was a fine event, and I chuckled with a new exhilaration as I thought of their expressions of surprise. And what of the stewards? Why, I could snap my fingers at them now. I had never seen them before: I was a lawful person, my passport was in order, I could laugh at them and swear I had never seen them before in my life. What were they talking about?

And they must have missed me by now. They would certainly realize someone had mysteriously disappeared. What had happened when David Lawson had been summoned, following the chief steward's report, to explain his reasons for fighting the Austrian?

Ha-ha, what a fine confusion there must have been, with the chief steward running around the vessel in despair, searching for me!

But wait....

I paused as I mounted the gangway to consider a new thought, and my blood surged wildly. The *Tahitien* was bound for Sydney, and I wished to go to Sydney. She could take me. I could travel on her. But with a ticket. Could I buy a ticket? I probably had enough money to buy a ticket. Sydney was not far now. Joyful gods, but what a magnificent enterprise, what splendid irony, to re-join *Tahitien* with a ticket, where everyone knew by now I had been a stowaway!

But the agency on shore was already closed, I knew. The bus from the airport had deposited the plane's passengers outside the office of TAI, and the Messageries Maritimes office was next door. It had been closed when we arrived.

Would it be possible, then, to purchase a ticket on board? Perhaps, if I avoided recognition until the thing was done. I was thoughtful, considering the chances, but there was only one thing to do, and that was try.

Mounting the gangway, I crossed the floodlit deck and entered the purser's office near by. A few passengers and two stewards stood in the spacious entrance foyer, but no one noticed me: and they would be first-class stewards, who had only seen me rarely. The purser was engaged in conversation with a stout civilian, but glanced up from his papers as I knocked.

"Pardon, monsieur," I began, edging into the cabin out of sight of passers-by. "I have just arrived in Noumea, and came directly to the ship, your office ashore was closed." I handed him my passport, opened to show the entry stamp put there hours before. "I was hoping I might purchase a ticket on your ship to Sydney. I hope I am not too late?"

He brushed my face with a glance of normal curiosity and took my passport.

"Australien," he murmured. "Well, I suppose we can sell him a ticket, perhaps?" He looked inquiringly at the portly civilian and, addressing me, went on, "This gentleman is the agent, it depends entirely on him. We have almost completed the papers, you understand. The vessel sails early in the morning."

The agent observed me with impatience, and nodded shortly.

"Yes, yes. But there is only fourth class, nothing else. You will have to travel fourth class."

He lied to my advantage. "A thousand thanks," I said gravely. "If you would be so kind. Ah, how much is the passage?"

"Twenty Australian pounds, and a few francs."

"I may pay in francs, of course?"

"Of course."

My heart was singing with happy triumph as I counted the money and handed it to him. God bless the luckless Austrian, he had done me a greater favour than he knew. I had sufficient and even a trifle left over. The ticket was made out and handed to me, with my passport, and my name and other details added to the inevitable list.

"You have your luggage?"

"Yes." The small brown-paper parcel in my hand.

"The fourth-class quarters are forward. Ask for the chief steward there, and show him your ticket. He will direct you to your berth."

Laughing to myself, I went down to the deck below and made my way forward. Dieu, but this was a happily ridiculous occasion: and I was on my way to Sydney? Why, all I had to do was sit down, and in four days or so the ship would be steaming through the Heads- lucky day. Life was a wonderful affair!

Weaving through familiar passages, I went to the galley and closets behind the fourth-class dining-hall, and the chief steward was there in company with Pencil-Moustache. Pencil-Moustache was standing at his ease drinking coffee, while the chief sat scribbling notes on a pad: P-M was the first to see me. His eyes grew wide and with the cup an inch from his lips he froze in the attitude of one just about to sip.

"*'Soir*," I said agreeably. "Is one of you chief steward?"

The chief looked up. An expression of stupefaction slowly assumed possession of his face, twitching small muscles. His mouth jerked open, but no words came forth. With a brave attempt to control laughter I coughed, and said again, "The chief steward? The purser said he would show me to my bunk."

I offered the ticket, placing it before him, but he ignored it.

"Sweet thunder," he cried, "what? But what are you doing here? Where did you—"

"I am a passenger, monsieur. I am travelling to Sydney. The purser said—"

"It's him!" P-M whinnied, spilling coffee. "By my own sacred mother...."

The chief rose to his feet, pale and fleshy face drawn with excitement, moist eyes swelling in their sockets.

"Ticket? You have a ticket now? What is your name?" He snatched up the ticket and scanned it. "Australian, yes, yes. Ha! No more David Lawson, eh? You disappear, someone takes your place, what happens? Hey?"

My broad grin refused to be controlled. "Don't know what you're talking about," I said agreeably. "You must be making a mistake. I've never seen you before."

"Hey? But from Tahiti? But I know, everyone knows: you travel from Tahiti on this ship. You punch the Austrian. You become six different people with six different names—" glancing anew at the ticket—"and none of them your own. Then suddenly you disappear, no one can find you. Where did—"

"You're mistaken," I said, shrugging. "I only joined the ship ten minutes ago. See!" I showed him my passport. "There is the entry stamp to New Caledonia, I've just arrived by air. Perhaps you confuse me with someone else?"

"Confuse? But—" He scrutinized me closely. Same face, same shirt, same jeans and sandals. "I know you, I talked with you, you ate at the second sitting. But where did you sleep? And no ticket at all, hey? And now you have another name, a quite different name. Sacred swine! And a ticket to Sydney. And you come here asking who is chief steward, hey? You don't know me yet?"

"Never saw you in my life. But you find some resemblance between myself and another person?"

"Resemblance?" shrilled P-M, but the chief signalled him to silence. A worldly man, the chief was rapidly regaining his self-possession as he shuttled facts and probabilities around inside his mind to form a pattern of intelligent deduction. He perused the ticket again to verify my name and the purser's signature, and his jaws worked on some imagined morsel as he stabbed at me with a speculative gaze.

"Resemblance," he muttered. "Yes, yes one might say so." What good would it do his reputation to admit, to higher authority, that he had permitted a stowaway to travel on the vessel under his very nose? That he had suffered the presence of an impostor at every meal, failing to detect him? And here was this assassin armed now with a valid ticket. What could be done against him, if he persisted in denials?

He handed the ticket to me. At least he would not be humbled by pretending to show me where Cabin 306 was.

"I believe," he said carefully, "that you might be able to find your own cabin. Meals are at the usual times. You may even possibly discover some of the passengers are familiar. But, please, it should not be necessary to amuse yourself by borrowing their names."

Ralph saw me as I entered fourth-class quarters.

"Hey, I thought you—"

"That's right. Where's Denny and Cliff?" It was apparent that the dormitories had been sealed off; comparatively few passengers continued on to Sydney.

"Er, in Cabin 301. But didn't you...."

His voice trailed away as I brushed past towards Cabin 301; they must have chosen to bunk with Lance when the dormitories closed. Pausing at the door, I glanced inside: Cliff was dozing on his upper bunk, Denny was on the bunk below, stretched out reading a book, Lance was pensively cutting his toenails. Two other men, Frenchmen and strangers to me, were occupied with open suitcases.

For a long moment I just stood there, so that the two Frenchmen glanced at me curiously; then, as Denny turned a page, his glance flickered towards me and was immediately riveted on my face.

"Well sufferin' hell," he murmured. "Look at what's arrived!"

Lance looked up, started with astonishment, and leapt up to shake

Deck scenes, fourth class on the Tahitien

*Aboard Tahitien. In the foreground is Cliff. From left to right are
Lance, author as stowaway, and Denny*

Author on houseboat

my hand and draw me in.

"You bloody beaut-ee! How'd you get here? Hell, they've been hunting all over the place. How'd you get to Noumea?"

"Plane." I laughed.

"Well, gee, I'll be a smothered uncle!" Denny said, and putting aside his book he kicked vigorously at the bunk above. "Hey, Cliff, wake up, get a load of what's turned up!"

The Frenchmen exchanged puzzled glances. Lance burst out laughing as I flashed the ticket to Sydney, and Cliff turned over growling. Suddenly he lifted his head, piercing me with his fierce, familiar scowl.

"What in the—" He propped himself up on his elbow. "Pete? Well, I'm buggered. Hey, you're back in Vila, what goes on?"

"Me, to Sydney. Decided life wasn't any fun without you characters," I said, laughing, "so I came back. Caught a plane from Vila. And look—" waving the ticket—"the nice man sold me a ticket. I'm a valid, lawful, paying passenger."

Then everyone was laughing and hurling facetious remarks and hooting, so that one of the Frenchmen nervously closed his suitcase and stowed it out of sight.

"Crys-sakes," Cliff cried, "those crazy stewards, they'll flip!"

"Ho-ho, they tried to accuse Dave of—ha-ha—funny? Hell! He told the chief officer to get stuffed. Ha-ha-ha!"

"Wait till the chief steward sees you. Gee I gotta be there."

"And Patsy and Marge, they were crooked as hell you didn't tell them. And those bloody stewards, when—ho-ho—when they see you at breakfast. Oh mother!"

"And that poor sonovabitchin' Austrian showing everyone his two gold teeth."

Rause came from a nearby cabin to see what was going on, and a great smile of welcome lit up his gentle face as he shook my hand. I was fond of Rause. Aye, fond of them all, these grand companions, my heart was full of glad affection for them all.

"How did you make out?" Rause wanted to know, and briefly I outlined the story.

"But can't they make trouble? When the chief steward sees you, he'll—"

"He already has. He was disturbed for a little while. He thought he recognized me. Then he seemed to decide it was perhaps better if he didn't."

"We've still got your typewriter," said Cliff, grinning. "And your blanket."

"Any food? I haven't eaten."

"Not a darn' thing."

"Sardines," Rause offered. "I've got sardines."

"Hell."

"Ask the chief," Denny suggested, chuckling. "He'd have some arsenic and ground glass."

"Aw, let's go ashore," Lance decided. "Hell, man, we've got to celebrate. Australian beer, in that wild honky-tonk."

"Yeah, eight shillings a bottle. Hot baby, but let's go wake up this hairy town! I got seven dollars left."

"Advance, men! Last night in port, let's hit the piss." They began searching for sandals and combing their hair. "Get Dave, Rause, and tell the girls."

Patsy and Marge embraced me and fed me on cold boiled eggs and olives and cheese, which they filched from first lounge tables, where officers were throwing a champagne party: and then we all trooped ashore, and the night was long and hilarious with revels in the taverns of Noumea.

There was, I discovered, no chain-gang in Noumea.

Tomaslov was a tall, young Yugoslav of extravagant good looks, acquainted with the prison and police of Noumea. He was only twenty-one, a native of Dalmatia's lovely city of Dubrovnik, but had escaped to Western Europe and emigrated to Australia three years before. His firm, square jaw had the strength of the stubborn Slav, his infectious laugh showed good white teeth; the flesh of his face was firm and tanned, level brows challenged the girlish beauty of his dark and long-lashed eyes, his hair was a thick mane of blue-black curls and ringlets sweeping low on the strong, clean forehead.

He had stowed away on a French ship leaving Sydney, but was caught and handed over to the gendarmes in Noumea; and, since he planned to try again as soon as possible, we discussed the matter together at some length.

"You see," he explained as *Tahitien* ploughed south and west towards Sydney, "this pretty girl in Sydney, she my sweetheart. Ah, but she too pretty, you know? So pretty, and I got big love for her, but she only sixteen years. Then one day she say, pretty soon now I have one baby. You know? She say I am the father, and I say, yes, I think so. So I say to her I am going to Melbourne for one week, and instead I go to Sydney docks looking for one ship. Ask plenty people, what that ship? Where she going? Then I pretend I am wharfie, and walk aboard one ship called *Caledonien*. Same like this, you know?"

"Yes, I know her." He seemed utterly without sympathy for the "sweetheart" he had left, and felt no need to justify his blithe desertion.

"In my pocket I only got two shilling left. I don't mind for that. I hide. Ship sail. I hide, steal food at night time, hide again. Pretty soon we come to Noumea, steward catch me."

He had not intended getting off there, but after two idle days he heard a group of girls laughing on the dock and he could no longer restrain himself. If he had wished, he could have walked boldly off the ship, but chose instead to leave by way of a porthole, squeezing through head first, at least twenty feet above the dock, so that he would plummet head first to the concrete.

A steward had seized him by the pants and dragged him back, possibly saving his life. He was locked up in the prison for twenty days—during which he could have earned three shillings a day, but refused, earning more at poker—and was then put aboard *Tahitien* and locked inside a cabin until the ship had sailed.

"But I try again," he assured me. "I know this kind of ship now. All the time I look, look, study where is best place to hide, best place to find food. Next time, maybe I get to Tahiti. Leave ship at Tahiti. I stay there short time, maybe long time; then I let gendarme find me. Gendarme say, who you? I say, I am Tomaslov from Yugoslavia, I am trying to find my way to Australia. Gendarme say, no, we send you back to Yugoslavia."

He laughed happily. "You know? Then they send me back, find me some passage back to Europe. Is good?"

"And your sweetheart?"

"Oh, she got father, mother," he said carelessly. "She O.K. You play poker?"

"Not with you. And there isn't any chain-gang in Noumea?"

"You mean, prison people walk about in chains to work? Oh no. Maybe long time before, not now. Is not so bad, that prison. But what you think? What the best way for hide on board these ship?"

I was silent for a time, thinking of the girl he had abandoned, and who would bear his child. But who was I to sit in judgement on a man called Tomaslov?

"Hide anywhere you like," I said. "But don't waste your time trying to hide from yourself."

The vessel travelled south and west four hundred miles each day, and winter's chill still lingered in the southern latitudes. Skies were clear, but the sun had lost its strength, and cold gusty winds swept the deck. Gods, who would have thought the Pacific could be so cold? I had no shoes, only thong sandals; no socks or underwear, no coat or cardigan; only a couple of T-shirts and my jeans, and swimming trunks. By cutting up my blanket and sewing it here and there with string, I tailored a curious cylindrical suit without sleeves, falling to my knees and slit on either side to the hips for easy walking.

People laughed, but their laughter was warmer than the chill of the glacial wind.

"What're you going to do, when you get to Sydney?" Denny asked. It was early on the morning of the last day of the voyage. Australia was in sight, a frieze of olive and ochre daubed with the reds of clustered rooves, hazed with industrial smoke and rimmed with a thin white line of surf.

"Do?"

I tore my hungry gaze away from the beauty of the land to blink at him in frank surprise. What would I do? Ghost of a feathered bunyip, my heart was swamped with love for my native country, an orchestration of gladness was berserk in my brain, a fever of excitement was coursing through my blood—was returning to Australia. Was there something else to do?

"Well," he said, unaware of my quickened pulse, "What I mean is, are you going to find work or something in Sydney?"

"Work?" I echoed in dismay. "Good grief, man, I've hardly got there yet." The very thought provoked a sensation of blistered hands. "I don't want to think about work, just now. I'm thinking about long week-ends at Spit Junction, and the flower-stalls in Martin Place, and Wynyard Station at five o'clock. And the harbour, Sydney Harbour...."

"I hear tell you've got a crazy bridge," said Cliff.

I laughed. "Aye, and the crazy bridge."

"And electric light, and paved roads?" he teased.

"And all the girls in grass skirts, dancing in the jump-up huts at King's Cross", remembering the Pole I met on Nevis.

"I've heard about that King's Cross. They reckon it's all right. And the koala-bear factory...."

"At Pennant Hills. And Taronga Park—ah now, there's a real zoo."

"And those Bondi trams," said Denny. "I hear they're pretty fast."

"Not really. Just a saying."

Collaroy, Crow's Nest, Cockatoo Island...ah, sweet familiar names!

"And Woomal...Woollal...."

"Woolloomooloo?"

"That's it. Woomalil....Aw hell!"

"And six-o'clock closing," I added. "All the bars close at six o'clock."

"Not now," Lance broke in, coming up to join us. "Been ten o'clock for years, now. Stone the crows, but you fellers'll have to come down to Melbourne. Sydney's only Sydney, but Melbourne, that's a real city."

I let it pass.

"Perth," I said. "Now there's a lovely city; and you won't find nicer people anywhere. And Brisbane. Warmer there. Warm climate, warm people."

Tasmania, Adelaide, Darwin, and the vastness of the Centre beyond the black stump—what richness there would be in discovering my own land! Long ago I had travelled her with a cigarette-swag and an eye for the passing train, through all the seven states and Tasmania: what joy there would be in wooing her once again.

Come back, my heart, from Martinique. Come back to Australia....

For the expatriate who returns to Sydney from the sea the great twin ramparts of the Heads reach out in embrace, enfolding him to the sweet and gaily coloured bosom of the harbour. *Tahitien* anchored in mid morning a mile or so inside, between Mosman and Rose Bay, while officials came aboard searching for folk who gibbered, or had spots, or familiar fingerprints, or had thoughtlessly borrowed passports from their cousins. Reporters hopefully hurried from deck to deck, passageways were stacked with improbable displays of cabin luggage, mandolins, pogosticks and parasols, model catamarans and inflatable giraffes, shrunken heads (genuine plastic) from Panama, and a thousand boxes and cases of every shape and size. Mothers clambered to and fro in a dither of excitement seeking agile children, despairing stewards fled here and there anxiously questing those who sought to escape without giving tips. The general effect, below deck, was that of a desperate colony of ants evacuating their nest in time of flood, and suddenly discovering there was nowhere else to go.

Tomaslov had escaped from stewards who wished to lock him up; it seemed that police would be waiting at the docks. He had chosen a stack of empty fruit-boxes deep in the bowels of the vessel near the cold-stores; he slithered into a niche, and I quickly arranged the boxes to hide him from any view. He would attempt escape at nightfall and go back to his girl.

Passengers formed queues in the first-class lounge. An official studied my passports with a speculative frown, examining the protective leather cover and its Moroccan title; another scrutinized my health certificate, recently brought up to date by careful use of a pen and the stamp-pad impression of a brandy-bottle seal.

"How much money do you have?" someone asked, and I searched the balding strip of goatskin which served me as a wallet. It held a little money, Conrad's address in St Vincent, a Hinano beer label with a dozen signatures, a newspaper cutting from *l'Information*, a carefully preserved sample of creased, but virginal letterhead from the *Vancouver Sun*, a licence to carry a pistol in Costa Rica, and the sketch of a handshake signal employed by members of a certain well-known lodge.

"Two pounds," I said. "Three dollars, ten pesetas, one escudo, and a quetzal."

He glanced up, and raked my unusual blanket costume with his sharp grey eyes.

"Crikey," he muttered with light scorn. "And they call it White Australia!"

The anchor was taken up, and *Tahitien* made her way deeper into the harbour; and the two Canadians, and Mike, and Ralph and Rause and others from across the great Pacific, exclaimed their admiration of this most beautiful of all the world's great shipping havens. Nests of yachts and pleasure craft rode trimly in green coves, bays and headlands were studded with villas and garlanded with evergreens and gardens; the massed red tiles and brick and swarming pastel tints of waterside suburbia flared against the sombre greens and greys of unkempt bush. The Domain came into view, rolling down in parklands to the harbour, and a hushed moment of almost pained surprise greeted the city's proud and vigorous skyline as it slid into view.

"Sweet Jerusalem," Mike murmured piously, remembering the indeterminate sprawl of Seattle. "But that's quite some city, eh?"

His tone suggested a current of secret resentment, and he might have added, "What right have these bums to a place like that?"

Cliff surveyed the scene with a puzzled scowl. "Crys-sakes, I never thought—But look at the goddam place, willya? Skyscrapers and all!"

Rause was silent, gazing at the spectacle with a mixture of admiration, anxiety, and childlike delight. Aye, and it was a sight for any stranger, this sunsplashed city set in splendour by jade and silver waters. Ralph was staring slack-mouthed, his spongy face seemed to sag as his eyes shuttled from point to point like disappointed ferrets.

"Yep, Sydney's all right," said Lance with quiet pride, and I sped him a friendly glance. One might forgive us if we were proud at the surprise of these North Americans: too many of them considered Australia, if they considered her at all, as a wilderness peopled by blacks and kangaroos and cute, little cuddly bears. A colony, no more; one of England's trash-cans, which contrived in some strange fashion to breed prodigious athletes, had summer in wintertime, probably dressed in sheepskins, and was saved from the Japanese by the United States Navy.

"Hey, lamp that goddam bridge! Caesar's mickey, just look at that, willya?"

A gust of astonishment passed around the deck.

"Let me tellya that's no small model, that baby's fully grown. What you guys call it? What's its name?"

Lance shrugged with affected nonchalance, but I knew he was bubbling with pleasure.

"*Mais c'est formidable!*" someone near by murmured.

"Just a bridge," he said. "No special name."

There were dozens like it, his tone implied: and to the Americans, accustomed to lavishing fine titles on any public construction larger than a privy, this was one of the unkindest cuts of all.

"What the hell!" cried Ralph, staring at something near Circular Quay. "What's that? That thing?"

He pointed to a curious structure with an unfinished roof of thrusting pods, squatting fatly on concrete piles at the tip of a parkland point. Well, what could it be? It looked like a cross between a switchback railway and a bed of enormous clams. I had never seen anything similar anywhere overseas.

"Hindu temple?" Rause suggested. It was more like the covered bazaars of Istanbul.

"A doohickey," said Denny. "A dragon-bellied doohickey, only it's upside-down."

"Nah," Lance declared, "I think I know what it is. It's the new opera house these Sydney gigs have built. It was in the papers. The architect went for a nit's tit, and when he came back someone had swiped the plans to build a revolving magpie trap. All he had left was his sheila's design for a cable-stitch sweater. You know, knit one, pearl two. Finished up like that."

We laughed.

"Opera house," someone murmured in unwilling fascination. "Man, oh man!"

Sydney, my Sydney—home! The end of the trail, the last port, the final and finest goal of all. Gateway to Australia, Mecca of east-coast urgers, paradise of jackeroos and stockmen: the city which smiles on the quick and the strong, and pushes the weak to the wall. Her heart is of bitter honey, her brain a cash register, her magic wand is a whip of tungsten steel. Her mantle is spun from illusion and sparkles with slivers of hope; her underclothes are of cheese-cloth begrimed with industrial soot and trimmed with gold. Proud, sly, corrosively plausible with leisurely zeal, she favours the man with the hottest dice, yet takes the foremost pew and prays aloud.

By all the gods that ever were, it was good to be back again!

Rause hurried away from the docks to find the first train south towards Tasmania, as if fearful of being seduced or lost amid the aggressive bustle of Sydney's streets. Mike had disappeared, David went off amid gay farewells in a taxi with two pretty girls, Patsy and Marge were spirited away by some tall, young man they had known overseas.

There were four of us left who met in the afternoon for a farewell drink. Denny and Cliff would stay with an aunt somewhere at King's Cross; when funds were on hand they would roar on north to Brisbane. Lance had wired for the fare home to Victoria, and would leave as soon as it came. We walked down Elizabeth Street, now laughing in our happiness at the moment, now thoughtful in the knowledge that companionship would end.

And ever and anon the four of us would pause to admire exciting points of passing interest: for the offices were closing, and the pavement was invaded by a host of pretty girls.

"Dames and more dames," said Denny happily. "And all white, too, all waiting for me. Girls?" he cried, waving roguishly to them. "Girls, I'm here, I'm here!"

"Some talent," Cliff agreed. He had a tendency to study attractive women with such intense inspection, from head to toe and back, that they would falter, glancing down to assure themselves they were adequately dressed and not by any dreadful trick wearing only a string of beads or a strip of vitreous cloth. Aye, there was pleasure in observing them, I had forgotten just how attractive Australian women were. Their manner of dress reflected conservative awareness of fashions which, overseas, had almost run their course; but the quality of their clothes mirrored a prosperous economy and in the art of cunning make-up, using fingertip control instead of trowels, they were as gifted and modestly inventive as most that one might find throughout the world.

But there seemed to be something missing from the street. What was it? I glanced around, mildly disturbed, but could not imagine what it was.

"The sheilas can wait for an hour or two," said Lance, grinning. "Let's have that beer."

We filed into a public bar behind him and were lucky to discover standing room by the counter. Minutes later the place was thick with business men swarming in for their after-office drink. Lance waved money in the air, making signals, and four beers arrived by magic in a slurrup of slopping foam.

"Bloody beaut," he said reverently, handing them around. We drank, with Cliff and Denny pensively savouring the taste.

"Not real bad," said Cliff as if surprised, and Denny nodded. "Good taste. Weak, though."

"That's what the bloody Yanks thought, till they found 'emselves flat on their orts after the fourth schooner. Melbourne beer's better, though." He drained his glass with a thirsty gulp.

Cliff gazed about him at the sterile appointments of a normal city bar: the bare concrete floor darkly stained, the antiseptic walls of tile scorning any ornament, the furnishings of chrome and glass and stainless steel behind the bar.

"Funny sort of joint," he remarked.

Lance glanced at him suspiciously. "Funny?"

"Yeah. Good idea, all standing up at a bar like this; but all these tiles and concrete. Looks like a clean public lavatory."

I burst out laughing at the pained astonishment on Lance's face, and he grinned crookedly.

"Modern bloody bar, that's what it is. Don't say things like that out loud or some ratbag's likely to drop you with a swift kingy. Come on, drink up, you're draggin' your flamin' feet."

A second round was ordered, and Denny's eyes twinkled with amusement as he watched the throng which pressed the bar, jealously nursing glasses of beer and abuzz with conversation. The perspiring barmaid was serving with all the damp economy of a whirling dervish in a birdbath. Australians, I reflected: scores of them, more than I had seen for years—grave, eager, brooding, laughing, well fed by the looks of them, and surely better clad than I. With their sombre suits they wore the confidence of men who had comfortable homes, and to whom famine and revolution were distant words used in foreign lands. They sipped their beer with the sanguine assurance of free men, to whom civil rights were as real and unquestioned as the concrete floor on which they stood, who already controlled tomorrow within the parenthesis of predictable routine. Were they happy, I wondered? The city had grown, and the trend was to urban life. What was it that persuaded untold millions to root themselves in suburbs around the world's great cities? What was the common denominator of the sum total who chose to devote their daily lives in allegiance to steel and bitumen and concrete? Did they know something, some common secret, which I had never learnt? Had I missed some whispered truth of great value?

Someone knocked Denny's arm, spilling half his beer.

"Bloody nong!" cried Lance. "You, fat man!"

The fat man turned slowly, head gently nodding from some kind of nervous tic, and balefully glared like a lazily angry bull.

"Gat vize," he rasped in heavy accent. "Knock your plock off!"

"You couldn't knock a cripple off a piss-pot!" Lance snarled. "Ignorant, bloody nong."

The fat man stared at him uncertainly for a moment and then looked away, head softly nodding. Denny studied his glass with raised brow, and decided to drink the remainder of his beer. Above the rumbling susurration of the public bar one was conscious of the street noises, the syncopated orchestration of a living, breathing city; grinding and whirring of traffic, slither and clack of feet, hissing of power brakes, of bubbles of laughter and shreds of sudden conversation sucked in through the door.

"The trams," I said abruptly. "They're missing. I couldn't place what it was. The trams have gone."

"'Struth, yes, years ago. "

Cliff had bought an evening paper from a thin, little newsboy who yelled, "Murderin Wagga, pa-apr!" several times and disappeared. He glanced at the first page, consumed by curiosity.

"What's a murderin' wagga?" Denny asked.

"Search me. One of them bunyips, maybe."

"Nah, you mug," said Lance. "That's a place. A town. There's been a murder in Wagga Wagga."

"In a whatta whatta?" Cliff was incredulous.

"Wagga Wagga, down south."

"Look," said Denny, pointing to a story about sharks. "Cool—an—gatta." He pronounced the word with slow relish, and looked up with a delighted smile. "Hey, cool, cool, Coolangatta-gatta, gatta-ta-ta-gatta!" He sang joyfully to himself and shuffled his feet with a bouncy rhythm.

"Murrum—bidgee," said Cliff, translating from the Wagga story; and he also began to twitch his feet and chant, with Denny softly clapping and adding ta-tas here and there.

"Murrum-ba! Murrum-ba! Murrum-ba-ba-bidgee, ba-ba, boo-boo-boo-ba!" The fat man turned around, and Cliff straightened up to scowl at him until he turned away.

"Crazy damn' names," he said. And then to Lance, in mime of his accent, "Drink yer grog, mite. Yer draggin' yer flymin' fite!"

"Garn, you bloody Canuck!"

Denny and Cliff were foreigners, then, but I was no longer so. What private impressions were they storing away, to be used in the manufacture of convictions later on? They would find their own Australia in their travels through the land; a continent of strange contrasts where indigenous and borrowed culture thinly overlay the primitive, as her cities thinly sprinkled her great coast; where individual brashness blends to social harmony, and bloody khaki in an athlete's cup is a soufflé of national pride.

Who were they, these Australians? I was one of them, and yet I was a stranger; how well did memory serve me—and how would they judge me? For I loved the memory, the clumsy and ill-defined picture I had preserved these many years, and shrank from the fear that the memory might be false, or that I might have become false, and wished that I might identify the memory, and myself, with them. Among them would I find myself intruding, that they were strangers all, that I had come home as an alien to unfamiliar folk in this loved, familiar land?

"Clean lavatory!" Lance commented in wonder. "But we're getting pretty good at civilizing mugs like you, with all the migrants to practise on."

"Darn' sure we never manage to civilize you Aussies, when you come to Vancouver." Cliff grinned. "Gee, you guys have a hairy reputation there!"

What of the memory that I had?

Beloved countryman: imperfect, as men are, and yet magnificently human as the progeny of pioneers can be. His personal independence spurred by isolation, ungentle in his desire for self-determination, he was quick to judge the stranger and wary of the foreigner, and as generous with his favours and his laughter as his fists. So memory pictured him. He was insecurely dogmatic in national vainglory, precipitate in defence of pride and selfishly impulsive in protection of his rights, colourless in politics and cooking, and curiously temperate in his recipes for living after dark.

The languid attitudes, the lazy smile, the watchful indolence so manifest on the surface were sufficiently well defined for some to acclaim it as a colonial characteristic; but it was only a social mask, an expedient deceit largely weakened by the erosion of Anglo-Saxon discipline; and turbulence lay close below the surface. Less easily provoked to passion than the Latin, less vicious in emotion than the Arab, less sensitive to slight than the Central European or the oriental, his impulse to individual aggression was yet too easily triggered by the accidental push, the upturned glass, the careless idiom: as if his cigarette lighter enshrined the Eternal Flame, reminding him—often enough against his will—that any personal challenge implied a sacred incitation to justify himself.

If this was the memory, what might reality prove to be?

"...call them kangaroos," Cliff was saying. "The first British territory they hit on the other side of the Pacific is Vancouver. So what do they do? They get jobs; six weeks, three months. Then, hop, they're off again to Toronto. Get jobs for a few months. Then, hop, they're off again to England. Never stay anywhere, just go from one springboard to the next. Tell you, it's getting tough for an Aussie kangaroo to get a job in Vancouver these days."

As he spoke, I was leafing through his newspaper. Murder in Wagga, forthcoming state election, star skater breaks leg, plan to net sharks, horse tramples jockey, more aid to schools. Ah, this lucky country! How many nations overseas, bloody with civil wars, riven in shreds by armed politics, fearful of threatened frontiers or frenzied with factional hatreds, oppressed by despots, or victims of plagues and hunger and judicial corruption and untold other evils—how many of those nations might envy the fortunate people where a murder in a country town was the headline of the day, and a broken leg was set in twenty-four-point type! There had been a time when I was bored with my own country, discovering monotony and tedium in her placid politics, her sedate elections, her social quietude, the inescapable constancy of her manners in cuisine, and clothes, in speech and song and architecture throughout three million square miles.

Blessed land…because this monotony, this quietude and constancy, these were the components of provincial harmony, the fringe benefits of national peace. It seemed I had lacked a yardstick to compare her with other lands.

Here, in my own land, there was peace.

"You two mugs really set on going north?" Lance asked.

"Brisbane," said Cliff.

"You'll pass through Coolangatta."

Denny began to shuffle his feet again, and commented, "Warmer up there, anyway. Too much like Vancouver down here." And addressing me, "What about you?"

"South."

"Hey? Isn't it colder down south, in this country?"

"Not far," I said, and grinned. "Place called Burradoo. By the Bong Bong River. In the shire of Wingecarribee between Wollongong and the Wollondilly."

Denny gave a thin, lopsided smile, and Cliff studied me with a worried frown.

"Aborigines'll get you." He tapped Denny, and began to jive while Denny clapped.

"Bong-bong, bo-bong-bong-carribee, do-do-dong dilly…." Lance and I watched helplessly. "Crazy names," he said at length. "I never did believe you guys down here spoke English."

A voice at my elbow intruded on my smile.

"Who's that drongo? A bloody Yank?"

"Drop dead," I said agreeably without looking around. "Someone made up a song by stringing names like that—"

"Hoy!" The owner of the voice thumped my shoulder, and I turned, feeling the burn of slow anger. With his long, thrusting jaw and small black eyes under beetling brows, he looked more like a grasshopper than anything I had ever seen outside a field of grass.

"You a bloody Yank too?" he asked.

"Poke your flamin' nose for you."

He laid his glass of beer on the counter and shaped up, shadow-sparring, tongue curling from one corner of his mouth, stabbing intensely at the air, feet executing an intricate little dance. At once it was evident that he was mocking me, and I laughed.

"The drongo's a Canadian, buddy. And don't hit me, you Aussies scare me to death."

"Canadian?" He paused, his quick little eyes lighting with interest. Advancing on Cliff and Denny, he insisted on shaking their hands, then peered at Lance. "You ain't no Canadian. You're a punchy digger. Shape of the skull."

He winked at me and went back to his beer. Cliff and Denny looked at me in mute inquiry, and I shrugged.

"A ning-nong," I said. "He likes Canadians. Doesn't know any better."

"Holy banana, what a hairy country," Cliff exclaimed, and glanced at his watch. "Hell, fellers, Denny and I have got to go."

We finished our beer and walked slowly out of the bar, pausing on the pavement outside. The breeze was cold, and I shivered. A chill shadow like a gust of grey snow passed through my awareness, and shrouded the moment with unease and faint misgivings. Ah yes: the cold climates, the struggle for warmth and shelter and food in wintry latitudes…the damp-frozen shoes, the crackly newspaper underwear, the crafty search at nightfall for such refuge as might offer. No wonder so many drifters kept to tropical lands…and I laughed at my foolishness, for now I was home and the lessons in survival lay behind me.

"Some time," they said, shaking hands with us.

"Sure, some time."

"You've got our addresses. Look us up if you come to Canada."

"Will do." Regrets were a fast current tugging something around inside my breast. "Luck, fellers. Best of good luck all the way to wherever you go."

"Yeah, guys, and the same to you. Crazy good luck. Well, bye now. Been good knowing you."

"Bye, fellers. Take it easy."

We stood there watching them as they strode off to where they had left their motor-bikes, and I wondered what would become of them, what might happen to them before they went back to Canada. Strange, I reflected, the role is reversed: for I am home, in my own country, and they are the travellers. They will move on to unknown destinations, exposed to the unpredictable, roaring along the highways to a thousand rendezvous with strange occasions.

Will my country be as good to them as foreign places have been to me?

A thin, young lad came down the street with a bundle of papers under his arm.

"Murderin Wagga," he cried. "Pa-apr!"

Printed in Great Britain
by Amazon

40526732R00178